Seeking Good Debate

Seeking Good Debate

Religion, Science, and Conflict in
American Public Life

Michael S. Evans

UNIVERSITY OF CALIFORNIA PRESS

University of California Press, one of the most
distinguished university presses in the United States,
enriches lives around the world by advancing scholarship
in the humanities, social sciences, and natural sciences. Its
activities are supported by the UC Press Foundation and
by philanthropic contributions from individuals and
institutions. For more information, visit www.ucpress.edu.

University of California Press
Oakland, California

Portions of chapter 5 and the appendix appeared in
"Who Wants a Deliberative Public Sphere?" *Sociological
Forum* 27 (4): 872–95. Portions of chapter 8 appeared in
"Supporting Science: Reasons, Restrictions, and the Role
of Religion," *Science Communication* 34 (3): 334–62.

Library of Congress Cataloging-in-Publication Data
Evans, Michael S., 1975– author.
  Seeking good debate : religion, science, and conflict in
American public life / Michael S. Evans.
      pages   cm
  Includes bibliographical references and index.
  ISBN 978-0-520-28507-1 (cloth : alk. paper)
  ISBN 978-0-520-28508-8 (pbk. : alk. paper)
  ISBN 978-0-520-96066-4 (ebook)
  1. Religion and science—Public opinion.   2. Public
opinion—United States.   3. Debates and debating—
United States.   4. Mass media and public opinion—
United States.   I. Title.
  bl240.3.e93 2016
  201'.650973—dc23   2015028380

Manufactured in the United States of America

25 24 23 22 21 20 19 18 17 16
10 9 8 7 6 5 4 3 2 1

In keeping with a commitment to support
environmentally responsible and sustainable printing
practices, UC Press has printed this book on Natures
Natural, a fiber that contains 30% post-consumer waste
and meets the minimum requirements of ANSI/NISO
Z39.48–1992 (R 1997) (*Permanence of Paper*).

Contents

Figures

Tables

Acknowledgments

I am deeply grateful to the many individuals and organizations whose generosity sustained this project. My greatest debt is to my research respondents, who invited me into their lives and communities, spent their valuable time talking to a curious sociologist, and asked nothing in return. There would be no book without them.

This book started as a dissertation in the University of California, San Diego, sociology department and grew to fruition in the Neukom Institute for Computational Science at Dartmouth College. At UCSD, John Evans saw the potential in my earliest ideas about this project and has never hesitated to be encouraging or critical at exactly the right moments ever since. John is a peerless and brilliant mentor. No amount of computation can calculate my gratitude for his guidance and support. Martha Lampland, Steve Epstein, Joel Robbins, and Bob Westman consistently provided valuable insight and wise counsel as the project developed. I continue to cultivate the many intellectual seeds that they planted in my work. At Dartmouth College, Dan Rockmore has been an unflagging supporter and catalyst of creative interdisciplinary research that starts conversations across boundaries. I am immensely grateful to be part of the Neukom Institute family.

Many other people have provided critical feedback, positive encouragement, and basic support along the way. Conversations with Alper Yalçinkaya, Louis Esparza, Lisa Nunn, Stephanie Chan, John O'Meara, Caroline Lee, Amy Binder, Isaac Martin, Andy Scull, Andy Perrin, Elaine

Howard Ecklund, Gary Adler, and Casey Oberlin have improved my thinking about this project at various stages of development. My parents-in-law generously provided a home base for South Florida fieldwork. My parents have inspired me at every step. There are so many others who have helped. Thank you. Thank you all.

Several organizations provided funding for data collection, writing, and the author's general survival. I thank them for their support. At UCSD, I received direct financial support from the Louisville Institute, Religious Research Association, Society for the Scientific Study of Religion, UC San Diego Science Studies Program, UC San Diego sociology graduate program, and the J. M. Hepps Fellowship. At Dartmouth College, I have been fully supported as a postdoctoral Neukom Fellow by the Neukom Institute for Computational Science, and graciously hosted by the Department of Film and Media Studies.

Portions of chapter 5 and the appendix have appeared in *Sociological Forum*. Portions of chapter 8 have appeared in *Science Communication*. I thank the editors and reviewers of these journals for helpful comments and suggestions, and the journals' publishers for permitting my reuse of material from those articles in this book.

Publishing a book is a team effort, but I especially thank Eric Schmidt for being this book's champion. Reviewers who read and commented on the full manuscript for the University of California Press improved the book considerably. I thank them for their efforts. I am also grateful to Maeve Cornell-Taylor, Rachel Berchten, Aimée Goggins, Steven Baker, and the rest of the team at UC Press for bringing this work from manuscript to finished product. Thank you all for making this book happen.

Finally, I dedicate this book to DT, who made it all the way, and to MK, who tried her best.

CHAPTER I

Rethinking Religion and Science

Is good public debate between religion and science possible? The dominant conflict narrative suggests that the answer is "no." Good debate is deliberative. Good debate happens when people and ideas are in productive engagement in public life. Good debate is not possible, the conflict narrative suggests, because religion and science will always be at war with each other.

Outrageous public statements reinforce the impression of conflict. Take, for example, debates over creationism, Intelligent Design (ID), and evolution. When the citizens of Dover, Pennsylvania, voted out their ID-supporting school board, televangelist Pat Robertson responded: "I'd like to say to the good citizens of Dover: If there is a disaster in your area, don't turn to God; you just rejected him from your city. And don't wonder why he hasn't helped you when problems begin, if they begin. I'm not saying they will, but if they do, just remember, you just voted God out of your city."[1] Likewise, biologist Richard Dawkins derides all who oppose evolution: "It is absolutely safe to say that if you meet somebody who claims not to believe in evolution, that person is ignorant, stupid or insane (or wicked, but I'd rather not consider that)."[2]

When public statements from religious leaders and scientists sound like the rantings of mad scientists and false prophets, it is easy to think that something about religion or science causes debate to go wrong. So we ask questions. The variety of these questions reflects the complexity of religion and science. Does faith conflict with reason? Is evolution a threat to biblical truth? Do scientists believe in God? Can prayer be evaluated through double-blind clinical studies? What grades do regular church attendees get in science courses? Do evangelicals know that the earth revolves around the sun, and not vice versa?

In asking these questions about religion and science, it is easy to forget that public debates involving science and religion are, first and foremost, public debates. By "public debates" I mean extended public conversations about important issues that occur primarily through mass media such as newspapers and television. Religion and science are not hermetically sealed in their own capsule. They are two out of many cultural institutions involved in the broader process of working out issues through public talk.

But what if public debate is itself the source of problems with religion-and-science debates? Religion and science may participate in public debate, but the whole point of public debate is to negotiate and manage the changing categories of social life. Public debate shapes what we can talk about, what we know about it, how we talk about it, and what we can do about it. In a fundamental sense, it is public debate that produces and reproduces religion and science in public life. Many people claim that religion and science cause problems for public debate. But it is just as possible that public debate causes problems for religion and science.

In the world of science and religion scholarship, few inhabitants write about religion and science as part of some larger process of American public life.[3] This book's novel contribution to religion-and-science scholarship is that it appears to be about religion and science, but it is really a book about public debate. I agree with most other scholars that there are problems in American religion-and-science debate. But I think that the problems stem from how public debate works, rather than from the relationship between science and religion.

I structure the analysis around a well-known problem of public debate: representation.[4] In theory, public debate is open to participation from anyone. But if everyone were to talk in public at once, the result would be cacophony, not debate. In practice, most significant and influential public debates occur in mass media, where elite actors define, present, and debate important issues before the widest possible audience. I call these elite actors "representatives." Representatives participate in public debate instead of, though not necessarily on behalf of, ordinary people. Representatives have unique power to influence our understanding of what is being debated, simply because they are the ones doing the talking in public.

Return for a moment to the quotes from Robertson and Dawkins. If this was a casual exchange between two somewhat inebriated bar patrons, quickly forgotten after a good night's rest, it would be unremarkable. But that is far from the case. Pat Robertson and Richard Dawkins are highly visible representatives in public debate. Mass media outlets distribute their words to a wide audience. Robertson and Dawkins could be engaged in a rich, deliberative, and thoughtful conversation about human origins. Instead, they are slinging personal insults and channeling divine threats.

Thinking about representation as a problem for public religion-and-science debate generates very different kinds of questions than those generated by the conflict thesis. How does representation shape public debates? How do representatives attempt to intervene in public debates? How do ordinary people evaluate representatives as good or bad? What does it mean that, for example, Pat Robertson and Richard Dawkins are seen as representatives of (respectively) religion and science? Do representatives of religion and science act differently than representatives from other domains of public life?

In what follows, I look at public debates about human origins, stem cell research, environmental policy, and the origins of homosexuality. I call these "religion and science" debates because they meet two conditions. First, these are all debates in which some people make claims based on religious authority. Second, they are also debates in which some people make claims based on scientific authority. This definition accounts for science and religion as parts of broader public debates, but avoids the all too common problem of selecting only those instances when religion and science already appear to be in conflict.

As with many controversial issues in American life, these religion-and-science debates ramify in complicated ways across the American cultural landscape. For example, arguments in debates about the origins of homosexuality also implicate hot-button political issues such as gay marriage, personal and professional issues such as the ethics of psychological treatment, and religious organizational issues such as the limits of congregational authority to resist denominational mandates against gay clergy. One social scientist with finite resources cannot possibly track all of the ramifications of these debates, or even identify and organize all of the possible data sources for a single debate. So this study is limited to a practical subset of what is available.

For information on debates and representatives, I constructed a data set containing thousands of articles from major national and regional newspapers in the United States within a ten year period, and analyzed these data using various forms of computer assistance. For questions about how ordinary people evaluate representatives, I interviewed sixty-two ordinary Americans across two different locations in the United States. Respondents varied in terms of religious background and affiliation and in terms of occupational commitments (e.g., scientific versus nonscientific job). While I briefly describe the various methods I used at appropriate points throughout the book, I have also included a detailed methodological appendix at the end of the book for reference. In all cases, respondents' names are pseudonymized to protect their identities.

I take a sociological approach to analysis in this book.[5] This means that I focus on what actual people say and do, rather than on how abstract ideas based on scientific theory or theology fit together. It also means that I do not attempt to arbitrate the truth or ultimate significance of claims involving religion or science. Such an approach may initially seem strange to some readers. For example, the history of the relationship between religion and sociology suggests that some religious persons might see sociological analysis as an attempt to undermine the validity of religious beliefs.[6] Similarly, the history of the relationship between the (other) sciences and sociology suggests that some science enthusiasts might see sociological analysis as an attempt to undermine the authority of science.[7] So, to address potential concerns up front, let me begin by laying out the reasoning behind my analytical approach.

RELIGION VERSUS SCIENCE?

Both religion and science figure prominently in American public life. Most Americans claim some sort of religious affiliation. Most Americans agree that America is a "Christian nation." Religious participation remains vibrant. Religious discourse permeates public discussion in settings ranging from alcoholism recovery meetings to presidential speeches. At the same time, most Americans have significant interest in science and technology. People regularly debate American competitiveness in terms of scientific and engineering education. Public respect for scientists remains high, and "scientific citizenship" is a key part of American identity.[8] To the extent that religion and science are important to Americans, it is no surprise to see that religion and science are part of public life. It would be surprising if they were not.[9]

At the same time, there is little consensus about what counts as religion and what counts as science. "Religion" in public discourse refers sometimes to institutions, sometimes to ideas, sometimes to practices, sometimes to people, and sometimes to all of these at once. It is sometimes any reference to moral principles, sometimes Christianity or Islam, sometimes what happens in churches, sometimes Protestantism or Catholicism, sometimes clergy, sometimes any reference to supernatural forces, and sometimes just "faith." "Science" also refers sometimes to institutions; other times to ideas, practices, or people; and still other times to all of these at once. It is sometimes any use of the scientific method, sometimes what happens in big labs and universities, sometimes particle physics or biology, sometimes scientists, sometimes any reference to natural forces, and sometimes just "reason." In short, the categories "religion" and "science," like many categories invoked to describe society, are messy, incoherent, and inevitably, inherently incomplete. So discussions about science and religion range widely, from concerns about what they really are, to how they are related, to how religion and science operate and affect broader social concerns.

THREE PERSPECTIVES ON RELIGION AND SCIENCE

Despite this range of definitions and interests, however, it is possible to talk about three major perspectives on religion and science that recur in popular and scholarly literature. Following convention, I call these three perspectives *conflict*, *complementarity*, and *complexity*. I note here that there is substantial slippage in the relevant literature between the claim that there is one single "religion and science" debate (with many manifestations) and the claim that there are many debates involving religion and science.

Conflict

For more than a century, the dominant perspective in religion and science has been the "conflict" or "warfare" perspective. First popularized by John William Draper in his book *History of the Conflict between Religion and Science,* the conflict thesis posits that science and religion are inherently contentious domains of human knowledge with mutually exclusive explanations for how the world works.[10] In this view, religion and science are essential and enduring categories of human life, extending back into antiquity and likely projecting into any visible human future. Citing such examples as the trial of Galileo, the "prayer gauge" debate, and the Scopes trial, scholars and popular sources attribute particular instances of conflict to an overarching and inevitable conflict between religion and science. The usual conclusion of these analyses is that science provides the superior explanation for how the world works and is therefore winning, or will win, its battle with religion.[11]

The conflict narrative imagines the world progressing toward total secular rationality. In this developmental view, societies become increasingly secularized as they become more modern.[12] Religion, as a primitive or irrational vestige of less developed societies, will be slowly eradicated by science, the paradigmatic rational epistemology. Rationality will displace irrationality. The future is secular.

In the more benign version of the conflict narrative, the displacement of religion by science is an evolutionary process. Rationality eventually wins out with the better form of knowledge production. Science's superior method of truth will, in the end, prove more durable. We need only wait for religion to play itself out. Although it is unfortunate that some people are still primitive and irrational, we can be generally tolerant of belief pluralism until our better future comes along.

In the most extreme, normative version of the conflict perspective, currently motivating the production of popular best sellers such as *The God Delusion* and *God Is Not Great: How Religion Poisons Everything,* there is no time to waste.[13] If the better future is rational and secular, then religion is not simply a vestige of past irrationality but an inimical force hostile to human flourishing. Even though science may win in the end, it is immoral and dangerous to allow that process to play out by itself. Science must defeat religion to produce a better world.[14] Anything less than the destruction of religion is a failure of humanity.

Despite the sometimes aggressive polemical language, conflict thesis proponents use "conflict" and "warfare" metaphorically. To the best of my knowledge, no respectable writer seriously advocates the genocide of religious people to advance the cause of science.[15] Even if they did, science has no armies, and such systematic violence would be difficult to mobilize. What is meant by "conflict" or "warfare" is not physical violence between armed bands of theologians and scientists, but rather confrontation between different perspectives. Conflict takes place in the public square, not on the battlefield. Battles are fought with words, ideas, policy, and laws, not guns, bombs, and assassination. This may seem obvious. But the fact that any proposed relationship between religion and science plays out primarily in the public sphere is of crucial importance to the argument of this book.

Complementarity

In the past fifty years, many scholars have challenged both the epistemological and the historical bases of the conflict thesis. From an epistemological perspective, theologians and scientists offer an alternative perspective often called complementarity. Like the conflict perspective, complementarity sees science and religion as essentially distinct realms of human understanding. Science is concerned with knowledge of the natural world. Religion is concerned with meaning and moral order. But in the complementarity view, this difference does not necessarily mean conflict. While conflict is one possible outcome, it can be avoided.

Under the aegis of complementarity there are differing normative prescriptions for avoiding conflict. For example, the "nonoverlapping magisteria" (NOMA) or "two worlds" approach, advocated by Stephen Jay Gould and Pope John Paul II, suggests that religion and science should be kept completely separate so that conflict will not occur over areas of epistemological jurisdiction.[16] This position resonates with debates over the separation of religion from politics.[17] Science is assumed to be a universally accessible way of knowing about the world, so it serves as the legitimate basis for government. Religion, by contrast, is plural and local, so it must be excluded from public deliberation over policies and laws that affect everyone.

At the opposite end of the normative spectrum, "dialogue" and "consonance" approaches suggest that religion and science should be in beneficial dialogue with each other, and even attempt to reconcile their differences, to best avoid conflict. Theologians, scientists, and organizations such as the John Templeton Foundation and the Metanexus Institute actively attempt to reconcile religion and science by highlighting similarities between the two, providing structured dialogues between actors affiliated with religious and scientific institutions, organizing public events to raise awareness of compatibility, providing personal testimonies of reconciliation between science and religion, and constructing systematic theologies that bring, for example, evolutionary theory and soteriology together into a coherent whole.[18]

Complementarity shares the conceptual model underpinning the warfare perspective, but does not assume inevitable secularization. Most proponents of complementarity are from vibrant religious traditions that bring the secularization thesis into question. Like the warfare perspective, complementarity sees potential conflict between religion and science as occurring primarily in the public square rather than through physical violence. Complementarity also sees peace as the normative ideal. For NOMA, peace is achieved and maintained in public life by means of a firewall between science and religion. Likewise, the dialogue and consonance approaches embrace the ideal of public debate as the place for productive deliberative engagement between religion and science (however defined). In all complementarity perspectives, the underlying motivation is to minimize conflict in public life.

Complexity

A more recent alternative to the conflict and complementarity perspectives comes from historians, who examine the specific circumstances of historical events commonly cited as religion-and-science conflicts. Instead of presuming an enduring epistemological conflict, the "complexity thesis" claims that instances of contention between religion and science are not necessarily conflict, not necessarily about religion and science, and most important, not indicative of any sort of larger pattern of conflict between religion and science. Instead, the complexity thesis claims that science and religion have no identifiable pattern of interaction.[19]

This claim has two parts. First, there is no way to demarcate religion and science. Historically and sociologically the boundaries of religion and science are not fixed and, in practice, move around so much that no overarching narrative can explain their connections. There are many times and places where religion and science either were not in conflict or were not even considered as separate categories. For example, in the nineteenth-century United States, Baconian Common Sense Realism emphasized science as part of God's revelation in nature.[20] And in Victorian England, some of the most ardent of "Darwin's defenders" promoted evolution as part of the divine plan for the world.[21]

Second, although conflict sometimes occurs that can be called "science versus religion," most episodes of conflict are local and contingent rather than universal and enduring. Local theological disputes or contentions over professional jurisdiction embody local concerns about power and authority that do not easily map onto a master narrative of conflict. So, for example, battles over Copernicus and Galileo are not episodes in the inevitable conflict between religion and science over the truth of the cosmos, but historically contingent conflicts over institutional authority.[22] Likewise, the Scopes trial was as much about conflict between conservative and moderate American Protestantism as conflict between Darwin and God.[23]

On its face, the complexity perspective is a ground-level attempt to debunk the conflict narrative by showing empirical examples that are contrary to what the conflict narrative would predict. However, this debunking is not just motivated by an overarching commitment to a position on religion and science (such as secularization). It is also motivated by concern for finding what is actually at stake in these conflicts so that future engagement can be more productive. Even though complexity does not share many assumptions about religion and science with the conflict or complementarity perspectives, it does share assumptions about the desirability of good public debate.

RELIGION AND SCIENCE AS A PROBLEM OF PUBLIC LIFE

While conflict, complementarity, and complexity differ in several respects, the more important point for this book is that they share three underlying assumptions. The first common underlying assumption is that religion and science encounter each other in the public sphere, not across a literal battlefield. The second is that the ideal for such encounters is deliberation or, in other words, that deliberative debate is good debate. The third is that good debate about religion and science is not just interesting in the abstract but also important to American society and meaningful to American citizens.

The Public Sphere

All mainstream perspectives assume that religion and science encounter each other in the public sphere. According to Charles Taylor, the public sphere is "a common space in which the members of society are deemed to meet through a variety of media: print, electronic, and also face-to-face encounters; to discuss matters of common interest; and thus to be able to form a common mind about these."[24] By "common mind" Taylor does not mean that everyone will agree on everything, or that total consensus is possible or even desirable. Rather, the public sphere is the space where people debate what kinds of things to talk about, how those things should be talked about, what kinds of things we can do, and what ways of doing things are generally acceptable.

Public debate thus shapes what we can talk about, what we know about it, how we talk about it, and what we can do about it. Given this power to shape imagination, thought, and ultimately, social activity, theorists of democracy agree that a good public sphere is central to a fair and just society that enables human flourishing for its citizens.[25] Public debate informs policy makers about issues of concern and provides public guidance and accountability for the formal exercise of executive and legislative power. For example, congressional leaders considering a tax increase need only watch the news or read newspapers to see a wide range of opinions, arguments, and reasons being discussed. Likewise, debates in the public sphere enrich the private lives of citizens by informing them about issues of broad concern and by demonstrating that a wide range of positions on any given issue is available.

I use the words "wide" and "broad" because they invoke the kind of ideal public sphere whose purpose is to maximize the range of possibilities for thinking and acting. This requires at minimum a space for discussion of issues where differences do not escalate into violence.[26] Generally speaking, the laws and police powers of the state provide a kind of backstop to the public sphere so that even people whose ideas are in serious conflict do not take up arms and assault one another.[27] Rather, they (in theory at least) take to the airwaves, the editorial page, the lectern, or even their local pub, to make arguments and claims that contribute to a multisided discussion of the issue with which they are concerned.

Beyond the minimal requirement of enforced nonviolence, the ideal public sphere provides access to all citizens.[28] This does not mean that access is equal or that every single idea will be heard by every single citizen. Rather, ideally, no unequal burden or constraint is imposed on particular groups of citizens based, for example, on wealth, racial background, sexual preference, or gender. In the ideal public sphere, anyone has as much of a chance to participate in public debate as anyone else. Of course, to the extent that inequalities exist in society, providing universal access to the public sphere may import those inequalities into public debate.[29] And obviously individual preferences regarding participation will vary. The key point, and the assumption shared by most, if not all, analyses of religion and science, is that the public sphere provides the arena for widely accessible nonviolent discussion of issues of concern, including (but not limited to) religion and science.

What Is Good Debate?

Discussion in the public sphere could unfold in many different ways. Participants might hold a public conversation in which they give reasons for their arguments and display a willingness to change their minds.[30] Participants might engage in agonistic conflict or contentious disagreement.[31] Participants might advocate for their position or interests in the public sphere without engaging with other participants.[32] Participants might "act up" in public to challenge dominant ideas about what should be debated at all.[33] All of these things might even happen at the same time.

But for scholars of religion and science, not all forms of debate count as good debate. Even though the various analyses of religion and science use different kinds of evidence and often come to different conclusions, they are all based (explicitly or implicitly) on a deliberative model of the public sphere. By "deliberative" I mean that participants in the public sphere encounter and engage one another with ideas, arguments, and claims.[34] This may at first seem like repetition of the previous point. But the emphasis here is on "encounter" and "engage." Good public debate occurs not just when people participate in the public sphere but also when they encounter and engage one another in the public sphere. Propositions about conflict, complementarity, and complexity are all propositions about how religion and science realize, or fail to realize, this deliberative ideal. Good debate is deliberative debate.

Consider Robertson and Dawkins again. Their statements in the public sphere are undoubtedly nonviolent participation. They are saying things in the public sphere. Other people can hear what they are saying and use that to inform their own decision making. However, Robertson and Dawkins are not actually encountering or engaging each other with ideas, arguments, and claims. To the extent that they acknowledge other persons or positions, such acknowledgment is simply prelude to derisory rhetoric and insults. This is participation, but it is not deliberation. So it is not good debate.

Conflict, complementarity, and complexity each draw on the deliberative ideal to suggest an answer to the question "Is good debate between religion and science possible?" From a conflict perspective, the answer is "no." Good debate is not possible because science and religion are at war. There is no interest in engagement. Religion and science are eternally and inevitably opposed. Further, for those working in a secularization mode, religion is an active problem for public deliberation because it benefits from subverting rational thought and argument. Religion cannot therefore legitimately participate in public debate. So the best thing to do is to wait out (or accelerate) the decline of religion so that the rational society can progress and a truly deliberative public sphere, based on shared public (secular) reason, can emerge.

From a complementarity perspective, the answer is "yes," and in the case of dialogue advocates, "yes, please." Deliberation is necessary in encounters between religion and science. Deliberative debate between science and religion generates and fosters productive relationships between two influential domains of society. In the NOMA model, deliberation clarifies the differences between religion and science. Such boundary work is key to maintaining the two magisteria as nonoverlapping, and thus crucial to keeping the peace. In the dialogue model, deliberation is necessary to identify common areas of concern and to move toward reconciliation between potentially conflicting viewpoints on those issues, again with an eye toward peace.

For complexity advocates, the answer is "yes, but not always, and not always in the same way." While deliberative debate is possible, whether or not deliberative debate is possible for religion and science is not a single, universally applicable question. There have been times when such deliberative debate has happened and other times when it has not. So it is at least possible. But look carefully at the underlying commitment to debunking the conflict narrative. That commitment is itself grounded in the deliberative ideal. If we are going to argue about religion and science, complexity advocates suggest, we should at least be having an informed debate about empirical cases rather than resorting to inadequate and counterproductive stereotypes left over from a previous century.

Why Does Good Debate about Religion and Science Matter?

All three major perspectives on religion and science are concerned about good debate. If the religion-and-science literature were just a few isolated pieces scattered across the scholarly landscape, we might shrug and move on. But this is not the case. Obviously, different disciplines vary across time in their interest levels in science and religion. For example, sociology began the twentieth century very interested in questions of religion and science, turned its attention elsewhere in mid-century, and only recently has experienced a resurgence of interest in religion-and-science questions.[35] But across disciplines, and throughout the past century, "religion and science" has been of enduring popular and scholarly concern. People are interested.

But why? As a recent book title asks about religion-and-science debate, "Why does it continue?"[36] There are many answers to this question. But one of the most obvious is that these debates are sustained and durable because many complicated social arrangements depend on how the debates unfold. For example, debates between creationists and evolution proponents are not just about abstract origin stories. They also concern the education of American citizens and the state's role in enforcing a particular view of the educated citizen. Debates about the efficacy of prayer and the health benefits of religiosity are important battlegrounds over the political authority of religion to influence the government, the role of science in determining good medicine, and the foundations of medical ethics. Abortion debates certainly involve issues of life and death, but historically they have also engaged "the role of women, the role of the state as a moral agent, . . . the right to privacy, the nature of democracy, and society's obligation to those in need."[37]

As entrenched institutions with connections to multiple sources of power, religion and science are also powerful sources of legitimacy. Empirically, debates become more significant when they draw on religion or science for legitimation. For example, patients with HIV/AIDS were largely dismissed as participants in debates about research and treatment until they appropriated the cultural authority of science.[38] Abortion is a prominent public issue in part because it is inextricably connected to religious "master frames" that claim transcendent truth about life and death.[39] Debates over homosexuality have become more prominent as participants have invoked scientific claims about a "gay gene" or the benefits of "affirmation therapy" to counter religious claims about the correct form of sexual relations.[40]

When we argue about religion and science, we are arguing about many other things at the same time. Science and religion debates are not simply objects of abstract interest or self-contained hermetic spheres of debate restricted to a few narrow or technical questions. Religion and science debates endure because they are important and influential more broadly in public life. They are important not just because they are about religion and science, but especially because they are also about many other things.

What I propose in this book is a basic shift in thinking about religion and science in public life. Instead of thinking about science and religion as a problem for public debate, we should think about public debate as a problem for science and religion. That is, if we think there are problems with religion-and-science debates (and every single perspective makes this claim), then I suggest that the problems lie in features of public debate rather than (necessarily) features of religion and science. If we want to know whether good debate between religion and science is possible, we need to consider the question of good debate.

REPRESENTATIVES AND PUBLIC LIFE

While debate certainly involves ideas, perspectives, and arguments, ultimately it is people who communicate ideas, articulate perspectives, and make arguments. People debate. So claims about the quality of public debate, however abstract or theoretical in their expression, are ultimately empirical claims about participants in public debate. At the risk of abusing one example, I point again to the opening quotes from Robertson and Dawkins. The question of good debate between religion and science, whatever else it might be, is an empirical question about what participants say and do in discussions involving religion and science.

Practically speaking, not everyone can participate in every discussion all of the time. Nor could we follow every discussion even if they did. So in this book I focus on representatives in public debate. Recall that by "representatives" I mean elite actors who define, present, and debate important issues before the widest possible audience, usually by contributing to general-audience mass media such as newspapers or television. Such access to general-audience mass media is highly restricted, so most Americans are not representatives in this sense. Rather, most Americans are ordinary people. By "ordinary people" I simply mean those persons who do not participate in public debate as it occurs in mass media. While there are many ordinary people in America, relatively few representatives participate in American public life.

Representing Religion and Science

In the most basic sense, representation is the "making present" or "representing" of something or someone that is not present.[41] To enable productive discussion on issues of interest to a large number of people, a relatively small group of actors represents the positions, opinions, and arguments of larger groups. Theories of representation are theories about the connection between ordinary people and elite representatives. The problem of representation is how do we get from a large group of interested people to an elite group of actors who have the power to participate in public debate?

In religion-and-science debates, ordinary people are often disconnected from elites. Formally appointed leaders such as church council members or clergy may have a different set of priorities than laypeople, because of different levels of personal commitments to social causes, or because their organizational duties may outweigh the need to represent ordinary believers, a situation commonly referred to as the "clergy-laity gap."[42] Elites might also leverage one set of issues and positions to gain power or elite standing, then change their minds or drift from their original positions so that the original set of issues is no longer salient, as with Christian politicians such as Jimmy Carter.[43]

The situation for science is similar. An entire scholarly subfield, called public understanding of science, exists solely to study the gaps between scientists and ordinary people.[44] Explanations for these gaps range from a "knowledge deficit" on the part of ordinary people to a "values conflict" between elite scientists and ordinary people.[45] At the same time that scientific elites emphasize the truth of claims about, for example, evolutionary origins or genetic markers for sexuality, ordinary people often operate with "vernacular knowledge" that is scientifically "wrong" but useful for building social relationships and communicating with other ordinary people.[46]

If the ideal of the public sphere is deliberative, and representatives are the ones who are supposed to be encountering and engaging one another in a deliberative public sphere, what does it mean that ordinary people and elite representatives are disconnected? What does it mean that Robertson and Dawkins, for example, are representatives of (respectively) religion and science? How do ordinary people evaluate representatives like Robertson and Dawkins? How does this evaluation shape public debate? How does it affect our understanding of what science and religion are doing in the public sphere?

The Good Representative

Representation has long been a central problem for political theorists. But until very recently, most normative theories of representation were grounded in empirical assumptions about elections and democracy.[47] When scholars talk about political representation, they usually mean electoral representation in democratic states.[48] Through the electoral process, ordinary people authorize, assess, and hold accountable representatives who speak or act on their behalf in the arena of institutional politics.[49] If an elected representative ceases to be a good representative, then he or she soon ceases to be an elected representative. So, in theory, representatives do what ordinary people want them to do.

But, in practice, electoral theories of representation fail to account for actually existing representatives in two ways. First, even for formal political representatives, there is often no electoral process, no authorization, and no accountability. For example, agents of international nongovernmental organizations, such as the Red Cross or Amnesty International, are generally recognized as representatives of prisoners of war or political prisoners, obviously without electoral authorization. World Trade Organization representatives are recognized as representatives of their respective countries but are neither elected by their countries nor particularly accountable to their country's populace. Subcomandante Marcos is widely recognized as a representative of the Zapatista movement, despite the fact that the entire existence of the Zapatistas presupposes an alternative model of political organization and action.[50] The only thing these representatives have in common is that some people see them as representative.

Second, representatives exist throughout society, not just in formal political institutions.[51] For example, in the controversy over creation and evolution, school board members, church officials, prominent scientists, and local government officials confront each other in courtrooms, marshal public support through interviews and opinion editorials, and petition curriculum committees.[52] In the controversy over human genetic engineering, scientists, bioethicists, theologians, philosophers, and politicians jostle for position on government advisory panels, institutional review boards, congressional committees, and the leadership of professional associations.[53] Clergy members make claims about the environment or sexuality directly from the pulpit, even as scientists publish scholarly articles and books on those same issues.[54] The only thing these representatives have in common is that they participate in public debates that occur in a variety of settings across American society.

So, what counts as a good representative in public debate? This is a complex empirical question. It is not simply a question of elections and their outcomes. To answer this question requires tracking what representatives in public debate actually do and say. But it also requires asking what ordinary people think about what representatives do and say. In public debate, what counts as a good representative depends on the connections between representatives and ordinary Americans.

Generally speaking, whether representatives are seen as good representatives or not depends on whether or not their words and actions align with what ordinary Americans expect from them. But since public debate shapes what we can talk about, what we know about it, how we talk about it, and what we can do about it, this evaluation process has specific consequences for religion and science. What people think about science and religion representatives in public debate shapes what they think about religion, science, and conflict in American public life more broadly.

How Representatives Matter

Representatives in public debate shape social life in two key ways. First, representatives shape the perception, formation, and organization of social groups. Pierre Bourdieu, drawing on a tradition leading back to Thomas Hobbes, theorized that representation is primarily a constitutive process.[55] Representatives do not just reflect the interests or identity of a territorially defined constituency, as in elections; they also create the symbolic meaning of a group membership, for members and for nonmembers. Subcomandante Marcos may be an exemplar to those within the Zapatista movement, but his main symbolic power is that he represents that group to observers across the world, who shape their own perceptions of, and actions toward, the Zapatistas based on what they know of Marcos.[56]

Such constitutive power has concrete effects. Groups organize based not only on support for or solidarity with their own exemplars, but also against those they perceive to be representative of their opposition. For example, American lesbian and gay activist groups changed their organization, frames, claims, and mobilization tactics in response to the rise and fall of Anita Bryant as a representative of the Christian Right anti-gay rights movement.[57] Similarly, mass media attention to one set of representatives rather than another effectively contained the Students for a Democratic Society (SDS) by shaping the public perception of SDS both for its members and for broader American society, resulting in the "unmaking" of the New Left.[58]

This matters for religion-and-science debates because it means that Pat Robertson and Richard Dawkins are not simply Pat Robertson and Richard Dawkins. They are part of a process that constitutes religion and science in the public sphere. When Robertson claims religious authority in public debate, he is in part defining for ordinary people what it means to be religious in that debate. When Dawkins claims scientific authority, he is in part defining for ordinary people what it means to be scientific in that debate. This does not mean that meanings transfer unproblematically from representatives to ordinary people or that such activity overrides all other available definitions of "religion" and "science." The point is that representatives in public debates about religion and science constitute (in part) what such debates are about, who is involved, what is at stake in each debate, and, most basically, what counts as religion and science in each debate.

Second, representatives shape what kinds of debate and discussion are possible. One way this happens is by shaping the content of the knowledge on which debate is grounded. For example, having representatives from the AIDS activist community involved in AIDS policy changed scientific knowledge about AIDS to include "lay expertise," rather than just clinical or experimental data, which in turn led to changes in AIDS policy making and substantive health outcomes.[59] Much of the recent dispute in the United States over such issues as climate change or Intelligent Design hinges on who is seen as speaking for scientists, with requisite attempts on all sides to prove that they are the real representatives of "scientific consensus."[60] And, more generally, because most scientific research builds on earlier research, established representatives of a particular position or field have a disproportionate effect on the content of subsequent scientific knowledge.

Representatives also shape discussion more directly by maneuvering to control debate in a way that favors their position. For example, the profession of "bioethicist" emerged from a jurisdictional battle among representatives over who could legitimately speak for ethics.[61] As a result, debate about ethics in science shifted from substantive rationality to formal rationality, excluding questions about ends in favor of questions about means. Likewise, important differences between the institutional position of representatives in Germany and the United States led to dramatically different types of public debate over abortion. In particular, those seen as representative by media in the United States are more likely to dominate debate, whereas in Germany those seen as representative of a political party, union, or organized religion dominate debate, regardless of media involvement.[62]

This ability to maneuver matters for religion-and-science debates because it means that representatives have an advantage in shaping subsequent debate, as they are the ones already prominent in public life. Such prominence can happen for many reasons unrelated to the quality of their arguments or their willingness to engage with other public sphere participants. For example, Pat Robertson benefits from the Christian Right's enormous investment of resources in media efforts over the past thirty years.[63] These efforts have targeted precisely the kind of attention that makes Robertson prominent in general-audience mass media. Even if a new representative appears in public debate and attempts to engage Robertson, that representative must do so, in part, on the terms set by Robertson. So representatives in public debates about religion and science do not just shape current debate; they also shape the possibilities for future debate.

BOOK OUTLINE AND PREVIEW OF FINDINGS

The basic plan of the book is to report what debates look like now, how representatives participate, how ordinary people evaluate them, why representatives do what they do, and what that means for what happens next. To anticipate the findings of the book, let me answer the main question first: Is good debate about religion and science possible? I say "yes." But it depends on aligning visions of good debate, not on aligning religion and science. In the chapters that follow, I break this answer down along a number of dimensions. Figure 1 provides a visual summary of the book's structure and argument.

Chapters 2 and 3 address the common claim that there is a problem with religion-and-science debates by analyzing four existing debates in American news media. Chapter 2 looks at debates over human origins and stem cell research, in which conflict is claimed to occur. Chapter 3 examines debates over the origins of homosexuality and environmental policy, in which encounters between religion and science might conceivably occur. Regardless of the issue at stake, public participants are rarely engaged with one another in discussion and argument at all. Religion talk and science talk tend to occur separately in mass media. Newspaper articles about science tend strongly to avoid religion, and vice versa. The most prominent representatives of religion and science in each debate, such as Pat Robertson or Richard Dawkins, simply promote their own agenda or engage historical figures that are not part of contemporary debate.

Religion and science representatives in existing debates are not engaged in deliberative talk. So what are they doing instead? And why does it matter? Chapter 4 uses data from the debate analysis and archival sources to show that for the most visible representatives in these debates, good debate means advancing an agenda. While a few representatives attempt to engage in more deliberative public talk, the highest-visibility representatives of religion and science (and other social institutions) consistently pursue advocacy rather than deliberative debate.

The obvious explanation for why representatives do what they do is that ordinary people want them to do it. Chapter 5 uses interview data to show that this is not the case. Representatives and ordinary people disagree over what counts as good debate. In contrast to

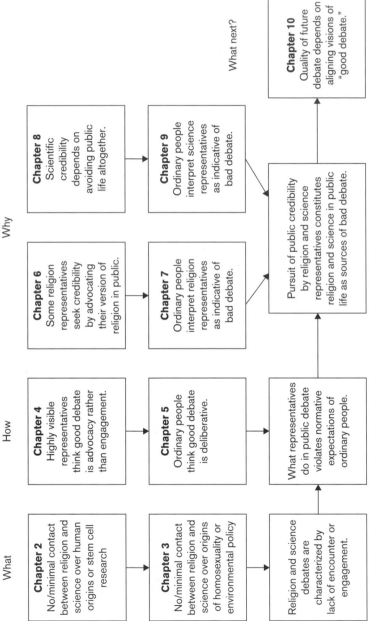

What

Chapter 2
No/minimal contact between religion and science over human origins or stem cell research

Chapter 3
No/minimal contact between religion and science over origins of homosexuality or environmental policy

Religion and science debates are characterized by lack of encounter or engagement.

How

Chapter 4
Highly visible representatives think good debate is advocacy rather than engagement.

Chapter 5
Ordinary people think good debate is deliberative.

What representatives do in public debate violates normative expectations of ordinary people.

Why

Chapter 6
Some religion representatives seek credibility by advocating their version of religion in public.

Chapter 7
Ordinary people interpret religion representatives as indicative of bad debate.

Chapter 8
Scientific credibility depends on avoiding public life altogether.

Chapter 9
Ordinary people interpret science representatives as indicative of bad debate.

Pursuit of public credibility by religion and science representatives constitutes religion and science in public life as sources of bad debate.

What next?

Chapter 10
Quality of future debate depends on aligning visions of "good debate."

FIGURE 1. Diagram of the book.

representatives, ordinary people think that good debate means engagement and deliberation. The key problem in these debates is that representatives participate in ways that conflict with what ordinary persons expect. The result is that ordinary persons negatively evaluate representatives and debates on normative grounds. For example, elected politicians are discounted in public debate because they are seen as incapable or unwilling to engage meaningfully with serious issues.

So why are representatives trying to get their way in the public sphere, rather than (or in addition to) some other setting? Drawing on theory from science and technology studies (STS), chapter 6 introduces the idea that representatives participate in the public sphere in order to pursue public credibility, which does not necessarily require deliberation. But not everyone pursues credibility in the public sphere. For example, the Religious Right pursues religious credibility in the public sphere, while the Religious Left does not. The historical domination of public debate by theologically and politically conservative religion representatives gives the Religious Right a structural advantage as those representatives continue to "own the space" of religion in public life.

Chapter 7 shows that the ways in which some people and not others pursue credibility in the public sphere shapes the possibilities for good debate in the future. Since Religious Right representatives are generally seen as working against good debate, they have poisoned the well of religion in the public sphere. Ordinary respondents, whatever their personal religious commitments, see all religion talk as inimical to good deliberative debate, no matter what its source. This effectively secular norm of public debate renders even moderate and liberal religious language and arguments either as not distinctively religious or as contrary to good debate.

And what about science? Chapter 8 shows that the dominant model of scientific credibility depends on separating the public credibility of science from any individual scientist. The result is that scientists generally do not pursue scientific credibility in the public sphere. But science remains a respected authority for ordinary Americans. With few exceptions, ordinary people are not "antiscience" in any meaningful way, even if they hold religious or other moral commitments that explicitly conflict with scientific claims.

Yet as chapter 9 demonstrates, this confidence depends on science remaining "faceless" in public life. Respondents largely endorse the public narrative of scientists as virtuous seekers of knowledge for whom participation in public life is a distraction or, at worst, corruption. Thus respondents see science as valuable, but generally disapprove of scientists in public life. In some cases, respondents think that science representatives are abusing the authority of science for their own personal gain. In other cases, such as that of Richard Dawkins, respondents think that scientists are trying to cut off good debate by deploying expert knowledge to silence opponents. Since public defense of science by science representatives runs counter to what ordinary people expect, science is particularly susceptible to challenge in public debate.

Chapter 10 returns to the opening question of the book. Good debate about religion and science is possible. But problems plaguing public debate about science and religion are deep-seated. Moreover, while there are identifiably different limits on future possibilities for religion and science to be involved in the public sphere, the root causes of problems lie in the structure of American public life and in the institutional histories that produce different versions of public credibility. But, ultimately, I think that our shared commitment to good debate in some form offers hope for our shared future.

CHAPTER 2

Considering Conflict

Human Origins and Stem Cell Research

Virtually everyone says that religion and science debates fail in some way to meet the standards of good debate. So in this and the following chapter I look at existing religion-and-science debates in order to establish what kind of debate is happening now. Is the general agreement over the quality of religion-and-science debates justified? If so, which explanation best accounts for the kinds of debates currently occurring? And what do debates about religion and science tell us about the public sphere more broadly?

In general, "public debate" is public talk as it occurs in the public sphere. But of course it is impossible to track all public talk, even about one issue. I address these questions by analyzing mass media newspaper coverage of four issues in which some participants make claims based on scientific authority and some participants make claims based on religious authority.[1] When I use the term "debate" with regard to an issue, I literally mean "the set of newspaper articles that discuss this issue." For example, the human origins debate is the set of articles from major U.S. newspapers that discuss human origins. (Such public debate is by definition "elite debate," and I use the terms interchangeably hereafter.)

The four issues that I selected are human origins, stem cell research, origins of homosexuality, and environmental policy. Each issue has both religious and scientific claims at stake. For example, human origins debate involves multiple religious claims about creation and divine intervention, as well as multiple scientific claims about human evolution. However, the kind of claims varies widely by debate. Sometimes religious claims derive from strict biblical literalism, as in human origins debate, but sometimes religious claims derive from complex theological analysis, as in the religious claim that homosexuality must be a choice because otherwise God has created sinners who cannot stop sinning. Likewise, each debate has broad policy implications. For example, environmental policy looks very different based on whether it is informed by scientific claims about anthropogenic climate change or by religious claims about the futility of intervening in a world destined for Armageddon.

While few would say that religion and science are always in conflict, there is general agreement that on some issues, substantive conflict occurs between some versions of religion and science. Human origins debate is often cited as an example of epistemological conflict in which exclusive knowledge claims from some religious and scientific sources compete for support.[2] Stem cell research debate is often cited as an example of moral conflict in which contested definitions of life, death, and personhood are incompatible with some religious beliefs.[3] Whether epistemological or moral, such conflict is an especially likely candidate for thwarting deliberative debate. So I begin with an analysis of these two debates, in which some conflict occurs.

HUMAN ORIGINS: A LIMITED ENCOUNTER

If you hear someone claiming that religion and science are in conflict, the chances are good that their illustrative examples come from debate over human origins. There is no question that visible moments of courtroom conflict, such as the Scopes trial, the rejection of "creation science," or the Intelligent Design trial *Kitzmiller v. Dover,* are part of this debate. But what part? If public debate involving religion and science fails to be deliberative, do these moments of conflict between religion and science make it so?

To answer this question about broader debate in mass media, I retrieved 3,241 relevant articles from major U.S. newspapers published from 1997 to 2007. Using a computational linguistics technique called *topic discovery,* I identified substantive topics of discussion in these articles, recorded how often each topic showed up in the articles, and calculated the probability that topics would be discussed together in any given article. Using another computational linguistics technique, called *named entity recognition,* I identified all personal and organizational names that occur in each of the articles and ranked each person or organization by how many articles mentioned the name. For each name, I also noted the other person and organization most commonly mentioned in the same articles with that name. Together, these methods identify patterns across public debate with regard to what is being discussed and who is (most often) participating.[4]

Mapping Debate by Topic

Some of the most basic claims about religion-and-science debates are actually claims about the arrangement of public talk. Take, for example, the claim that Intelligent Design is a site of conflict between science and religion.[5] This is actually a strong claim about the arrangement of public talk. Intelligent Design necessarily implicates talk about religion and talk about science. If this is true, it should be difficult to construct an account of Intelligent Design (e.g., a newspaper article) that does not also discuss both religion topics and science topics. So, when an article in mass media is about Intelligent Design, it will also be about other topics that are identifiable as religious or scientific. If it is not, further explanation is required. By mapping the distribution of discussion topics in public debate, we can evaluate whether such claims are justified.

Figure 2 maps discussion topics in the debate about human origins.[6] The more prominent topics in this debate are indicated by larger type sizes. The largest two topics by far are "Scientific Perspectives on God" and "Evolution in Schools?" The next most prominent topics are "*Kitzmiller v. Dover*," "ID and Discovery Institute," and "Human Genetic Evolution." After that are the less prominent topics "Biblical Creationism" and "Darwin's *Origin of Species*," followed by many other topics that show up even less frequently.

The distance between any two topics in figure 2 corresponds to the likelihood that an article discussing one topic also discusses the other topic. The closer two topics appear on the map, the more likely they are to be discussed together in any given article. So, for example, an article that discusses "Human Genetic Evolution" is highly unlikely to also discuss "Supreme Court and Religion." But an article that discusses "Biblical Creationism" is highly likely to also discuss "Darwin's *Origin of Species*." Note that some of the most prominent topics (by far) are highly unlikely to occur together in public debate.

The overall pattern in figure 2 is one of separation between religion and science in debate over human origins. On the left (especially upper left) of the topic map are several topics that concern issues internal to, or

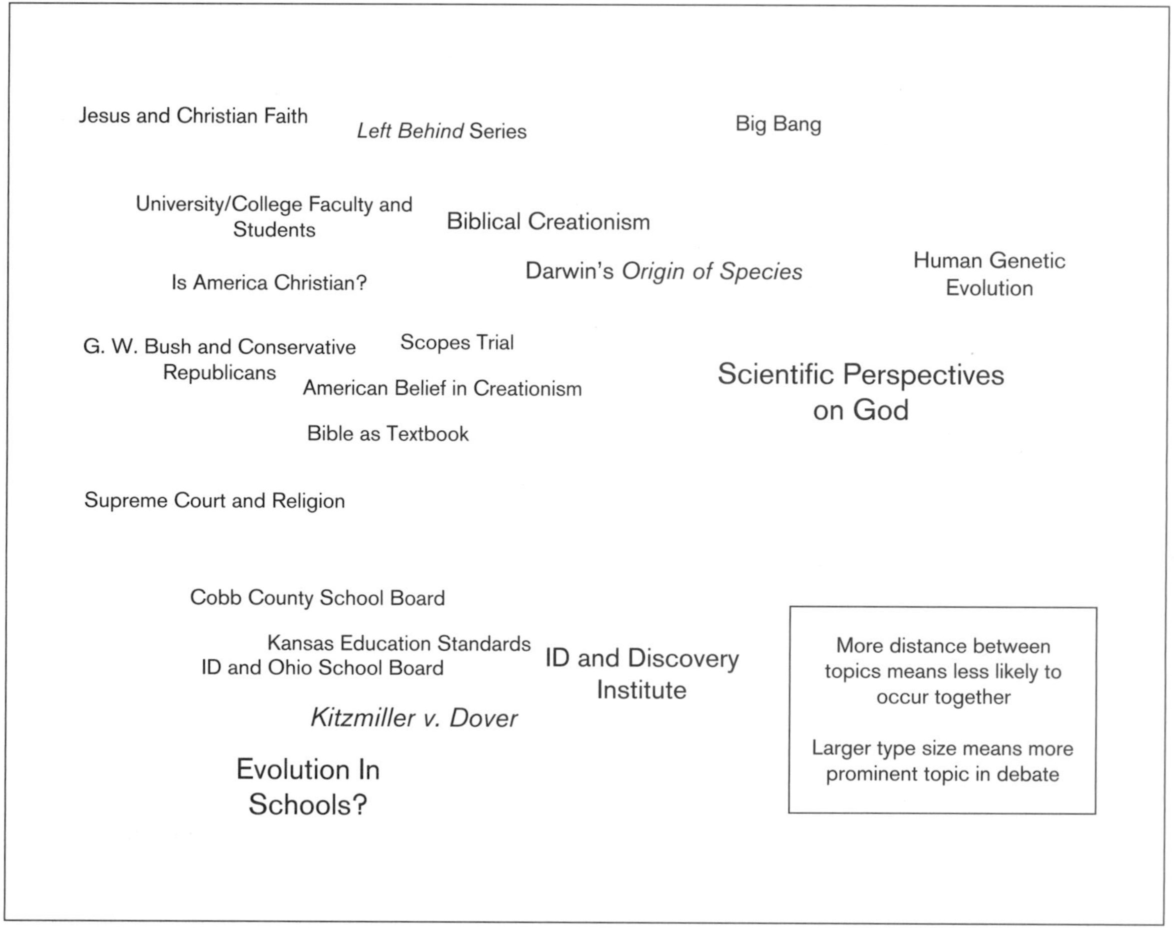

Jesus and Christian Faith   *Left Behind* Series   Big Bang

University/College Faculty and   Biblical Creationism
                Students
                                                                Human Genetic
            Is America Christian?   Darwin's *Origin of Species*   Evolution

G. W. Bush and Conservative   Scopes Trial
          Republicans   American Belief in Creationism   Scientific Perspectives
                                                                      on God
                        Bible as Textbook

Supreme Court and Religion

Cobb County School Board
        Kansas Education Standards   ID and Discovery
ID and Ohio School Board   Institute

            Kitzmiller v. Dover

            Evolution In
            Schools?

More distance between
topics means less likely to
occur together

Larger type size means more
prominent topic in debate

FIGURE 2. Topic map: human origins debate.

characteristic of, religion. For example, "*Left Behind* Series" refers to evangelical Christian novels about the End Times as prophesied in the Christian New Testament's Book of Revelation, while "Jesus and Christian Faith" is self-explanatory. These religion topics tend to involve one another in public debate. A document about the topic "Is America Christian?" is likely also to discuss "American Belief in Creationism" or "G. W. Bush and Conservative Republicans." It is especially unlikely to focus on "Human Genetic Evolution." For the most part, discussion of one religion topic is more likely to involve discussion of a related religion topic.

On the right side of the figure are several obviously scientific topics. "Human Genetic Evolution," "Big Bang," and "Scientific Perspectives on God" are closest to the topic "Darwin's *Origin of Species,*" but they are farthest away from topics about religion, education, and church (see upper left of figure 2). Discussion of evolution as it relates to other scientific issues is largely self-contained. To the extent that God or religion figures in this discussion, it is about what scientists think about God and religion, rather than engagement with explicitly religious topics such as "Jesus and Christian Faith." Discussion of "Human Genetic Evolution," while relatively prominent overall, is much more likely to occur with discussion about what scientists think about God and religion than it is to occur with discussion about teaching evolution in schools.

At the center bottom of figure 2 are topics about the teaching of evolution and Intelligent Design in public schools.[7] This part of the map includes the most prominent topic in the entire debate, "Evolution in Schools?" Note that most of the topics are about specific instances (e.g., court cases such as *Kitzmiller v. Dover*) when Intelligent Design proponents have attempted to introduce their own materials into local school science curricula. Although several of these topics contain references to evolution or science, they are distinct from scientific discussion of these issues. That is, discussion about teaching of evolution in schools is separate from scientific discussions about human origins (and related scientific issues). Articles about any of these specific topics are likely to involve discussion of related legal topics, but as the distance indicates, they are not likely to involve discussion of the science topics depicted on the figure's right side.

What does this pattern of separation between religion, science, and legal topics mean? Recall that deliberative debate minimally requires encounter and engagement. As figure 2 illustrates, encounter and engagement do not generally happen for religion and science in human origins debate as a whole. A limited encounter does occur, as articles about biblical creationism are more likely to also discuss Darwin's *Origin of Species* than to discuss any other topic.[8] But aside from this limited encounter over the truth of two competing claims, the three topic areas tend to be self-contained discussions. Science topics tend to involve other discussion of science or scientists. Religion topics tend to involve other discussion of religion. And discussion of what to teach in schools tends to involve discussion of related legal cases rather than discussion of religion or science topics. Even though discussion about teaching evolution in schools and discussion about scientific perspectives on God and religion feature prominently in the debate about human origins, they tend to do so separately, and rarely mix in actual debate.

Mapping Debate by Representatives

Looking at the overall distribution of public debate over human origins, it appears that religion and science are mostly separate, rather than engaged. From this perspective, debate generally fails to be deliberative, not because of instances of conflict, but because the preconditions for deliberative debate simply do not occur. No encounter, no engagement, no deliberative debate. But even if this is true for debate as a whole, it still could be the case that the most prominent representatives, the ones whom people are most likely to see, are actually encountering and engaging one another in smaller parts of public debate. Looking at topics alone would not show this, so we also need to look at what the top representatives in human origins debate are doing.

Table 1 reports the top ten representatives in this debate, ranked by the number of individual newspaper articles in which their name occurs. The most striking feature of this top ten list is that more than half of the most prominent representatives in current public debate are dead—in most cases, long dead. Charles Darwin, the naturalist whose books *The Origin of Species* and *The Descent of Man* laid the foundation for an evolutionary theory of human origins, clearly dominates. John Scopes, William Jennings Bryan, and Clarence Darrow, all key figures in the famous 1925 Scopes Monkey Trial, figure prominently in the debate. So too does Stephen Jay Gould, science popularizer and highly cited evolutionary biologist,[9] and Galileo Galilei, the late-sixteenth–early-seventeenth-century astronomer and physicist whose support for Copernicanism drew the attention of the Catholic Church.

The living representatives are a diverse bunch. George W. Bush, a recent U.S. president, is only somewhat less prominent than Charles

TABLE 1   TOP TEN REPRESENTATIVES IN THE HUMAN ORIGINS DEBATE

Person	No. of Articles	Person Most Often Occurring With	Org. Most Often Occurring With
Charles Darwin	≥ 500	John Scopes	Discovery Institute
George W. Bush	≥ 450	Charles Darwin	Discovery Institute
John E. Jones III	≥ 190	Charles Darwin	Dover Area School District
John Scopes	≥ 175	Charles Darwin	U.S. Supreme Court
Michael Behe	126	Charles Darwin	Lehigh University
Eugenie Scott	122	Charles Darwin	NCSE
Stephen Jay Gould	110	Charles Darwin	Harvard University
William Jennings Bryan	100	Clarence Darrow	ACLU
Galileo Galilei	97	Charles Darwin	Catholic Church
Clarence Darrow	92	William Jennings Bryan	U.S. Supreme Court

Darwin in this debate.[10] The remaining representatives in the top ten are participants in the controversy over teaching Intelligent Design in schools. John E. Jones III, a U.S. district judge, presided over the *Kitzmiller* case, which ruled against the introduction of Intelligent Design materials in Dover, Pennsylvania, science classes. Michael Behe, a biochemist and senior fellow at the Discovery Institute, advocates Intelligent Design. Eugenie Scott, a physical anthropologist and former executive director of the National Center for Science Education (NCSE), has consistently fought against the introduction of creationist or ID materials into science classrooms.

If we ignored the long-dead representatives, we could probably come up with a way to link some of these representatives with the topic map in the previous section. Stephen Jay Gould, for example, publicly expressed views about the place of religion in the world and the relation of religion to science. Such discussion maps approximately onto the prominent topic "Scientific Perspectives on God." Likewise, the several representatives in the controversy over ID in the classroom map onto the prominent topics "*Kitzmiller v. Dover*," "ID and Discovery Institute," and "Evolution in Schools?"

But what of Galileo? Galileo predates Darwin, so he obviously has not taken sides when it comes to Darwinian evolution and biblical creationism. Neither does he have much to say about what to teach in American public schools, whether America is a Christian nation, or the qualities of the *Left Behind* series. So what is Galileo doing in debates over human origins? There seems no obvious correspondence with the substantive topics being discussed in human origins debate.

For that matter, what of Charles Darwin? If you look only at the top representatives in table 1 without reference to the topic map, you might say that the human origins debate is just one giant discussion about Charles Darwin. Darwin is the person most commonly occurring with almost every top representative. The main exception is Darwin himself, who occurs primarily alongside John Scopes (the Monkey Trial defendant). The only other exception is Clarence Darrow, the defense counsel in the Scopes trial, who occurs primarily with William Jennings Bryan, the trial's prosecutor. Looking at top representatives in the debate, it appears that Charles Darwin is a sort of central core of debate, even though many of the topics in the map, whether scientific (e.g., Big Bang) or religious (e.g., *Left Behind* Series) do not have substantive connections to Charles Darwin's historical scientific claims.

What Representatives Do

Obviously Charles Darwin and Galileo Galilei are not personally participating in public debate over human origins. What is happening is that living representatives are invoking the names of dead representatives to help make a case for their agenda or position. Despite the wide range of substantive topics, Darwin, Galileo, John Scopes, Stephen Jay Gould, and other deceased representatives show up consistently across debate as living representatives invoke them. These deceased representatives are recognized and often esteemed exemplars. Attaching them to a claim, whether as friend or enemy, can make the claim more credible.[11]

Drilling down to the individual news articles that make up the data set, this pattern becomes clear. For example, opponents of Intelligent Design gain advantage by linking ID efforts to failed past efforts to change science curricula in schools, such as "creation science." Invoking Galileo and the Scopes trial transforms a local school board dispute over evolution in the classroom into the latest instance of how religion tries to leverage power to stop science, just as the Catholic Church did to Galileo, or as Protestant fundamentalists did to John Scopes (and, by extension, Charles Darwin). At the same time, ID proponents such as Discovery Institute fellow John West also invoke Galileo and the Scopes trial to transform the dispute into an issue of government overreach and censorship: "The effort to try to suppress ideas that you dislike, to use the government to suppress ideas you dislike, has a failed history. . . . Do they really want to be on the side of the people who didn't want to let John Scopes talk or who tried to censor Galileo?"[12]

The invocation of representatives as exemplars works for some living representatives, as well. Take George W. Bush. Looking at specific mentions in articles, it is clear that some mentions are made simply because Bush is a reference point for government and lawmaking. But many, and perhaps most, of the mentions concern comments he made about creationism. For example, when asked directly whether he believed that the Bible is literally true and a guide to science, Bush replied, "I think that for example on the issue of evolution, the verdict is still out on how God created the earth. . . . I don't use the Bible as necessarily a way to predict the findings of science."[13] Throughout the debate, Bush is invoked by supporters as representative of their own position, and by opponents as the representative of their (perhaps idealized) opposition.

More important here, though, is what is not happening. The most prominent representatives, the ones whom people are most likely to see in public debate, are not actually engaged in debate with one another over substantive topics. They are, first and foremost, engaged in a struggle to define the debate on their own terms.[14] This struggle does not require engagement with other representatives and, in practice, may require avoiding such engagement altogether. Eugenie Scott, for example, regularly portrays ID efforts as the latest in a continuing series of efforts to defeat science, no different than "creation science" or similarly religious efforts.[15] This is not a consideration of the substantive merits of Intelligent Design. Nor is it an engagement with ID proponents. It is a dismissal of the topic altogether as unworthy of engagement.

Let's return to the now familiar examples of Pat Robertson and Richard Dawkins. Both of these representatives show up prominently in public debate over human origins (Robertson more than Dawkins, but both are in the top thirty by article mentions). When Pat Robertson makes his statement about God's judgment on the citizens of Dover, Pennsylvania, he is referring to the Intelligent Design decision. But he is not actually debating Intelligent Design. Instead, he is staking out the position that debate should really be about what God wants people to do. Likewise, when Richard Dawkins makes his statement about people who do not believe in evolution, he is not actually debating evolution. Instead, he is staking out the position that evolution is beyond question, so we should be debating what to do about religious resistance.

Representatives in the human origins debate may make specific claims about, for example, biblical creationism, what to teach in public schools, or scientific perspectives on God. But they are primarily participating in the public sphere in order to advance an agenda or to advocate for a particular position. Understanding this point helps align the information from analysis of topics with that from analysis of top representatives. The agenda or position that representatives are advocating need not require engagement with other representatives. It may be about the fundamental legitimacy of a topic, the virtues of supporters, the historical precedents of an issue, or the qualities of the representative doing the talking.

It is true that there are some instances of conflict in debate over human origins. But this does not mean that the rest of human origins debate is deliberative. To the contrary, engagement of any sort between religion and science in this debate is unusual. In general, talk about religion and talk about science tend to be separate. And the most prominent representatives are not actually engaging one another in debate. They are advocating their positions and pursuing their agendas. Human origins debate is a limited encounter between religion and science. But, oddly enough, the few instances of conflict may be the only substantive engagement between religion and science in this debate.

STEM CELL RESEARCH: DEBATE BY PROXY

Stem cell research provides another case in which conflict is clearly part of public debate. Unlike human origins debate in which exclusive knowledge claims compete to explain reality, stem cell research debate involves moral conflicts in which scientific and technological claims invoke contested definitions of life, death, and personhood. There is no question that these claims involve substantive moral conflicts for at least some religious believers.[16]

But does this moral conflict translate into a problem for public debate? If so, how? And if so, does moral conflict present a different problem than epistemological conflict? To answer these questions about broader debate in mass media, I retrieved 2,605 relevant articles from major U.S. newspapers published from 2002 to 2007. As with human origins debate, I identified and mapped topics of discussion across the entire debate, and identified and ranked all persons and organizations mentioned in these articles.

Mapping Debate by Topic

If there is an obvious and direct engagement between religion and science over stem cell research, what we would see in a topic map is science topics and religion topics in close proximity, either directly to one another or to a topic over which they are debating. An interesting variation in stem cell research debate is whether the alleged encounter is based on moral concerns over similarities to abortion or on other grounds.[17] For example, if religion and science are engaging each other over moral issues, then religion topics and science topics should occur in close proximity to topics associated with moral concerns, such as discussions about abortion or bioethics.

Figure 3 shows the topic map for stem cell research debate. As before, larger type size indicates higher prominence in debate. The most prominent topic by far is "Human Embryonic Stem Cell Research" (hereafter "Human ESCR"). The next most prominent is "Party Politics." These are followed by "Religious Morals in Public Life," "Taxes and Health Care," and "Catholic Views on Abortion." The remaining topics vary slightly in prominence, as indicated by type size.

On the left side of figure 3 are several closely arranged topics related to science. The most prominent topic in this area (and the entire debate) is the science topic "Human ESCR." Articles that are about human ESCR are most likely to also discuss other closely related science topics, such as "Human Cloning" or "Bone Marrow Cancer Treatment." Discussion of these topics centers primarily on the technical or scientific aspects of various forms of research related to stem cells. Similar scientific research or techniques, such as in vitro fertilization, also tend to be discussed in the same articles. Discussion of these topics is unlikely to involve nonscience topics, such as "Party Politics," and least likely to involve discussion of religion topics, such as "Evangelical Christians" or "Vatican II."

On the right side of figure 3 are several closely arranged topics related to religion. This area also contains one of the most prominent topics, "Religious Morals in Public Life." Articles about this topic are more likely to also discuss "Vatican II," "Catholic Views on Abortion," or "Evangelical Christians." This makes sense, as these topics relate to denomination or group-level variations on (for example) "Religious Morals in Public Life." But while discussion of religion might also involve political topics, it rarely involves scientific or technical topics such as "Human Cloning" or "Human ESCR." As with human origins debate, most religion talk is distinct and separate from science talk. Discussion of religion topics tends to involve discussion of other religion topics.

At the top center of figure 3 is the highly prominent topic "Party Politics," which might reasonably be called a prominent outlier. "Party Politics" embraces inside-baseball discussion of what Republicans and

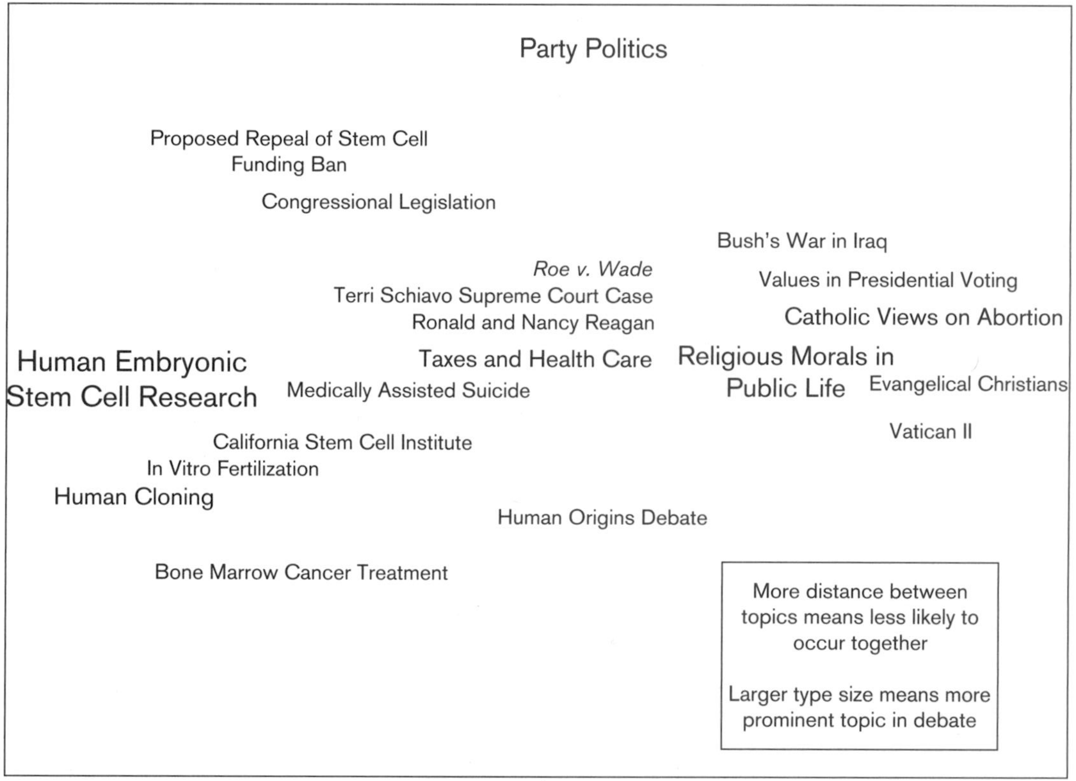

FIGURE 3. Topic map: stem cell research debate.

Democrats (primarily) are up to in their political moves. Articles regarding "Party Politics" are usually about little else. But note that "Party Politics" is very far away from obviously scientific or obviously religious topics. If an article about party politics is also about something else, that something will most likely be a related politics topic, such as "Congressional Legislation" or "Taxes and Health Care," but not "Bone Marrow Cancer Treatment" or "Evangelical Christians."

Many topics in stem cell research debate are equally likely to involve politics and religion topics or science topics, or both. For example, articles about "Proposed Repeal of Stem Cell Research Funding Ban" or "Medically Assisted Suicide" are just as likely to also be about "Party Politics" as about "Human ESCR." Articles about "Bush's War in Iraq" are equally likely to also be about "Party Politics" as about "Evangelical Christians." An article about "Taxes and Health Care" is equally likely to also be about "California Stem Cell Institute" or "Catholic Views on Abortion." And topics such as "Terri Schiavo Supreme Court Case" and "Ronald and Nancy Reagan" are about equally likely to involve religion, science, and politics topics.

Finally, near the bottom center of figure 3 is the infrequent topic "Human Origins Debate." As might be expected, "Human Origins Debate" is equally likely to occur with religion topics or science topics. But note that this is not two topics with competing claims (as in "Darwin's *Origin of Species*" and "Biblical Creationism" in human origins debate). People are not actually debating human origins. They are invoking the human origins debate as an example of conflict between religion and science. So, while "Human Origins Debate" is equally likely to involve religion or science topics, it does not indicate a substantive encounter between religion and science in this debate.

What patterns can we see in this topic map? If we momentarily disregard the topics in the center of the map, the overall pattern of separation between religion and science is easy to see. And, as expected, moral concerns emerge in several topics. But such topics tend to involve religion rather than science. In stem cell research debate, as in human origins debate, religion and science are not directly encountering one another. The more interesting pattern is that a variety of topics are equally likely to implicate religion topics, science topics, and politics topics. This raises the possibility that even though religion and science are not directly encountering one another, they might be engaged in a sort of encounter by proxy in which both religion and science are equally implicated in the discussion of other political issues.

Mapping Debate by Representatives

So, what is going on in this debate? On one hand, science and religion topics appear to be separate, as in human origins debate. No encounter, no engagement, no deliberative debate. On the other hand, encounter and engagement could be happening over certain political issues. The topic map shows that science and religion are sometimes involved in these discussions, but how they are involved is less clear. As before, we need to look at what top representatives, the representatives whom people are most likely to see, are doing when they participate in this debate.

Table 2 shows the top ten most visible persons in stem cell research debate. Two things immediately stand out. First, most of the top representatives in this debate are involved in institutional politics at the highest levels of the U.S. government. George W. Bush, Bill Clinton, and Ronald Reagan are former U.S. presidents as well as former state governors. John Kerry, Mitt Romney, and Sam Brownback are all former presidential candidates. Bill Frist was the Republican majority leader in the U.S. Senate during most of this period. Nancy Reagan was the First Lady during the Reagan presidency and, notably, the motivating force behind the U.S. government's "Just Say No" campaign.

Second, U.S. president George W. Bush dominates this debate, even though others are also prominent. Bush shows up in (at least) every other article in the debate. Even John Kerry, Bush's Democratic opponent in the 2004 U.S. presidential election, appears in less than half as many articles as Bush does. Bush and Kerry are obviously a step above the rest, however. Pope John Paul II, the formal leader of the worldwide Catholic Church and the only explicit religion representative in table 2, shows up in almost one out of every ten articles, but still comes nowhere close to Bush and Kerry.[18] Terri Schiavo, a Florida patient at the center of a right-to-die controversy, garners only half as many mentions as the pope. Note that there are no obvious science representatives in the upper echelon of representatives.

At the top level, this debate involves mostly politicians and a pope. The co-occurrence information in table 2 further reinforces the picture of politician dominance in general, and Bush's dominance in particular. The top ten representatives in this debate tend to occur with Bush. The exception is Bush, with whom Kerry shows up most often. In other words, Bush is so prominent in stem cell research debate that no matter who is mentioned in a news article, they are likely to be mentioned with George W. Bush. Note also that, in contrast to human origins debate,

TABLE 2   TOP TEN REPRESENTATIVES IN THE STEM CELL RESEARCH DEBATE

Person	No. of Articles	Person Most Often Occurring With	Org. Most Often Occurring With
George W. Bush	≥ 1,300	John Kerry	U.S. Congress
John Kerry	≥ 600	George W. Bush	Catholic Church
Pope John Paul II	≥ 250	George W. Bush	Catholic Church
Bill Clinton	≥ 200	George W. Bush	U.S. Congress
Ronald Reagan	≥ 200	George W. Bush	Republican Party
Bill Frist	≥ 150	George W. Bush	U.S. Congress
Terri Schiavo	135	George W. Bush	U.S. Congress
Nancy Reagan	127	George W. Bush	U.S. Congress
Sam Brownback	125	George W. Bush	U.S. Congress
Mitt Romney	106	George W. Bush	U.S. Congress

there are only a few different organizations. The Catholic Church, Republican Party, and U.S. Congress are implicated along with the top ten representatives in this debate.

What Representatives Do

What explains this dominance of institutional politics and this particular configuration of representatives and organizations among the most prominent in stem cell research debate? Drilling down to individual articles, it appears that stem cell research is a kind of litmus test for faith and politics. Politicians who profess religious affiliation, which is to say most U.S. politicians, are asked about, and talk about, their position on stem cell research in religious terms. In general, proponents of stem cell research use science talk and downplay religion. Opponents of stem cell research use religion talk.

Religion talk in stem cell research debate involves placing the issue firmly within existing religious debates about human life and personhood.[19] When Pope John Paul II shows up in stem cell research debate, he is talking about stem cell research as similar in moral terms to abortion or euthanasia, as an intervention into qualities of human personhood, rather than similar in technical terms to, say, in vitro fertilization. The explicitly religious topics derived from topic discovery map onto the American religious traditions that have traditionally opposed abortion and euthanasia: Roman Catholicism and evangelical Protestantism. Pope John Paul II shows up because he is the most prominent public religious figure to have a stake in opposing abortion and euthanasia, which he (as head of the Catholic Church) attaches to stem cell research debate.

Even though they do not use words like "God" or "Christian," many prominent politicians also justify their opposition to stem cell research by invoking general moral claims about the "sanctity of life" that locate the issue within a religious framework.[20] Mitt Romney, a self-identified Mormon, dismissed pro–stem cell research arguments as governor of Massachusetts when he wrote, "Lofty goals do not justify the creation of life for experimentation and destruction."[21] Likewise, Sam Brownback, a conservative Republican who openly identified as evangelical, proposed a cloning ban similar to the stem cell funding ban in his speech at the 2004 Republican convention: "A fundamental principle of our democracy and our Republican Party is respect for the inherent dignity, equality and sanctity of every human life. . . . We do not measure the value of a life by wealth or social status. We believe that every person is beautiful, unique, and has great purpose. Every life must be honored and protected."[22]

By contrast, representatives who support stem cell research tend to make moral claims about the potential medical benefits offered by scientific research. Nancy Reagan, for example, publicly advocated for stem cell research that would alleviate the suffering of those with degenerative diseases, such as her husband, Ronald Reagan. But these representatives do not typically debate the scientific or technical aspects of research. Rather, they mobilize science as an alternative to mobilizing religion in arguments about the moral implications of stem cell research. When Bill Frist publicly changed his position from opposing to supporting public funding for stem cell research, he also changed his public justification, moving from a "sanctity of life" position to emphasizing the potential of scientific research to bring about treatments and cures for significant diseases. And at the same 2004 Republican convention where Sam Brownback proposed a cloning ban to preserve sanctity of life, Nancy Reagan's son Ron Reagan Jr. argued that Ronald Reagan would never have allowed religion to shape his political position on something with the potential to save lives.

Whatever the personal beliefs of representatives might be, this selective deployment of religion in public debate is so patently political that it even provokes criticism from competing representatives. For example, after signing into law a ban on government funding for stem cell research, George W. Bush was widely accused of using generic moral language (e.g., "sanctity of life") to mask a religious agenda intended to attract and retain evangelical Christian voters. Similarly, after expressing public support for stem cell research as a presidential candidate, professed Catholic John Kerry was heavily criticized by Catholic bishops who suggested that he be denied Communion or even be excommunicated from the church for violating official church doctrine in the service of political ambition.[23]

What the most prominent representatives do in stem cell research debate is mobilize either religion or science, but not both, to make moral arguments that justify their political positions and advance their agendas. Stem cell research debate is actually the politics of "for" and "against." Politicians for stem cell research largely draw on arguments about the benefits of scientific research for American citizens. More commonly and more visibly, politicians against stem cell research largely draw on religious arguments about the similarity of the stem cell research issue to other issues of life and personhood, such as abortion and euthanasia. Proponents talk science. Opponents talk religion. But all are talking about the politics of moral issues.

It is true that there are some instances of moral conflict in debate over stem cell research. But, as with human origins debate, these instances of conflict are not subverting an otherwise deliberative debate between religion and science. Religion and science remain largely separate in public debate. In theory, political conflict could overcome this separation by bringing religion and science together into debate over moral issues. In practice, the most visible representatives reinforce the separation of religion and science by linking them to political differences. The apparent proxy encounter turns out to be the residue of representatives drawing on science and religion separately for moral justification of their political agendas.

RELIGION, SCIENCE, AND CONFLICT

Scholars generally agree that religion and science debates fall short of a deliberative ideal. When we think about *how* religion and science debates often fail to be deliberative, the obvious candidate is conflict. But existing debates over human origins and stem cell research, debates in which we know that some conflict occurs, seem to display a pattern of separation. When people talk about religion, they generally do not talk about science. When people talk about science, they generally do not talk about religion.

So, scholars are right. These debates fail to be deliberative. But the interesting thing is how they fail. These debates fail to be deliberative because the basic conditions for deliberative debate simply do not occur. Rather than being the exceptions in an otherwise deliberative debate, the few recognized instances of conflict are actually exceptions to a pattern of separation. In human origins debate, there is one limited encounter over biblical creationism and Darwin's theory of evolution. And in stem cell research debate, moral debates over political issues sometimes involve both religion and science, though not equally. The unexpected plot twist is that instances of conflict in these debates are the few instances when the basic conditions for deliberative debate happen at all.

CHAPTER 3

Potential Encounters

Origins of Homosexuality and
Environmental Policy

In religion-and-science debates in which most people would say that some conflict occurs, there is a general pattern of separation between religion and science. Even more surprising is that instances of conflict appear to form the only substantive engagement between religion and science in these debates. Instead of being the exception to otherwise deliberative debate, conflict appears to be the only situation in which the basic conditions for deliberative debate even occur.

But is this separation unique to the issues in which conflict is generally thought to exist, or is it part of a broader pattern across debates involving religion and science? After all, it is possible that human origins debate and stem cell research debate, however large and well known, are unusual or even unique cases. Without comparing them to other debates, we run the risk of taking two possibly unusual examples as the basis for broader claims about religion and science.

To address this possibility, I analyzed mass media newspaper coverage of two additional issues: the origins of homosexuality, and environmental policy. Both of these are issues in which some participants make claims based on scientific authority, while other participants make claims based on religious authority. In each case, there is the potential for debate of the sort claimed by almost everyone writing about religion and science. So, how do these debates happen? How do they stack up against the deliberative ideal? And are patterns in these debates consistent or inconsistent with patterns observed in the previous debates?

ORIGINS OF HOMOSEXUALITY: SCIENCE AND EVERYTHING ELSE

Debate over the origins of homosexuality—that is, over what makes a person gay or straight—might seem at first an unlikely place to look for public debate about religion and science.[1] But sexuality has long been an issue in which public figures have made claims from religious and scientific authority alike. Christianity, for example, has long wrestled with the question of homosexual orientation and behavior (which are often distinct in religious discourse). Since medieval times, prominent religious representatives have made public claims intended to keep scientific and medical information out of the process of determining whether homosexual orientation and behavior are sinful.[2]

By the same token, natural philosophers and, later, scientists have consistently attempted to draw on scientific evidence to determine what makes someone gay or straight. For example, scientists have claimed that there is a "gay gene" that determines the direction of human sexual attraction.[3] Such a finding would potentially settle key religious questions about whether homosexuality is a sinful choice or a natural aspect of God's creation. Moreover, in terms of public policy, more is arguably at stake in the issue of sexuality than in issues such as human origins, as questions around the malleability of sexuality implicate questions of justice with regard to legal rights to marriage, adoption, immigration, inheritance, health care, and employment.

Yet the first thing that you notice when you look at public debate about the origins of homosexuality is that there is not much of it. Using the methodology outlined in the appendix, I retrieved only 362 articles for the period from 1997 to 2007, despite multiple inclusive search criteria. By way of illustrative contrast, I retrieved 3,241 articles about human origins from the same period. While this is a debate with a great variety of stakes, and it is of great concern to religious organizations, gay advocacy organizations, activists, politicians, and many ordinary people with wide-ranging experiences of sexuality, it does not translate into anything like significant coverage in general-audience mass media.

MAPPING DEBATE BY TOPIC

Given the historical and political dimensions of this debate, we would probably expect religion topics and science topics to occur together on a topic map. Given the wide variety of political implications in this debate, we might also expect various political or legal topics to appear on the map. And to the extent that this debate is primarily an encounter between religion and science over the origins (and implications) of sexuality, we would expect that other topics would equally implicate both science and religion topics.

Figure 4 shows the topic map for this debate. The most prominent topic by far is "Christian Homosexual Change Groups," which is clearly a religion topic. Two of the other four most probable topics are clearly science topics. One is "Genes and Sexual Orientation," the other "Genes and Human Behavior." The remaining two most prominent topics do not explicitly indicate religion or science content. "Talking to Parents" and "Homosexuality in Montgomery County School Curriculum" are prominent and implicate a wide range of other topics, but are not specifically religion or science topics.

Unlike human origins debate, religion topics and science topics, while separate, are not entirely self-contained discussions. More precisely, as figure 4 illustrates, religion topics are mixed in with a variety of topics not obviously about religion or science. So, while "Christian Homosexual Change Groups" and "Talking to Parents" may be the most probable topics, they tend to share space with many other topics in these newspaper articles. For example, news stories about the Montgomery County sex-ed curriculum often also discuss the Christian viewpoint on whether homosexuality can be changed.[4]

Note, however, the obvious separation of the science topics "Genes and Sexual Orientation" and "Genes and Human Behavior" from everything else. This is a striking finding. Discussion of genetic research tends to be self-contained, or related to discussion of similar research into DNA or in neuroscience. Discussion about science topics is far more likely to implicate discussion about other science topics than it is to touch on topics related to religion, personal narrative, and so forth. Looking at specific articles, this distinction is clear. Articles about the possible discovery of a "gay gene," for example, tend to discuss competing scientific studies and treat the issue only as a debate internal to science.[5]

What figure 4 shows is that public talk about the origins of homosexuality is basically split into two disconnected discussions. One is a rich discussion about homosexuality, change, morals, persons, religion, politics, and policy, an interchange in which each of these topics implicates several other topics. The other is a highly constrained discussion about scientific findings regarding genetics and behavior in articles that

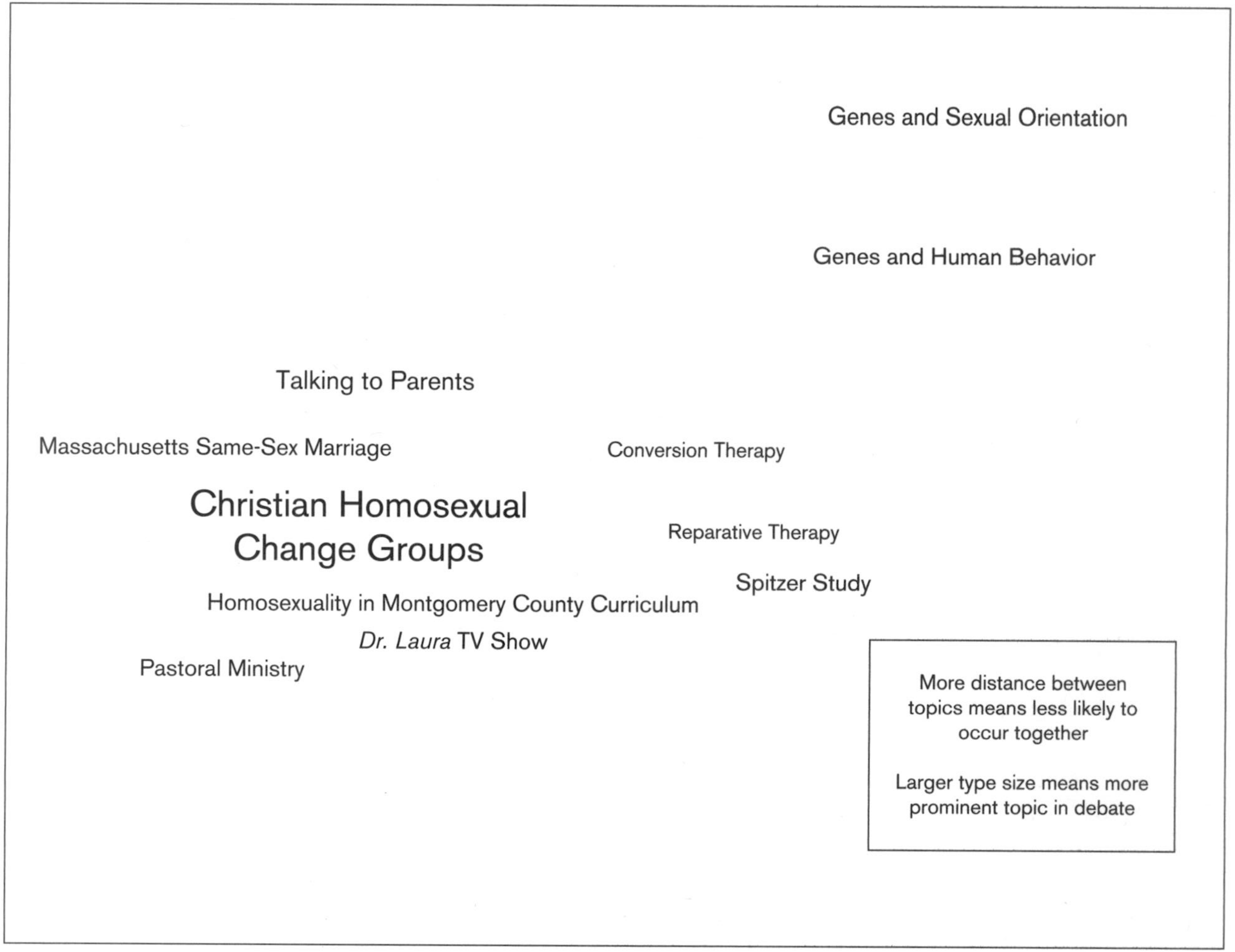

Genes and Sexual Orientation

Genes and Human Behavior

More distance between topics means less likely to occur together

Larger type size means more prominent topic in debate

Conversion Therapy

Reparative Therapy

Spitzer Study

Talking to Parents

Massachusetts Same-Sex Marriage

Christian Homosexual Change Groups

Homosexuality in Montgomery County Curriculum

Dr. Laura TV Show

Pastoral Ministry

FIGURE 4. Topic map: origins of homosexuality debate.

rarely implicate topics beyond the internal scientific discussion. Of course, this is not to say that no article ever is about both, for example, "Conversion Therapy" and "Genes and Human Behavior." Looking at every article will eventually turn up a story about the "gay gene" that also mentions, for example, the Family Research Council, a conservative religious organization that grounds its critique of homosexuality in concerns about the traditional family.[6]

But the important point here is that there is no general way to portray this debate as an encounter or engagement between religion and science. This debate is better described as "science and everything else," where "everything else" contains more or less related topics ranging from the political (Massachusetts Same-Sex Marriage) and religious (Pastoral Ministry) to those not explicitly religious or political (Talking to Parents, Conversion Therapy, Reparative Therapy). But this is not "science *versus* everything else." Discussion of science topics is simply separate from discussion of everything else.

Mapping Debate by Representatives

Table 3 shows information on the top ten representatives for this debate. In descriptive terms, the most visible persons in this debate are a radio talk show host (Schlessinger), a U.S. president (Bush), two Christian ex-gay activists (John and Anne Paulk), a gay activist (Besen), a conservative Christian political activist (Falwell), a conservative Christian moral activist (Dobson), a genetic scientist (Hamer), a proponent of "reparative therapy" (Nicolosi), and a victim of tragic antigay violence (Shepard). Most are people who have some sort of stake in this particular issue, but the stakes vary widely. Many are clearly associated with religion and at least one (Hamer) is associated with science.

The first thing to note is that even the representative who appears in the most articles is still only mentioned in thirty-four out of a possible 362 articles—hardly a dominant position in the debate. Based on visibility rankings, no one is especially central or dominant in public debate over the origins of homosexuality, at least in the sense of showing up more often than other representatives.[7]

Aside from the obviously much smaller scope of this debate, another important difference lies in the co-mentions of other persons and organizations with the top representatives. In debates over human origins or stem cell research, one main person, such as Charles Darwin or George W. Bush, tended to be mentioned alongside other top representatives.

TABLE 3   TOP TEN REPRESENTATIVES IN THE ORIGINS OF HOMOSEXUALITY
DEBATE

Person	No. of Articles	Person Most Commonly Occurring With	Org. Most Commonly Occurring With
Laura Schlessinger	34	Joan Garry	Paramount
John Paulk	30	James Dobson	Focus on the Family
James Dobson	24	John Paulk	Focus on the Family
George W. Bush	22	John Kerry	American Psychological Association (APA)
Jerry Falwell	21	Pat Robertson	Exodus International
Wayne Besen	20	Gary Cooper/Michael Bussee	Exodus International
Anne Paulk	20	John Paulk	Exodus International
Dean Hamer	20	George Rice	National Cancer Institute
Joseph Nicolosi	20	Clinton Anderson	APA
Matthew Shepard	19	Trent Lott	Family Research Council

According to the pattern here, much of the interaction appears to happen around the organizations Focus on the Family and Exodus International, and among John Paulk, Anne Paulk, James Dobson, Jerry Falwell, and Wayne Besen. But several top representatives, such as Laura Schlessinger and Dean Hamer, seem to be involved only in isolated encounters with other representatives.

What Representatives Do

So, what explains this pattern? Looking at individual articles reveals that this debate is mostly a series of controversial incidents that drew media coverage. Take, for example, talk show host Laura Schlessinger ("Dr. Laura"). When Paramount announced a new *Dr. Laura* TV show, organizations such as the Gay and Lesbian Alliance against Defamation (GLAAD) drew public attention to Schlessinger's previous statements that homosexuality is "deviant," "destructive," and a "biological error."[8] Schlessinger is thus visible because of an isolated controversy in which she made offensive comments that drove media-focused activist responses against her sponsoring organization.

Similarly, a specifically scientific controversy involved Dean Hamer, a genetic scientist at the National Cancer Institute who published (with coauthors) a 1993 article apparently identifying a "gay gene."[9] In 1999, neurologist George Rice of the University of Western Ontario failed to reproduce the results, sparking public discussion and pushing Hamer to defend his study. This prompted several other articles, especially in science and technology sections of the newspapers, that reviewed the controversy and presented both Hamer's and Rice's research in scientific perspective. The story gained traction as a public spectacle in which scientists argued with other scientists.

But take away Laura Schlessinger, Dean Hamer, and George W. Bush (who must campaign on every issue against his electoral opponent, John Kerry), and what you are left with is a few organizations and a few prominent representatives arguing with one another about whether homosexuality can or should be changed. On one side are Focus on the Family, Exodus International, and the Family Research Council, all of which are grounded in conservative Protestant theology and doctrine, and all of which take (or took) the position that homosexuality is wrong (or bad) and should be changed.[10] On the other side are Human Rights Campaign and Truth Wins Out, which, respectively, advocate for equal rights based on sexuality and actively track and oppose the so-called "ex-gay" movement.

Much of this debate actually hinges on one specific incident. Wayne Besen, at the time a spokesperson for the Human Rights Campaign, released a photo of John Paulk at Mister P's, a widely known gay bar in Washington, D.C. At the time, John Paulk was the manager of Focus on the Family's Homosexuality and Gender Department, the elected chair of Exodus International's board of directors, and the most visible person (along with his wife, Anne Paulk) cited by these organizations as an exemplar of a successful Christian "ex-gay" conversion. John Paulk's links to Focus on the Family implicated James Dobson, a clinical psychologist and public moralist who constantly mobilizes arguments against homosexuality on his widely carried radio show. John Paulk's links to Exodus International also called into question the truth of the "ex-gay" claim writ large, prompting Joseph Nicolosi and the National Association for Research and Therapy of Homosexuality (NARTH) to mount a defense of their approach to "conversion therapy," and prompting Besen to point to the departure and subsequent commitment ceremony of early Exodus International leaders Gary Cooper and Michael Bussee.

Not all of the people in this debate are such active participants. The two most obvious examples are Jerry Falwell and Matthew Shepard, who are invoked in many different discussions of sexuality, including but not limited to the Paulk scandal. Whenever persons who oppose Dobson, Nicolosi, and others mobilize rhetoric that paints religious groups as conservative, angry, hostile, or even hateful, they invoke Jerry Falwell as the exemplar of such groups, with Pat Robertson also often getting added for additional illustration of the claim.[11] Matthew Shepard, a victim of antigay violence, serves as an exemplar for the treatment of gay people by others in society. So, when Senate Republican leader Trent Lott claimed that homosexuality was a sin of addiction like alcoholism or kleptomania, many of the responses cited Matthew Shepard's death as evidence for why Lott's comments were nonsensical. Shepard, like Falwell, is generally invoked by other representatives in order to advance their agenda.

There is significant potential for encounter and engagement between religion and science in public debate over the origins of homosexuality. But in existing debate, the pattern of separation is even clearer than in human origins or stem cell research debates. Scientists argue with other scientists in science places, and religious people argue with gay people wherever they can, because they have a stake in changing them. Religion is involved in a wide variety of other discussions. But science is almost completely isolated from those discussions. Even more dramatically than in the debates previously discussed, the general pattern is separation between religion and science.

ENVIRONMENTAL POLICY: RELIGION AND EVERYTHING ELSE

The final debate to consider in this study is debate about environmental policy. As with debate over the origins of homosexuality, debate about environmental policy involves public claims based on religious and scientific authority alike. For example, scientists regularly claim that immediate intervention is necessary to halt the anthropogenic aspects of global climate change.[12] At the same time, religious representatives and even some politicians claim that God is in control and that scientific consensus about anthropogenic climate change is therefore completely irrelevant to environmental policy.[13] These are explicitly competing claims about environmental policy that derive directly from science and religion, with wide-reaching implications for politics and policy.

Debate over environmental policy also provides an important contrast to debate over the origins of homosexuality. Both debates offer opportunity for encounter and engagement between religion and science. But maybe size matters. It is possible that there is separation between religion and science in debate over the origins of homosexuality simply because the debate is so small. Small debates have fewer opportunities for encounter, and a few such incidents significantly shape the debate. So it is possible to object to the findings from debate over the origins of homosexuality by saying that the separation between religion and science reflects the scarcity of opportunity. Maybe the potential encounter has not been realized yet, but if the debate were larger (if it became a more prominent issue, for example, or if we waited long enough), perhaps we would see the encounters or engagement that create the conditions for deliberative debate.

Looking at debate over environmental policy helps respond to this objection. Debate over environmental policy focuses on climate change. But it also touches on many other related issues, such as conservation, regulation, and energy infrastructure. As a result, debate over environmental policy is huge. With 4,236 articles in the data set, it is by far the largest of the four debates in this book.[14] If religion and science offer potential encounter in public debate, such a large and complex debate should provide more opportunities for such an encounter. A pattern of separation between religion and science across this huge debate would add even more weight to the argument that separation between religion and science is normal, rather than exceptional, in these debates.

Mapping Debate by Topic

There is a pattern of separation between religion and science across this huge debate. Figure 5 shows that religion topics and science topics are as far apart as it is possible to be on the map. In the articles, discussion of religion, particularly evangelical Christianity, is almost completely disconnected from discussion of other topics. Note that both religion and science topics are featured prominently in this debate, so it is not simply a matter of misjudging the extent to which this is a religion-and-science issue. The most prominent topic, as indicated by type size, is "Climate Change Scientists," followed closely by "Federal Environmental Policy." The next most prominent topic is "Evangelical Christians," followed by "Global Warming" and "Coastal Sea Level."

On the left side of figure 5 are many science topics, including "Climate Change Scientists," the most prominent topic in debate. That topic includes discussion about what scientists say about climate change, not simply information about the scientists themselves. The most closely related topics are also obviously science-related. So, while many articles in the debate are about "Climate Change Scientists," they are also often

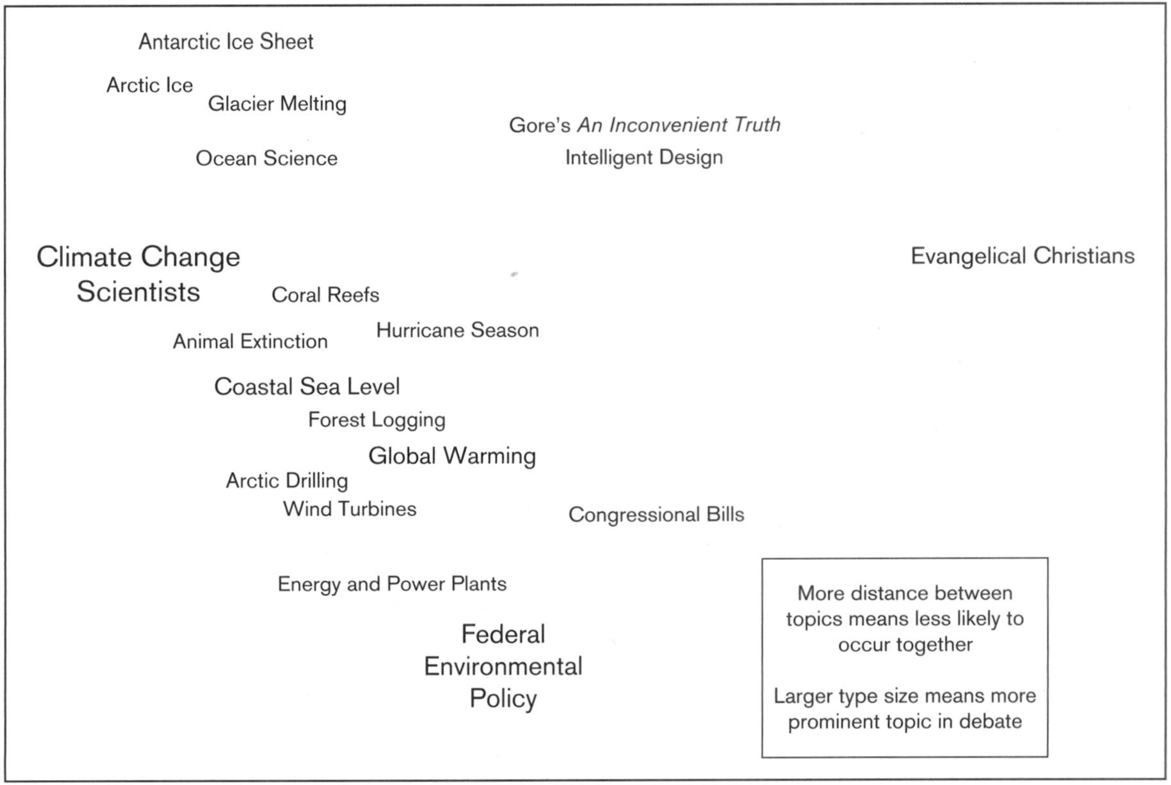

Antarctic Ice Sheet

Arctic Ice   Glacier Melting

Ocean Science

Gore's *An Inconvenient Truth*

Intelligent Design

Evangelical Christians

Climate Change
Scientists

Animal Extinction   Hurricane Season

Coastal Sea Level
Coral Reefs

Forest Logging
Global Warming

Arctic Drilling
Wind Turbines

Congressional Bills

Energy and Power Plants

Federal
Environmental
Policy

More distance between
topics means less likely to
occur together

Larger type size means more
prominent topic in debate

FIGURE 5. Topic map: environmental policy debate.

about "Animal Extinction," "Ocean Science," or "Coastal Sea Level." Likewise, and more obviously, an article about "Antarctic Ice Sheet" is highly likely to also address "Arctic Ice" or "Glacier Melting."

These science topics on the left are distant from the prominent political topic "Federal Environmental Policy" at the bottom of figure 5. Many articles about "Federal Environmental Policy" also discuss "Energy and Power Plants" or topics related to legislation (Congressional Bills), rather than, say, "Glacier Melting" or "Coral Reefs." Similarly, topics about infrastructure or regulation, such as "Arctic Drilling" or "Forest Logging," are more likely to occur with other policy-related topics, such as "Wind Turbines," than with "Ocean Science" or "Glacier Melting."

But, in general, figure 5 shows that science topics and policy topics are intermixed in public debate. Discussion of "Arctic Drilling" does not, for example, usually implicate "Arctic Ice" or "Glacier Melting." But it does implicate "Global Warming." Note the topic distinction between "Global Warming" and "Climate Change Scientists." Articles about "Climate Change Scientists" tend to also address science topics such as "Coral Reefs," "Animal Extinction," or "Ocean Science." Articles about "Global Warming" tend also to touch on more direct policy topics, such as "Wind Turbines" or "Forest Logging." So "Global Warming" bridges scientific and political discussion. The related topics, mostly about regulation of and infrastructure in industries with environmental impacts (logging, drilling, energy production), reinforce an impression that science and policy topics are mixed together in public talk.

What is striking about figure 5 is the position of the only obvious religion topic, "Evangelical Christians." While this topic is prominent in the debate, it is entirely disconnected. No other topic is close enough to it to reasonably claim a high likelihood of occurring with it in an article. Articles about evangelical Christians are mostly just about that topic. If such articles discuss other topics, those topics are probably not science-related. In fact, the topic least likely to occur with "Evangelical Christians" is "Climate Change Scientists," the most prominent science topic. So, even though it is one of the most prominent topics, "Evangelical Christians" is entirely isolated from other discussions.

The pattern in figure 5 is one of complete separation of religion talk from other talk in debate over environmental policy. As with debate over the origins of homosexuality, there is no general way to portray this debate as encounter or engagement between religion and science. But in this case it is religion that is isolated from an otherwise rich discussion of scientific and political aspects of environmental policy. This debate is better described as "religion and everything else" or, even more accurately, "evangelicals and everyone else."

Mapping Debate by Representatives

Table 4 reports information on the top ten representatives in debate over environmental policy. The top six representatives are all either current or former politicians, as might be expected given the profusion of policy topics on the topic map. Bush and Clinton are former U.S. presidents and state governors. Al Gore served as vice president to Clinton and ran against Bush as the Democratic presidential candidate in 2000. Arnold Schwarzenegger served as California governor. John Kerry served in the U.S. Senate and ran against Bush as the Democratic presidential candidate in 2004. John McCain serves in the U.S. Senate and ran as the Republican presidential candidate in 2008.

The remaining four representatives appear to be split between religion and science. Despite the possibility for wide-ranging involvement from across the religious spectrum, all three religion representatives in the top ten are conservative religious leaders active in political discussions. James Dobson, founder of Focus on the Family; the late Jerry Falwell, founder of the Moral Majority; and Pat Robertson, founder of the Christian Coalition, all speak (or spoke) out regularly on political issues from an explicitly conservative religious standpoint. And even though the topic map shows significant discussion of science topics, the only scientist among the top ten representatives is Lonnie Thompson, a paleoclimatologist specializing in ice core analysis.

Just as in stem cell research debate, George W. Bush is by far the most prominent representative and the one most likely to be invoked alongside other representatives. But in contrast to the debates previously discussed, Al Gore is more prominent in this debate than any other politician besides Bush. In fact, he is more prominent than Kerry and Bill Clinton combined. Gore is also prominent on the topic map (Gore's *An Inconvenient Truth*). And when Lonnie Thompson, the only science representative in the top ten, shows up in public debate, he is mentioned primarily alongside Gore.

Table 4 also shows that religion representatives in this debate largely co-occur with one another, with their political advocacy organizations, or with elected representatives. They do not co-occur with scientists at the top level, a pattern consistent with the separation from scientific discussion on the topic map. What is interesting is that they appear to

TABLE 4   TOP TEN REPRESENTATIVES IN THE ENVIRONMENTAL POLICY DEBATE

Person	No. of Articles	Person Most Commonly Occurring With	Org. Most Commonly Occurring With
George W. Bush	≥ 500	Bill Clinton	EPA
Al Gore	≥ 220	George W. Bush	U.S. Congress
Bill Clinton	≥ 140	George W. Bush	EPA
Arnold Schwarzenegger	127	George W. Bush	Sierra Club
John Kerry	73	George W. Bush	EPA
John McCain	63	George W. Bush	U.S. Congress
James Dobson	59	George W. Bush	Focus on the Family
Jerry Falwell	49	Pat Robertson	Republican Party
Pat Robertson	48	Jerry Falwell	Christian Coalition
Lonnie Thompson	43	Al Gore	Ohio State University

be engaging in political advocacy even though, according to the topic map, discussion of religion in this debate generally does not involve any particular political issue or discussion.

What Representatives Do

The participation of most politicians in this debate is easily explained. Bush, for example, participates directly in debate over environmental policy as a politician campaigning for the U.S. presidency. Like other politicians, such as Kerry or Gore, he promotes his agenda and distinguishes his position from political opponents. As the sitting president during this time frame, Bush is also the symbolic target of efforts by others to advance their agendas. He is not just "Bush" but also "the Bush administration." For example, when McCain and Schwarzenegger separately sought to enact state and federal legislation that increased restrictions on emissions, they attacked the perceived failures of "Bush's" Environmental Protection Agency (EPA).

Gore is a different story. Certainly Gore is a former politician, but that did not put him in the top ten for, say, stem cell research debate. Looking at individual articles, it is clear that Gore's participation as an environmental activist vaults him to prominence in this debate. His nationwide campaign to raise awareness of human contributions to climate change drew significant media attention, both on its own and as the subject of the hugely popular (and Academy Award–winning) documentary *An Inconvenient Truth*. The movie's popularity also explains the prominence of scientist Lonnie Thompson, who served as a scientific advisor and whose findings are featured prominently in the film. Gore has paramount standing in this debate (and not others) because he actively promoted an environmental policy agenda both during and after his career in electoral politics.

What, then, of the religion representatives? How is it possible for politically active conservative religion representatives to be among the most prominent, but have religion talk generally separate from science and policy talk across debate as a whole? The answer is that, by and large, the three religion representatives are talking about why the environment should not be an issue for Christians. They are engaged in an internal discussion with other evangelical Christians about the appropriate level of political involvement on the issue. For example, Jerry Falwell said: "I believe that global warming is a myth. And so, therefore, I have no conscience problems at all, and I'm going to buy a Suburban next time. It is God's planet, and he's taking care of it. And I don't believe that anything we do will raise or lower the temperature one point. The whole thing is created to destroy America's free enterprise system and our economic stability."[15] And in an open letter condemning the National Association of Evangelicals (NAE) for taking a position on climate change, James Dobson and other evangelical Christian representatives wrote: "[Some people] are using the global warming controversy to shift the emphasis away from the great moral issues of our time, notably the sanctity of human life, the integrity of marriage and the teaching of sexual abstinence and morality to our children."[16]

Clearly, anyone could say such things. But the prominence of these religious leaders in debate comes from their political influence.[17] For political positioning, and perhaps for electoral politics, it matters what evangelical Christian leaders say about an issue. Politicians, especially those in the Republican Party, court the evangelical vote.[18] But the important point here is that they are not engaging science and deliberating about the environment. If they talk about "global warming," for example, it is to dismiss it for religious reasons, not to engage in substantive discussion about science. Such statements have political implications and therefore receive media attention, but they are not based on engagement with science either by topic or in representative terms.

Debate over environmental policy, like that over the origins of homosexuality, contains the potential for encounter or engagement between science and religion. But, here too, religion and science remain separate. Prominent political figures are mostly involved with an array of political battles over regulation and remediation of environmental issues. To the extent that science representatives show up, it is in service of these political battles. Liberal or moderate religious figures are simply insignificant in the debate. Conservative religious figures who have a history of political activism are arguing with one another over whether or not to be involved in political battles over the environment, but their participation is completely separate from everything, and everyone, else. So, while debate over environmental policy differs in size and scope from the other debates in this study, the pattern of separation between religion and science is entirely consistent with the other three debates. Even without conflict, the basic encounter and engagement necessary for deliberative debate between religion and science do not occur.

RECONSIDERING RELIGION AND SCIENCE DEBATES

In debates over human origins and over stem cell research, widely recognized instances of conflict are actually exceptions to a more general pattern of separation between religion and science. If we looked only at those debates, we might conclude that conflict is the cause of that separation, or at least an important factor. But looking at debates over the origins of homosexuality and over environmental policy, we see the same pattern of separation. Debate over the origins of homosexuality is "science and everything else," with science talk confined to internal argument among scientists over genetic sources of homosexuality. Debate over environmental policy is "religion and everything else," with religion talk confined to internal argument among evangelical Christians about whether or not to engage in political activism.

So, to answer the opening question of this chapter, the pattern of separation between religion and science occurs broadly across debates. It is the same pattern whether or not there are well-known instances of conflict. It is the same pattern whether or not that conflict is epistemological, as in debate over human origins, or moral, as in debate over stem cell research. The same pattern appears whether debate is small and focused, as in debate over the origins of homosexuality, or large and complex, as in debate over environmental policy. We find the same pattern whether we look broadly at all discussion in these debates or look closely at the most visible representatives. With very few exceptions, religion and science are separate in public debates.

When we think about how deliberative debate between religion and science might fail, it is easy to focus on encounters that go wrong or to point to specific instances of conflictual or contentious engagement between religion and science representatives. Such situations happen sometimes. But focusing on the quality of such encounters misses a much larger problem. Religion and science representatives generally do not encounter or engage each other in the first place. In theory, they could be encountering other representatives and engaging in deliberative debate. In practice, that does not happen.

Put another way, what is wrong with these debates has much to do with how religion and science representatives participate in public debates, but it does not have much to do with how religion and science representatives engage each other. This suggests a basic shift in thinking about religion and science in public life. Instead of focusing on the quality of rare encounters between religion and science representatives, we need to look instead at how they generally participate in public debates as representatives in the public sphere.

CHAPTER 4

Representatives and Good Debate

Religion and science representatives are not generally engaging each other in public debates involving religion and science. Across these debates, whatever the issue, religion talk tends to be separated from science talk. This is surprising. While everyone agrees that there are problems with religion-and-science debates, no one has previously suggested that they are bad because of a more general problem with how representatives participate in public debate, rather than a problem between religion and science.

But what is the problem, exactly? We know that the basic conditions for deliberative debate between religion and science do not occur in these debates. We know that separation, rather than conflict, is the usual condition. But knowing that there is separation between religion and science does not mean that we automatically know how such separation happens. Maybe representatives are actually trying to encounter and engage one another, but something is preventing them from doing so. Maybe representatives are not actually trying to encounter and engage one another at all, but are doing something else instead. Or maybe some representatives sometimes try and fail, and other times do not try. Any of these situations (or all of them at once) would fit the pattern of separation.

To find out how this separation, this basic failure of deliberative debate, occurs between religion and science in public debate, we need to know how representatives in these debates participate. What are representatives doing? What do they think that they are doing? Are they trying to be deliberative and failing? Or are they doing something else entirely? Are religion and science representatives behaving in distinctive ways, or are they simply doing what other representatives do? And, most fundamentally, what counts as good debate in representatives' estimation?

Put more bluntly, what kind of debate do representatives want? To address this question, I analyzed biographical and textual data for a sample of forty-three elite representatives from different categories (e.g., religion, science, politics) and with varying levels of visibility in these debates.[1] In plain English, I looked at public information for evidence that would show what kind of debate each representative sought to achieve in public life. To be clear, not all representatives make a statement like "I think we should have good debate, and it looks like this example." And it is difficult, if not impossible, to discern particular intentions of representatives in these debates. So, rather than try to ascribe motives or intentions, I simply classify with regard to their apparent goal. When they do things in public life, what kind of debate are they trying to achieve?

Two distinct approaches emerged among the representatives in the sample. In one approach, which I call *public crusade,* what constitutes good debate is advancing a moral agenda and excluding from public talk those who disagree. In the other approach, which I call *elevating the conversation,* what constitutes good debate is expanded public talk that does not necessarily advance a specific substantive agenda. Perhaps surprisingly, there is no obvious categorical difference between the prominent religion representatives, science representatives, and other kinds of representatives. Visibility matters most. Higher-visibility representatives tend to take a "public crusade" approach, while the "elevating the conversation" approach occurs almost exclusively among lower-visibility representatives.

I illustrate these approaches with six examples of representatives who participate in these religion-and-science debates. These examples help to show that the differences in approach to good debate do not map directly onto differences between religion and science. Rather, they tend to divide along lines of prominence, though not directly. Among more prominent representatives, what constitutes good debate is success at promoting their own agendas and excluding those who disagree. Among less prominent representatives, both approaches occur. While some less prominent representatives pursue "public crusade," for others what constitutes good debate is the expansion of public conversation, even if it means that their preferred moral agenda or substantive position is not specifically advanced. The key observation is that, while both approaches occur among lower-visibility representatives, higher-visibility representatives are almost exclusively engaged in public crusade.

GOOD DEBATE AS PUBLIC CRUSADE

What constitutes good debate for higher-visibility representatives is what I call public crusade. Historically, the Crusades involved religious motivations for military quests to reclaim formerly Christian lands and convert, or eliminate, those persons with whom the Christian church disagreed. To varying extents, "crusade" is a fitting description for current efforts by representatives in public life to advance their moral agenda and convert persons to their point of view. While not always explicitly motivated by religion, representatives who engage in public crusades unconditionally advocate a position or package of positions in public life. From this perspective, public debate that distracts from the crusade's mission should be avoided or suppressed.[2]

Jerry Falwell: A Paradigmatic Case

Take, for example, the late Jerry Falwell. In the 1970s Falwell, a church pastor in Virginia, became convinced that America had departed from the Christian moral path of its founders and that active religious involvement in politics would be the only effective way to militate against further decline. As Susan Friend Harding observes, Falwell applied the conservative Protestant notion of "witnessing," that is, persuasive talking intended to convert nonbelievers, to public life.[3] In Falwell's own words: "If the leaders of Christendom in this nation don't stand up against immorality, we can't expect anyone else to lead. I believe it is the duty of gospel preachers to set the pace. When sin moves out in front, preachers and Christians everywhere must speak out. I will as long as I have breath."[4]

In 1979 Falwell founded Moral Majority, a political organization for conservative Protestants. Through Moral Majority Falwell sought to implement laws and policies based on conservative Protestant moral teachings. Similar efforts had worked locally on specific issues such as gay rights and on single issues nationally such as gender rights.[5] Falwell sought national political influence across a broad range of issues, such as abortion, homosexuality, stem cell research, and the "traditional family."

To overcome the decentralized organizational structure of conservative Protestantism, Falwell emphasized setting aside the debates over religious issues that separated denominations and congregations in the first place. For Falwell, debate was not productive; it was divisive. In the formative meeting of the Moral Majority, he emphasized the importance of a united front for effective political intervention: "I know that under normal circumstances most of us wouldn't even speak to each other. But these aren't normal circumstances. We've got to work together to save this nation. Afterward we can go back to arguing amongst ourselves."[6]

Scholars of electoral politics credit Falwell's Moral Majority with the swing of many conservative religious voters from Carter in 1976 to Reagan in 1980, and with the persistent alliance of Republican national politics with conservative Christian moral issues throughout the 1980s.[7] Moral Majority formally dissolved at the end of the 1980s. But Falwell continued his crusade for explicitly Christian moral laws and policies until his death in 2007. In part he remained influential because of his ongoing connections to later generations of Christian political activists. But he continued to gain media attention by saying outrageous things in public to draw attention to his moral agenda. As he put it in 2000:

> Once you reach the place where your words are respected, then what you say does have impact. Occasionally, I'm accused of saying things that I didn't say. But usually, I'm guilty and by intent, I say what I believe. If it isn't controversial, it isn't worth talking about.[8]

And in 2006:

> A pastor has to be media-savvy if he's going to reach everybody. I don't mean to be ugly and harsh, but to be forthright and candid. And the result is that people that don't like you start listening.[9]

Falwell provides a paradigmatic case of the "public crusade" approach. Until his death he remained committed to advancing a set of moral positions in public life. As a religious "witness," he did not need to engage in debate with other representatives, because he was telling people what he believed to be right. They could convert, or not. As the founding of the Moral Majority illustrates, debate could only interfere with the crusade. Freed from the need to debate, Falwell could then say or do whatever he liked as long as he deemed it useful for drawing attention to his moral agenda.

Variations on a Moral Theme: James Dobson

Like Falwell, James Dobson is involved in many debates in this study. For Dobson, a psychologist with a Ph.D. from the University of Southern

California, the American family is under moral threat. The only way to stop that threat is to reclaim or convert as many people as possible to a traditional view of the family (heterosexual, not divorced, strongly authoritarian). In 1977 Dobson founded Focus on the Family "to spread the Gospel of Jesus Christ through a practical outreach to homes."[10] The Focus on the Family organization publishes books and produces media programming (e.g., the daily radio show *Focus on the Family*) to advance Dobson's moral agenda. Popular books, such as *Dare to Discipline, Love for a Lifetime,* and *Love Must Be Tough,* offer practical advice for dating, marriage, and family relationships, primarily by suggesting a return to Dobson's moral ideal of traditional family relationships. In 1981 Dobson founded the Family Research Council, a lobbying organization focused on issues such as student prayer in public schools, heterosexual-only marriage, pornography, abortion, and stem cell research, to advance his moral view of the traditional family through influence on elected public officials rather than just ordinary people.

Dobson thus appears to be engaged in almost the same approach as Falwell: a well-organized public crusade to intervene in public life over moral issues grounded in conservative Christian doctrine. When speaking to religious media, such as the magazine *Christianity Today,* Dobson uses explicitly religious talk, as one would expect from a religious crusader. For example, in a 2004 Q&A with *Christianity Today,* interviewer Stan Guthrie asked what would happen if the American family failed. Would Focus on the Family close up shop? Dobson replied: "The family is created and ordained by God. It will never fail, but it can suffer great harm as a result of man's efforts to redefine it. Love for God and for our neighbor demands that we protect people from this harm."[11]

But unlike Falwell, Dobson does not simply speak in public as a religious crusader. Despite being touted as the most influential evangelical in America, Dobson often consciously uses generic moral language not necessarily tied to a particular religious tradition.[12] He speaks in terms of "values," or of families, lives, and relationships. This language is a kind of "moral Esperanto" that provides common ground with many people who are not conservative Christians or even religious at all.[13] In theory, "values" are not the sole purview of conservative Protestants.[14] So, for example, when asked about supporting pro-life politicians, Dobson could have talked about whether they were Godly or in keeping with biblical requirements, but he instead replied in more generic moral terms: "And why would we not support someone who does line up with our values system, when we would have to literally hold our noses to support somebody that contradicts those values? And we have seen elections—they're very dynamic, they're volatile, they change."[15]

Such generic moral language is uncharacteristic of Falwell's "witnessing," as it passes up an opportunity to speak in explicitly religious terms, offering instead a set of publicly accessible reasons that do not depend on religious commitment.[16] Yet Dobson goes even further beyond religious talk, drawing on language from behavioral science in addition to, or rather than, generic moral language. For example, when asked by CNN's Larry King about the origins of homosexuality, Dobson did not use religious language or even generic moral language, favoring instead a behavioral science justification of his moral position: "It usually comes out of very, very early childhood, and this is very controversial, but this is what I believe and many other people believe, that i[t] has to do with an identity crisis that occurs too early to remember it, where a boy is born with an attachment to his mother and she is everything to him for about 18 months, and between 18 months and five years, he needs to detach from her and to reattach to his father."[17]

Given the apparent openness to different kinds of talk, Dobson may appear to be more interested in debate, and even deliberation, when compared to the exclusively religious Falwell. But all of this talk, no matter what its underlying justification, goes toward one end: advancing Dobson's moral agenda in public life. More ways of talking are more ways to convince people to follow the crusade. Bringing in different kinds of reasons is simply another way of subverting potentially divisive debate, particularly in the political arena. Dobson's use of generic moral talk and science talk partly undercuts any competing arguments from nonreligious perspectives. It also suggests that Dobson's single moral vision is supported from multiple directions. At its core, Dobson's approach to representation is only a slightly more clever version of Falwell's approach. And as with Falwell, Dobson is not actually interested in engaging in debate with other representatives, only in a public crusade to reclaim lost moral territory and convert people to his cause.

Politics as Public Crusade: George W. Bush

George W. Bush provides an illustration of the public crusade approach that is not simply about religion or science. Unlike the previous examples, Bush is a successful product of the American electoral system, having campaigned for and won both state-level and national-level executive offices. Winning elections is, of course, a successful strategy for gaining prominence in public life. However, the concern here is with Bush as representative, that is, as a public figure who organizes his public life around a particular vision of what that life ought to be. Many people win elections, but not all organize their public lives for the same reasons.

Like other public crusaders, Bush participates in public life out of a moral conviction that something has gone wrong in American society. From Bush's perspective, the main problem of American life is dysfunctional politics grounded in a lack of principled action. His response is to pursue principled decision making as a political leader. As he explained in 2007: "I think it's very important for people—for a president to make decisions based upon principles. You know, you can be popular, but you may be wrong. And I would rather, when it's all said and done, get back home and look in the mirror and say, I didn't compromise the principles that are etched into my soul in order to be a popular guy. What I want to do is solve problems for the American people and yield the peace that we all want."[18]

Yet the principles to which Bush refers are not grounded in a desire for engagement with other representatives or expansion of public talk. Quite the opposite. In Bush's view, commitment to principled leadership requires disregard for different and possibly conflicting points of view, whether from other elites or from ordinary persons. Engaging other representatives in debate is actually an obstacle, in that it detracts from strong principled actions. When Bush speaks of good debate, it is debate that occurs after the real action has already taken place. Debate is what people do after leaders do the right thing. For example, when asked about polls showing public dissatisfaction with his leadership, Bush replied:

> Polls are nothing more than just, like, a puff of air. What matters is results. And, ultimately, people will be able to make, you know, an objective judgment of a president and his administration and, in this case, a country's commitment. And so [what] I care really about is the results of the programs. I hope by now people have learned that I'm not one of these guys that really gives a darn about elite opinion. What I really care about is, are we saving lives? And in this case, we are.[19]

As an inhabitant of elected higher office, Bush could not avoid all debate. The United States is not a dictatorship. The separation of powers in American politics structures some encounters and engagement as part of policy making. For example, spending allocations proposed by Congress require presidential approval. Likewise, a declaration of war by the president requires the approval of Congress. But in cases in which principled leadership encountered the structural requirement for debate (however minimal), Bush presented the case for debate as something that would always happen and could therefore be set aside in the national interest. While some debate in politics cannot be avoided, unity should triumph over debate: "I think it's important for me to continue to reach out to the Democrats, and will—and Republicans, for that matter—and explain the strategies and the way forward, but also to explain to them that presidents and Congresses will be dealing with this ideological struggle for quite a while, and therefore it makes sense to work together now to help not only us succeed, but help them succeed."[20]

For Bush, the "way forward" is his way, based on his own moral convictions. Yet some of Bush's language might suggest that he is open to debate. For example, when asked in Texas, a largely religious and conservative state, about whether Intelligent Design should be taught in schools, Bush seemed to be advocating public debate as important:

> I think—as I said, harking back to my days as my governor. . . . Then, I said that, first of all, that decision should be made to local school districts, but I felt like both sides ought to be properly taught . . . so people can understand what the debate is about. I think that part of education is to expose people to different schools of thought, and I'm not suggesting—you're asking me whether or not people ought to be exposed to different ideas, and the answer is yes.[21]

But it is clear that this apparent openness to debate is simply part of the greater strategy. While Bush suggests that learning about debate is an important part of education, he is not actually interested in that debate. As a public crusader, Bush is remarkably consistent in suppressing alternative viewpoints in public talk whenever possible. He is not advocating actually having a debate, since that would mean weakening his principled leadership. Instead, he is trying to make room in policy for an otherwise unpopular position that he personally holds. Apparent openness to debate is an attempt to convert opponents to his point of view: "Well, I think you can have both [evolution and creationism]. I think evolution can—you're getting me way out of my lane here. I'm just a simple president. But it's, I think that God created the Earth, created the world; I think the creation of the world is so mysterious it requires something as large as an almighty, and I don't think it's incompatible with the scientific proof that there is evolution."[22]

Like other public crusaders, Bush adheres to a moral vision of the world as fallen or broken, in this case because of unprincipled and therefore dysfunctional politics. His remedy is principled leadership. This approach dismisses debate as inimical to the exercise of good moral leadership. Where possible, alternative perspectives should be disregarded. Debate can take place after the fact, but not as part of policy making. When debate is unavoidable, it should be minimized in favor of unity behind a principled leader. And while advancing a moral agenda sometimes means talking as though debate were important, actual debate is undesirable.

Removing the Religion Barrier: Richard Dawkins

Richard Dawkins, an evolutionary biologist and former Oxford University professor, constantly talks in public, primarily to criticize religion. His book *The God Delusion* basically claims that religion is a consensus delusion, grounded in contagious false beliefs, that prevents human flourishing. This is of course a moral position, and by speaking in public, Dawkins advances his moral agenda, much as seen in the examples discussed above. For Dawkins, the very existence of religion in public life is objectionable:

> Disagreements between incompatible beliefs cannot be settled by reasoned argument because reasoned argument is drummed out of those trained in religion from the cradle. Instead, disagreements are settled by other means which, in extreme cases, inevitably become violent. Scientists disagree among themselves but they never fight over their disagreements. They argue about evidence or go out and seek new evidence. Much the same is true of philosophers, historians and literary critics.[23]

Dawkins objects to religion because, in his view, it interferes with the scientific inquiry that produces valid knowledge. Science has a reliable process for disagreement and debate that can ground nonviolent, reasonable debate. I use the word "reasonable" here to indicate Dawkins's commitment to evidence and process rather than faith or revelation. According to Dawkins, unlike religion, the process of scientific inquiry can provide common grounds for human progress:

> Not everybody can evaluate all evidence; we can't evaluate the evidence for quantum physics. So it does have to be a certain amount of taking things on trust. I have to take what physicists say on trust, for example, because I'm a biologist. But science [has] a system of appraisal, of peer review, so that I trust the physics community to get their act together in a way that I know from the inside. I wish people would put their trust in evidence, not in faith, revelation, tradition, or authority.[24]

Obviously Dawkins engages in controversial and outrageous public talk in order to discredit religion. But most of his talk concerns indicators of disbelief in scientific conclusions. So, for example, Dawkins famously wrote, "If you meet somebody who claims not to believe in evolution, that person is ignorant, stupid or insane (or wicked, but I'd rather not consider that)."[25] For Dawkins, a person's position on evolution indicates whether or not that person meets the prerequisites for participation in public life. Notably, a religious person can participate in public life if she or he believes in evolution:

> Well, evolution is different about this, because there are a large number of evolutionists who are also religious. You cannot be both sane and well educated and disbelieve in evolution. The evidence is so strong that any sane, educated person has got to believe in evolution. Now there are plenty of sane, educated, religious people: there are professors of theology, and there are bishops; and so obviously they all believe in evolution or they wouldn't have gotten where they have because they would be too stupid or too ignorant. So, it is a fact that there are evolutionists who are religious and there are religious people who are evolutionists.[26]

But for Dawkins, religion that is friendly to scientific inquiry is the exception rather than the rule. Instead, most religion impedes the progress of scientific inquiry. To achieve a better world, religion hostile to such good debate must be defeated:

> If only such subtle, nuanced religion predominated, the world would surely be a better place, and I would have written a different book. The melancholy truth is that this kind of understated, decent, revisionist religion is numerically negligible. To the vast majority of believers around the world, religion all too closely resembles what you hear from the likes of Robertson, Falwell or Haggard, Osama bin Laden or the Ayatollah Khomeini. These are not straw men, they are all too influential, and everybody in the modern world has to deal with them.[27]

Dawkins holds a clear idea about, and preference for, public talk that excludes religion. By "good debate" he means nonviolent reasoned discussion about issues of concern, grounded in evidence produced through trustworthy processes. The process of scientific inquiry is ideal for anchoring such debate. But the dominant forms of public religion, he argues, work against good debate. For example, disbelief in evolution marks a religious denial of available evidence. Getting rid of religion is necessary to institute the broader scientific process of reasonable debate based on evidence rather than revelation. The point is for science to win in public life, in order to solve problems and improve society.

While they vary in important ways, different representatives from a variety of backgrounds engage similarly in "public crusades" in public life. In this approach, what constitutes good debate is advancing their moral agenda. This means conversion rather than encounter or engagement. While it is not always practical to avoid debate, it is preferable to avoid or suppress public debate. To put the approach in its most basic form, representatives who engage in public crusade just want to get their way.

GOOD DEBATE AS ELEVATING THE CONVERSATION

The phrase "elevating the conversation" comes directly from one of the approach's practitioners in debates over environmental policy. In the "elevating the conversation" approach, representatives look for ways to intervene usefully and selectively to improve existing debate. For representatives who take this approach, what constitutes good debate is inclusive public talk that incorporates a variety of different perspectives in order to produce useful policy outcomes. The problem is that debate is sometimes uninformed, which makes reasoned deliberation more difficult. Ignorance makes debate worse. Representatives in this category recognize a gap in information and seek to improve debate by filling that gap with expert knowledge. The point of this approach is to elevate existing conversation by increasing information and encouraging deliberation.[28]

Expanding Possibilities: John Haught

One example of a representative who seeks to elevate the conversation is John Haught, a professor of systematic theology and former director of the Woodstock Theological Center at Georgetown University. Haught intervenes primarily in debate over human origins. As seen in chapter 2, such debate is the site of one specific conflict between biblical creationism and Darwinism. Whereas public crusaders such as Falwell, Dobson, or Dawkins attempt to exclude their perceived competition from public life altogether, Haught attempts to bring different perspectives together productively.

Haught's theology combines Pierre Teilhard de Chardin's process theology with an evolutionary account of human origins. In Haught's kenotic theology of evolution, God is self-emptying. Divine love becomes creative force in the world, not as a direct act of creation that shapes the world in specific ways, but as an enabling force that fuels the growth of the world. The details of this theology are complex, but the bottom line is that Haught provides an account of God and the world that describes evolution and other related natural processes as expressions of creative power emptied from God into the world. Haught thus offers a theological alternative to the conflict model of religion and science.

Despite his religious affiliation, Haught sometimes appears to be taking sides against religion. For example, Haught served as an expert witness in the *Kitzmiller* Intelligent Design case, in which he testified that ID was religious in origin and therefore should not be taught in science classes. The National Center for Science Education recognized Haught's efforts with a "Friend of Darwin" award. But Haught does not see this as opposing religion. Instead, he is opposing bad debate. For Haught, deliberative debate means better understanding, not just of the opposition but of one's own position:

> In my theology of evolution I ask: What might the Darwinian understanding of the life story mean when viewed from the perspective of Christian faith, and what are the implications of evolution for understanding the content of faith? For me, what comes out of this kind of reflection is that I can't think about God the same way after Darwin as I did before. The conversation with science allows us to dig deeper into the meaning of our faith traditions. What difference does it make to our understanding of God that the world's life-story comes about by evolution rather than by instantaneous magical interventions?[29]

Haught grounds his criticisms of human origins debate in a normative vision of informed, deliberative debate. From Haught's perspective, these debates are not as good as they could be. The problem is that the conflict narrative drives nondeliberative participation based on ignorance of theological possibilities that bring religion and science together in productive dialogue. Such possibilities exist, and as a theological expert he has created some of those possibilities himself. Yet ignorance persists, even among other experts. For example, in speaking of the new atheists (e.g., Richard Dawkins, Sam Harris), Haught laments:

> My chief objection to the new atheists is that they are almost completely ignorant of what's going on in the world of theology. They talk about the most fundamentalist and extremist versions of faith, and they hold these up as though they're the normative, central core of faith. And they miss so many things. They miss the moral core of Judaism and Christianity—the theme of social justice, which takes those who are marginalized and brings them to the center of society. They give us an extreme caricature of faith and religion.[30]

But Haught does not restrict his criticism to the new atheists. He also criticizes religious participants in human origins debate. Either because they are not aware of possibilities or because they are not committed to the ideal of deliberation in public debate, religious participants sometimes work against good debate. For Haught, this is as big a problem as any caused by the new atheists: "But when any Christians reject evolution these days, one may presume that they usually, though not always, do so on the basis of a literalist style of biblical interpretation. It's this that concerns me. Combined with the principle of private interpretation of Scripture, biblical literalism can end up short-circuiting the process of public debate, justifying almost any domestic and international policies one finds convenient."[31]

Haught obviously measures his criticism in terms of how people subvert public debate for their own purposes. Yet he cannot simply make theological expertise available. Not all people are experts. And if people are already unwilling to deliberate, then adding more information means only increasing the number of things that they do not deliberate about. Haught's approach, then, is to convince elites that productive alternatives exist. Ideally such knowledge will trickle down through public conversation into ordinary people's understanding. But Haught recognizes that elevating the conversation solely through theological intervention in elite public debate may not work. When asked about the future of science- and religion dialogue, he replied: "I'm not terribly optimistic that much is going to happen on a broad cultural level, but I am optimistic that both scientists and theologians will see more importance to the conversation than they have up to this point. In a secondary way, once more people start talking about issues in science and religion, this may have an effect on education and on culture, but I don't see this happening overnight. I'm hopeful, but I'm not optimistic."[32]

Haught's vision of deliberative public life goes unrealized in the debates that he observes over human origins. His expert theological knowledge allows him to recognize a lack of information in these debates, and provides him with the intellectual resources to contribute expertise that should, in theory, elevate the conversation about human origins. He does not advance a particular moral agenda, and he works within existing debate. These two distinctions mark Haught's approach to representation as different from the "public crusade" approach. But Haught also recognizes that "elevating the conversation" is an, at best, diffuse, indirect, and partial approach to changing public debate.

Improving the Signal: Gavin Schmidt

Like Haught, Gavin Schmidt, a research scientist in climatology at the NASA Goddard Institute for Space Studies,[33] sees current public debate as underinformed and therefore not as good as it could be. As a scientific expert in climate modeling and climate change, Schmidt's concern is that debate about the environment is increasingly distant from scientific evidence. From Schmidt's perspective, this is not simply ignorance on the part of participants. Rather, participants looking to improve their political position pollute debate by illegitimately claiming scientific authority for their public talk:

> It's clear that there are a lot of people who talk about politics who are neither interesting nor objective. When it comes to discussing what to do about climate change, it appears to be a fact of life that people will use the worst and least intelligent arguments to make political points. If they can do that by sounding pseudoscientific—by quoting a paper here or misrepresenting another scientist's work over there—then they will. That surprised me before I really looked into it. It no longer surprises me.[34]

From Schmidt's expert perspective, people are not informed enough about current scientific findings to distinguish between good and bad science. Obviously Schmidt has positions on the importance of scientific evidence and what the correct understanding of climate science ought to be. His activity could be seen as a public crusade to convert others to his point of view. However, like Haught, Schmidt emphasizes good debate as more important than political victory. The goal is not to win an argument and get your way, but to enable a better debate than what is happening now, even if that means that you might ultimately be disadvantaged in a competitive public arena. Good debate, meaning informed and deliberative debate, is most important. "I don't advocate for political solutions," he said. "If I do advocate for something (and if you put your voice into the public sphere, then it has to be to advocate for something. Why would you do it otherwise?), [m]y advocacy is much more towards having more intelligent discussions, which is completely naive and stupid and I realise that."

Schmidt participates in environment debate by presenting data and providing additional resources to elevate the conversation about climate change. Unlike public crusaders who seek only to convert others or exclude them from public debate, Schmidt rarely presents arguments against those who disagree. Rather, he promotes the use of scientific evidence. For example, Schmidt is a permanent contributor to RealClimate.org, a website that provides summaries of scientific findings on climate science, answers frequently asked questions about climate science, and engages in public conversation through blogging and commentary. Schmidt uses his particular expertise to provide resources and interact with interested persons in order to improve the quality of debate:

> Over the past five years, I have spent a lot of time building up resources. We spend a lot of time building background for journalists, staffers, and for science advisors of various kinds. We're building up resources that people can use so that they can tell what is a good argument and what is a bad argument. And there has been a shift. There has been a shift in the media; there has been a shift in the majority of people who advise policymakers; there has been a shift in policymakers. This kind of effort—and not just by me, but also by other equally concerned people—has had the effect of elevating the conversation.

But, like Haught, Schmidt has doubts about whether the approach of elevating the conversation will actually work to improve debate. From Schmidt's perspective, there are too many people with interests in bad debate. Bad debate is politically useful, as it creates confusion and breaks apart competing political interests. So elevating the conversation may not actually be a solution to achieving good debate:

> The problem is that the noise serves various people's purposes. It's not that the noise is accidental. When it comes to climate, a lot of the noise is deliberate because if there's an increase of noise you don't hear the signal, and if you don't hear the signal you can't do anything about it. Increasing the level of noise is a deliberate political tactic. It's been used by all segments of the political spectrum for different problems. With the climate issue in the US, it is used by a particular segment of the political community in ways that is [sic] personally distressing. How do you deal with that? That is a question, which I am still asking myself.

Like John Haught, Gavin Schmidt understands public debate as something already happening. It can be better or worse. Schmidt's scientific expertise provides insight into problems of uncertainty over what counts as good scientific information. He recognizes that some persons exploit this uncertainty to subvert debate. But rather than trying to fight political battles, Schmidt emphasizes "elevating the conversation" by contributing his scientific expertise to the areas where that knowledge can (perhaps) make a difference. While he is not necessarily optimistic about the efficacy of this approach, he persists because it does not detract from good public debate even if others try to do so.

Both John Haught and Gavin Schmidt take positions in their respective debates. However, they do not necessarily take a position against anything but uninformed, nondeliberative debate. "Elevating the conversation" means adding better information, not striking out against those who disagree. Unlike those who engage in the public crusade approach, representatives who seek to elevate the conversation are committed to deliberative debate and are not looking to convert others. In the elevating-the-conversation approach, representatives use their expertise to improve the debate that is already happening. They understand good debate to be informed and deliberative. And they work to increase information and deliberation in debate, even as they express doubts about whether anything at all will change.

REPRESENTATIVES AND GOOD DEBATE

What constitutes good debate for representatives in these religion-and-science debates? There is no single answer. Representatives have different ideas about what good debate is and whether it is desirable. Two approaches show up consistently across the four debates in this study. First, in the "public crusade" approach, representatives seek to advance a moral agenda and convert people to their point of view. This requires avoiding debate when possible, and suppressing debate when necessary, in order to minimize opposition to their crusade. Second, in the "elevating the conversation" approach, representatives seek to improve existing debate. This requires using expert knowledge to identify weaknesses and make useful contributions to debate, even if those contributions might not make a difference.

But, perhaps surprisingly, the distribution of these approaches actually has more to do with visibility than with any categorical distinction or membership based on religion or science. "Public crusade" can be found anywhere, but it is prevalent among the highest-visibility representatives in the sample. In contrast, "elevating the conversation" is almost exclusively found among the lowest-visibility representatives in the sample. Given that science representatives tend to have lower visibility, while religion representatives tend to have higher visibility, it is tempting to say that science representatives are more inclined toward deliberative debate, while religion representatives are less inclined. But at the same levels of visibility, science and religion representatives look alike in their approaches to public debate. Higher-visibility science representatives (e.g., Richard Dawkins) take the same public crusade approach as religion representatives. Similarly, lower-visibility religion representatives (e.g., John Haught) take the same elevating-the-conversation approach as low-visibility science representatives.

In short, the most visible representatives in these debates, whatever their affiliation, participate in ways that are most inimical to deliberative debate. While this may not be generalizable to all representatives in all debates, it does actually account for many of the most visible representatives in these debates. Of course, it is not clear from this evidence whether the public crusade approach actually works better than elevating the conversation for making representatives more visible in mass media. But, setting aside the empirical fact that most methods for gaining public visibility do not actually work consistently, the question here is not about how representatives become visible.[35] Rather, the question is whether representatives, whatever their ultimate goal or purpose, approach public life in a manner consistent with normative preferences for deliberative debate. The short answer is that, in general, they do not.

This finding is crucial for understanding how and why people think that these debates are bad. Recall that most scholars and popular authors attribute the lack of quality in these debates to the relationship between religion and science. A bad relationship between religion and science, the theory goes, is imported and reproduced in public debate. Problems of public debate simply reflect problems between religion and science. Yet, even setting aside the absence of such a relationship in public talk, the findings here point in a different direction.

Certainly problems of public debate are directly attributable to the behavior of the representatives in public life. But *most* representatives are behaving in ways inimical to deliberative debate. It is just really unusual for representatives to seek out, and develop, the encounters and engagement that mark deliberative debate. So the problem in these debates is not the relationship between science and religion. The problem is more general. What representatives do impedes, to a greater or lesser degree, the deliberative debate that almost everyone studying religion and science, and many normative theorists of democracy, hold up as ideal. This is especially true of higher-visibility representatives.

If academic scholars and democratic theorists were the only ones frustrated by this behavior, seeking good debate would simply be an academic exercise. But what representatives do in public life has constitutive effects. Public debates are important because of their implications for broader talk among ordinary Americans. Debates in public life provide topics, arguments, and stories for conversations at the dinner table, the pub, and the water cooler. So what does it mean that the most visible representatives concerning these issues are also the least likely to engage in deliberative debate? What are the implications for the vast majority of Americans who are not academic scholars and democratic theorists? Is it even a problem? Do ordinary persons even want deliberative debate?

CHAPTER 5

Ordinary Americans
and Good Debate

For the most visible representatives in religion-and-science debates, good debate means trying to get your way. This approach obviously conflicts with what scholars of religion and science, and many normative democratic theorists, think is good debate. Trying to get your way does not require encountering or engaging other representatives, so it does not foster deliberative debate. Clearly these two notions of good debate are at odds. And on its face, this seems a problem. Actually existing debates are not as good as they could be, and representatives are to blame.

But consider an alternative explanation. Maybe scholars of religion and science (and many normative democratic theorists) are the only people who think that good debate is deliberative debate. After all, the public sphere is part of democratic society. It is possible that representatives seek to get their way for reasons that are entirely democratic. Maybe representatives are doing exactly what ordinary Americans want them to do. If that is the case, then scholars of religion and science might be right that these representatives, and these debates, fail to be deliberative, but this failure is not actually a problem for the vast majority of Americans who are not (officially) academic researchers or democratic theorists. Instead, what representatives do reflects what ordinary Americans want.

This alternative explanation seems to be supported by studies of what American voters, or at least potential voters, want from their elected officials. Studies of electoral politics show that voters consistently prefer representatives who help them get their way, and vote based not only on direct substantive political similarities or interests but also on evaluative "shortcuts" such as candidate gender, race, and religion.[1] To the extent that this is true for the broader arena of public debate, prominent representatives seeking to get their way should be evaluated positively by ordinary Americans. What ordinary Americans think is good debate should align with what representatives think is good debate.

But is this actually the case? Surprisingly, existing empirical studies provide no obvious answer. The link between representatives and ordinary persons in public debate is rarely, if ever, considered as a set of empirical questions about what ordinary Americans want.[2] As a result, many key questions remain unanswered. Does the behavior of representatives in public life matter to ordinary Americans? Why are representatives important? Do ordinary people actually think that there are problems with representatives in these debates? If so, what are the problems that they see? And, most important, what kind of debate would they prefer to see?

To find out what counts as good debate for ordinary Americans, I engaged in semistructured individual interviews with sixty-two respondents from a variety of religious and scientific backgrounds.[3] I started each discussion with open-ended questions about how respondents understood each religion-and-science debate. I then asked respondents to participate in a variety of evaluation exercises. By "evaluation" I simply mean how and why persons recognize something as good or bad.[4] Respondents evaluated anonymized résumés and quotes from representatives. They discussed various representatives by name. They even constructed an ideal committee of representatives for each issue. And as they evaluated representatives in these debates, their own preferences about representatives and about public debate emerged.

HOW ORDINARY PEOPLE SEE DEBATES

Before seeing any names, résumés, statements, or any other potentially guiding information, respondents told me what they thought about each debate in terms that made sense to them. How they talked about a debate varied. Sometimes respondents preferred to describe groups of people, such as "scientists" or "creationists." Sometimes respondents described debate in terms of positions, such as "pro-evolution" or "pro-environment." Sometimes respondents simply did not say anything at all (e.g., "I don't know enough about it, really.") And, like many responses to open-ended questions throughout the interview, substantive answers sometimes emerged only in dialogue or following a prompt or challenge on the part of the interviewer, rather than being clearly presented in finished form.

But while respondents varied in their specific approach to describing what debates are about, they consistently distinguished between debates that are about religion and science and debates that are about something else entirely. In almost every case, respondents described human origins debate and stem cell research debate as some variation of religion and science, whether as specific persons ("creationists versus scientists") or in more general terms ("religion versus science"). And, in almost every case, respondents did not see debates over the origins of homosexuality or environmental policy as religion-and-science debates. Debate over the origins of homosexuality was seen primarily as "religious people versus gays" or "no conflict/don't know." Environmental policy debate, by contrast, was seen as multisided, with the sides varying among politicians, scientists, environmental activists, religious persons, and corporate industry.

Given that I selected each of these debates based on the involvement both of religion and of science, the fact that some debates were seen as between religion and science while others were barely seen as involving religion and science at all is a basic refutation of the idea that religion and science are inherently conflictual or opposed.[5] But the more important point is that respondents' internal maps of what debates are about aligned neatly with the distribution of prominent representatives in those debates. This is instructive for our understanding more generally of the role of representatives in public debate.

Religion-and-science Debates as Religion and Science

The vast majority of respondents understood human origins debate to be some version of "creationists versus scientists" or "religion versus science." For example, Jennifer described it as a "kind of a science-versus-religion debate" where the "most vocal" participants "are the fundamentalist Christians basing their [position] on the Bible." Jennifer specifically recalled going to a religious school as a child where "they were teaching us that it was exactly 4,004 years before Christ that the world was here and dinosaurs are a myth put there by God to confuse people and scientists are wrong and that kind of thing." She also noted that members of a local religious community consistently challenged her "friends who teach biology in schools" whenever they taught concepts related to evolution. After relating these various anecdotes, she summarized human origins debate as "scientists versus fundamentalist Christians."

Jennifer is hardly alone. Nor is her approach to answering the question unusual. Respondents often drew on personal experiences with their friends, neighbors, and co-workers, as well as what they saw in newspapers or on television, to describe what the debate is about, who was debating, and what the overall debate tended to look like. Respondents also tended to describe debate in multiple ways in response to prompting. So, for example, Yuri described human origins debate as occurring among a variety of creationists, including "Christian pastors" and "Jewish rabbis," but she observed that people arguing "for the evolution part [are] mostly people who [don't] believe in God." She explicitly admitted that her framing of the debate reflects her knowledge of the creationist position, and allowed that her "bias come[s] in because I'm not as harsh as how I view the evolution people."

While there was some variation in how respondents described and articulated their understanding of human origins debate, clearly respondents consistently see it as some version of religion-and-science debate. Whether they described it as creationists versus scientists, creationists versus atheists, or simply religion versus science, respondents see this debate as structured entirely by a conflict in some form between religion and science. This is consistent with what the epistemological conflict model would predict. Respondents described competing claims about human origins, with science offering an evolutionary account and religion offering a creationist account that cannot both be true.

As with human origins debate, the dominant mode for describing stem cell research debate was in religion-and-science terms. But in contrast to human origins debate, stem cell research debate appeared to be understood primarily as an issue of moral positioning. Note that there were several variations that described stem cell research debate as expression of moral objections. Zoe, for example, said, "Some people don't believe that we should have that right to genetically manipulate or clone or whatever, but other people believe that it's part of progression, it can help cure illnesses and diseases, so why not continue on that research?" In discussing who is involved in the debate, she specified "the very religious people, they definitely are the people who are very against it and think it's against God, think it's unnatural," while "people who are more scientifically inclined want to do everything they can to cure diseases and fix things and make a better future." Like Zoe, many respondents saw stem cell research debate as religious people making moral claims about science, even while recognizing potential benefits of scientific research. Max, for example, cited a study that he read in which a child had "had an IQ of maybe 40," but "after injecting fetal stem cells into his brain, he was able to tie his shoe, hold his defecation, and actually communicate." But Max quickly pointed out that there are many moral issues involved that have to be worked out: "If you're going to be using fetal stem cells and you could say, well, then people will just have babies for stem cells. But then you're like, well, you can only use aborted ones. Well, then people will have abortions for stem cells. So then it becomes a moral issue."

Similar to human origins debate, the stem cell research debate provoked respondents to describe debate in primarily religion-and-science terms. However, this was not because of competing epistemological claims, but rather because of moral claims seen to originate in religious traditions competing with moral claims implied by the science of stem cell research.[6] As Erika put it, the debate is really about what to do given "the scientific research that's taken us into uncharted waters." In most cases, respondents understood this debate to be primarily about religion making moral claims to which science must, in various ways, respond. While the resulting "religion versus science" description was consistent with what a conflict model might predict, the reasons for that description were not expressed in terms of epistemological conflict. Even so, respondents saw both debates in religion-and-science terms.

Religion-and-science Debates as Something Else

In debates over environmental policy and the origins of homosexuality, while religion and science participate, debates were not seen as primarily between religion and science. Only three respondents explicitly talked about the origins of homosexuality in religion-and-science terms. Morris, for example, had talked about this debate "in Sunday School class" and basically thought that it is about whether being gay is "biological or choice." For Morris, those who are arguing are "scientists of course, geneticists and whatnot, as opposed to those who are religious conservatives." But for the most part, respondents saw debate over the origins of homosexuality as a conflict between religious people and others. Barry, for example, said that it "is more of a religious debate on whether being gay or straight is correct from the point of view of—I don't want to say going to heaven or hell, but from a religious standpoint, is it acceptable." Clarifying who might be debating, Barry said, "I think it is the Catholic church that is doing most of the debating, and

I think they're debating with the gay community but much more so with themselves about the apparent kind of hypocrisy of—now, I'm not an expert on the Bible but what it says to be—love thy brother and yet don't love thy brother if they're gay." For Barry, debate over the origins of sexuality is rooted in a religious issue that manifests as debate over how to treat gay people in society.

Although respondents consistently identified religion as important, they usually imagined the other "side" or "sides" not as scientists or even science more generally, but as gay persons. For example, Sterling described the debate in terms of gay persons defending themselves against (primarily religious) people who are trying to limit them. Sterling has "a family member who's gay, if that matters," and noted that "the gay advocacy groups are very strongly vocal" and "trying to make the point on this issue." He thought that "the only people arguing against them are just people that are just saying, 'That's wrong,'" which fortunately is not "a huge vocal opposition." Similarly, Anita saw gay persons as defending themselves in public debate against moral attacks. In Anita's terms, gay people "want to be accepted by society, be recognized," but must defend against "the other side," which consists of "people [who] are raising their children, and they have a concern [about gay people]."

Debate over the origins of homosexuality was not generally understood in religion-and-science terms. But it was sometimes not even considered in debate terms. Alexander, for example, while admitting that "this [debate] is something I'm not so familiar with," nonetheless suggested that it is probably about personal experiences, in which "some people believe that there are things that you learn, how you're raised, and that's how you come about, that's what you become," while "other people believe that you are born with the God-given destiny, and that's where you live." For Alexander and several others, the debate is not so much an overarching conflict as a discussion about how to make sense of one's own experiences and beliefs. But whether framed as conflict or not, this debate did not prompt respondents to describe it in religion-and-science terms, despite the involvement of both religion and science in public talk about the issue.

Debate over environmental policy was primarily seen as a multisided debate with extensive political and activist involvement. As with the origins of homosexuality, while some respondents described the debate in religion-and-science terms, most did not. No clear consensus emerged. For most respondents, the debate is about some combination of politics, science, religion, industry, and activism. What that combination includes varied considerably among respondents, but rarely did anyone consider this to be a religion-and-science debate. To the extent that there is common ground in respondents' perceptions, it is that environmental policy debate is an arena for different interest groups to promote their agenda, with religion and science not registering among the most prominent groups. Harvey talked about watching specials on the History Channel and how "Gore is so prominent," but said that when it comes to debate, he "usually hear[s] it through whatever political lies are said," and that "political parties at large pretty much bring the thing up every once in a while as an issue to try to attract votes when the elections are on." Scott similarly described this debate as being among "folk that have an economic interest, folks that have, I guess I would say, a moral interest from the standpoint that their personal morals motivate them to become involved because of a perceived injustice, and people that have not so much an economic interest in the results of the argument skewing one way or another, but rather folks that have an economic interest in there being an argument at all."

Even when respondents recognized that environmental policy debate could potentially center on religion and science, they pointed out that it generally is not a religion-and-science debate in practice. Leo, for example, said that "there isn't a whole lot of people left who don't see climate change as an issue" and that "there's very few who deny that it's even occurring." Even "younger Christians, especially in the evangelical sector, are seeking solutions to climate change trying to reverse." When I asked him where the older religious persons, especially evangelicals, stand, he replied: "I just don't think it's that big of an issue. Older evangelicals are more concerned with moral issues, for example, abortion, homosexuality, whereas younger evangelicals have a different focus on social justice, sound environmental policy, things like that." For Leo, even if older religious people could in theory make this more of a religion-and-science debate, they do not do so, because they are arguing about other issues. As with the origins of homosexuality debate, respondents simply did not see environmental policy debate in religion-and-science terms.

Representatives as Boundary Markers

All of these debates involve religion and science. But not all are seen as debates between religion and science. Whether they are seen as religion-and-science debates or not depends on the distribution of representatives (and, to a lesser extent, on the distribution of talk). The most prominent representatives in human origins debate are scientists or religious leaders closely associated with conflicting positions, in this case evolution and creationism. The most prominent representatives in stem cell research debate are religious leaders and politicians making moral claims against science that are grounded in religion talk. Both of these debates have visible religion and science representatives. Both are seen as religion-and-science debates.

Similarly, the most prominent representatives in debate over the origins of homosexuality are various religious leaders and gay and ex-gay activists who primarily take pro-gay positions grounded in political discourse or anti-gay positions based on religious belief. The most prominent representatives in environmental policy debate are a mix of political actors and religious leaders who sometimes use religion talk, but do so primarily to align with business interests or to minimize the importance of the environment issue entirely. Both of these debates have a range of representatives who are not clearly religion and science representatives. Both are seen as something other than religion-and-science debates.

There is an inescapable alignment between the mental maps of debate that respondents hold and the maps of public talk produced by the distribution of prominent representatives. Obviously it is not the case that every respondent has a master list of prominent representatives to which they refer in describing these debates. But what ordinary persons understand debate to be is entirely predictable with reference to the most prominent representatives who show up in these debates. In this sense, prominent representatives serve as boundary markers for the substantive content of public debate.

But respondents also expressed their thoughts on the debates in terms of the quality of representatives in those debates. For ordinary people, debates are not abstract ideas. They are the product of particular people talking in public. Put simply, what people think about these debates is actually what they think about representatives in these debates. Debates are what representatives do. If we want to know what counts as good debate for ordinary Americans, we have to understand what counts as a good representative for ordinary Americans.

HOW ORDINARY PERSONS EVALUATE REPRESENTATIVES

So how do ordinary Americans evaluate representatives in these debates? Across all interviews, respondents applied what I call a *deliberative frame* to evaluate representatives. By "deliberative frame" I mean that respondents primarily evaluated representatives in terms of openness to multiple perspectives, respect for conflicting positions, and commitment to ongoing discussion. In each dimension of evaluating a representative, respondents mobilized a deliberative frame. Evaluation sometimes appeared to be based on shortcuts grounded in, for example, apparent identity or interests that seem unrelated to norms of public debate. However, respondents primarily used such shortcuts to assess the open- or closed-mindedness of a representative. The assessment of deliberative potential outweighed agreement with the representative's position or resemblance to the representative's apparent constituency.

Evaluating Résumés

In the résumé portion of the interview, respondents reviewed anonymized résumés of selected representatives that included information such as age, education, nationality, employment history, publications, religious affiliations, and awards. Not every respondent gave the same importance to each factor in the evaluation process. The consistent finding is that, whatever factors they think are important, respondents negatively evaluated those résumés that they thought signaled closed-mindedness. For example, Samuel assessed as follows the résumé of a prominent author and "family values" activist affiliated with the conservative Christian group Focus on the Family: "Yeah, this one would be in opposition to [gays]. It's pretty cut and dried, just based on the books that he's written. Again, focusing on the American values. So it's more the traditional versus opening up to other options. So, yeah, I would definitely think that, because of his religious background."

Note that this evaluation process was directed toward a deliberative ideal, not just against religion in particular. Samuel is himself a committed Catholic. The concern was about "opening up to other options," and the "traditional" commitment to "American values" seemed to Samuel to indicate a fixed perspective or apparently illiberal commitment to one point of view. Similarly, in evaluating the résumé of a prominent, award-winning endowed professor of science, Holly expressed concern about "closed-minded" perspectives: "He's a researcher, obviously. He represents more science-based, probably more closed-off science-based population as opposed to researchers. [I mean] just a more research-based closed-minded population that don't necessarily look at all the facts and think that perhaps only their viewpoint and their research is the most that matters."

Likewise, respondents positively evaluated those who appear open-minded or objective, including some scientists and religious moderates. In assessing the résumé of a conservative Christian broadcaster and activist, Lydia responded: "This is also a really bright person. And this is really a passionate person. I wouldn't say fundamentalist—she's not fundamentalist—it's not that. She's sort of—this is the woman who's trying to bridge the gap between [one side] and [the other side]. She's coming up and trying to talk really intelligently about it."

Similarly, Barry invoked a number of identity-related factors in his positive evaluation of a research psychologist's résumé:

> [B]ecause this person is an author of scientific papers on sexual orientation, I'm assuming this person has researched sexual orientation and has a more balanced view of it. Now there are things that might counter what I'm saying here. Traditionally an older population is not always as open to diversity. [This representative] is associated with the Presbyterian Medical Center. In my experience religion fosters a more conservative attitude towards the gay community but I'm not going to assume that because I've had a lot of friends myself who are very religious yet very open to the gay movement.

Evaluating Statements

In the statement part of the interview, respondents evaluated anonymized comments that representatives had actually made in public debate. In evaluating these statements, respondents negatively evaluated language that took a strong, fixed position or specifically targeted someone else's position. For example, Harvey evaluated a statement claiming that environmental problems are an offense against God: "I think this is a rather narrow-minded view, and it's anti-environmentalist. This guy will take a crap in his kitchen and make a statement like that and call it an offense against God."

Respondents were particularly sensitive to tone in statements made by representatives. For example, in responding to a comment from a prominent scientist about how people who don't believe in evolution are ignorant, stupid, or insane, Morgane disagreed with the claim about evolution, but expressed greater concern about the tone of the statement: "Well, I disagree with this statement wholeheartedly, of course. And this person is obviously not just an evolutionist, but somebody who lacks any kind of integrity or compassion or just basic communication skills." In evaluating a statement from a prominent conservative religious activist referring to the "homosexual agenda" as "a beast that wants our kids," Arthur sarcastically replied, "That's not inflammatory at all. This person is obviously rabid." And Daniela said:

> I strongly disagree with this. I don't know—I think it's because of the word "beast." Well, it really—I think a lot of the ways the really conservative religious people in this particular debate really shoot themselves in the foot [is] by using words like "beast." And the way they frame this . . . I mean, they use words that make them seem nonhuman. Just like in war, all right, the way the military community would talk about the enemy in ways that are nonhuman to make them easier to kill.

To be clear, respondents who mobilized instances of the deliberative frame were doing so in addition to, or in spite of, any substantive agreement or disagreement. Daniela is a neuroscientist, but she also disapproved of the "ignorant, stupid, or insane" statement, even though it comes from a scientist. Dwight, who is staunchly pro-evolution, evaluated the "ignorant, stupid, or insane" statement similarly to Morgane, who opposed evolution: "That is a little harsh. I like to think that I'm not that judgmental about them. They have a belief or disbelief in evolution, and there's reasons behind it, and the best you can do is to try and understand those reasons."

Don, who personally thinks that homosexuality is biological and unusual, nonetheless objected to a statement calling homosexuality a "biological error" on the grounds that it is unnecessarily hostile: "Whoa. I don't agree with this. There's two words you can take out and I might. I think it's biological but I don't think it's an error. You take the 'error' words out, and there's some truth to it. Who would say that? Somebody that was homophobic."

Though less commonly, respondents also positively evaluated statements that were explicitly open to different conclusions or cognizant of alternative positions without condemning them. For example, Solomon positively assessed a statement made by a senior fellow at a conservative think tank: "This could have been a scientist; it could have been a spiritual leader . . . 'spiritual' there meaning a grounded person. This is the statement that comes closest to my opinion, and I think this is a person who came to this conclusion by perhaps his own experiences or observations. But this is a person who would be open to, again, listen[ing] to the other points of view. This is a person who you'd want to have in a group discussion to introduce mutual ideas." And Ian evaluated a statement by a prominent conservative Christian activist: "At least I can respect this person. Mainly from his tone of voice. He believes. It makes it an opinion on his part rather than an edict, which I respect. I disagree with it. It probably represents a church group as well."

Obviously respondents used shortcuts, but note that they were not consistent in their use of shortcuts in evaluating résumés and statements. Religion did not always mean negative assessment, for example. Disagreement did not always mean disapproval. Agreement did not always mean approval. Clearly what respondents saw as deliberative or as signaling openness to multiple perspectives varied considerably. The robust qualitative finding is that respondents evaluated representatives using a deliberative frame.

Appointing Hypothetical Committees

In the committee part of the interview, respondents suggested who would be good representatives on a committee that would hold the ideal debate about each topic. This part of the interview was entirely open-ended. The point was to see how respondents made their choices. Respondents populated committees in a variety of ways, naming particular persons (e.g., "Bob Newhart"), unidentified members of a social group (e.g., "a scientist"), or some combination (e.g., "my minister, a scientist, and James Dobson").

But even with this diversity of selections, respondents consistently justified their choices with reference to the deliberative frame. This occurred in three different ways. First, respondents selected individuals that they judged to be personally open-minded and respectful of other positions. Second, respondents constructed committees that, as a whole, reflected their preference for inclusion of multiple perspectives and for ongoing discussion. Finally, respondents paid particular attention to the ways that any committee would relate to a broader audience, rather than just to a select audience of elites or like-minded people.

Several respondents appointed representatives to their committees based on personal qualities they judged to be consistent with the deliberative frame, such as open-mindedness, neutrality, or willingness to have conversations with people who disagree. In many cases these representatives were either popular activist media figures, such as George Clooney or Oprah Winfrey, or moderate religious leaders, such as the Dalai Lama. Charles, for example, explained his choice of Dr. Drew Pinsky, host of the talk show *Loveline*: "Well, Dr. Drew, I think, because I really like what he has to say about sexuality and different kinds of viewpoints about it. I think he has a really good way of articulating different arguments and doing it in ways that people aren't necessarily put off by it, even if they disagree."

Both Erika and Damien (in separate interviews) picked representatives a bit closer to home, but for similar reasons:

Erika: I know I would put my friend on it. She's a Methodist minister. Because she's very strong in her views and her views are very well considered. She's—has a real interest about people and life, has a large exposure to different kinds of people.

Damien: I think I would put my pastor in there. I'd put him in there because I think he's absolutely willing to engage in the talk and also like—also be like—not seek to punish or to treat [the other side] as outcasts or anything by any means . . . there's no sense of condemnation or anything like that, and I think—to me that's a really important thing. So [the committee] wouldn't make policies that are exclusive.

Respondents also emphasized inclusion of multiple perspectives in the overall committee composition. They favored representatives who would keep discussion going rather than ending debate, even if this means that no one wins the argument. For example, while the specifics of the representatives and issues were not always the same and the "sides" in each debate varied, both Miley and Amanda clearly expressed an underlying commitment to a deliberative frame. Asked about a (hypothetical) committee to decide what would be taught about human origins in schools, Miley responded: "Okay, well, I don't know specific people. I'd probably try to have it as even as possible, maybe two religious people; I'm not exactly sure who. Two scientists, scientific people that have studied evolution and have all the evidence for it, then maybe one kind of neutral—not so much neutral, but who could get facts from both." And on the issue of origins of homosexuality, Amanda offered a more sociological perspective on representation, but still favored deliberation as the guiding principle: "Okay, I would like it to be evenly representative. And I don't think, you know, necessarily the supposed 10 or 13 percent of the committee being as in the population, but more like fifty-fifty representing heterosexual and homosexual perspectives. And I'd like it to be split genderwise as well, equally. But not all like the guys, straight guys and then you know what I mean? I'd like it to be so that there was some good equity there."

Respondents also picked committee members who they judged would help extend the conversation to a broader public audience. Sometimes this meant selecting ordinary people who they thought might talk to other people more easily. For example, in selecting members for a committee on environmental policy, Judith offered the following choice: "I want an electrician, just because I think that would help understand everything more. So when we present to the people our ideas, there's gonna be someone that can explain every facet of this new engine, of this new whatever. So these aren't necessarily gonna be famous people. I want to understand why this works and how it will be better. I need someone that can in laymen's terms describe it to us because I don't think people are getting on board for this stuff." But on another issue, Judith gave a slightly more cynical take on the deliberative frame during her committee selection: "I would have it be a balance, if you will. Have someone on there that I know would disagree, just to kind of, at least, appease some people and reach more people. I'd probably pick Ronald Reagan; he's my right-wing guy. Now I need females. Maya Angelou because she's so eloquent. And Ayn Rand. Really mix it up."

As Judith's statement indicates, even though respondents often held strong positions on particular issues, their commitment to the deliberative frame (whatever the motive) could override their temptation to "stack the deck" in favor of their own position.[7] Raymond, for example, did not select his committee based on issue agreement, but on his assessment of whether his committee members would be acceptable within a deliberative frame: "Well, the Falwells and the popes and the Pat Robertsons and the George Bushes probably would certainly not be there. I might have Al Gore there just because I respect his clear-mindedness about things. And even if he took a position that I might not agree with, I would be interested to know why I don't agree with him, you know, why he—because I think his words are reasonable, well reasoned, so I might have Al Gore on there."

Sometimes respondents admittedly stacked the deck in favor of their own position by selecting committee members who would agree with their own point of view. But this was by far the exception rather than the rule. And even in these cases, respondents tended to justify their choices in terms of inclusion or open-mindedness. Take, for example, Pamela's committee on the issue of human origins, which emphasized her desire to include a range of backgrounds:

> Well, I would stack the deck on my committee and make sure that all of them believed in Jesus Christ . . . because of the impact of the nature of what they're going to decide. I would want somebody on the committee who represents a broad spectrum of background, maybe has experience in a number

of different facets of life, or a number of different fields of life, or a number of different experiences in life. I mean they all should have some variety of background.

And Josefina excluded people with whom she disagrees from a committee on environmental policy, primarily because she does not see them as open-minded participants:

> I don't think anybody on the, speaking from, you know, thinking that morality and environment can't go hand-in-hand, I don't think anybody like that should be on the committee. Conservative Christians . . . I don't want somebody like Susan Sarandon who causes so much tension on the topic. I want somebody that's kind of a neutral figure but a face that people recognize and can talk about the environmental issues in a tone where everybody can understand it.

Despite commitments to a particular position in debate, respondents justified their choices with reference to the deliberative frame, either by appointing individuals whom they judged to be open-minded and inclusive, or by ensuring that the committee as a whole reflected a wider range of perspectives. Even when they stacked the deck in favor of their position, they included a range of other viewpoints as well. Their use of interests in evaluation, then, was not simply to reconstruct debate to favor their own interests. Rather, they used their knowledge of representatives to construct deliberative debate that brings together many different perspectives. They sought to maximize, rather than narrow, the scope of debate.

THE ELECTORAL DISCOUNT

The deliberative frame raises an interesting question about politicians in public debate. We know that Americans vote for politicians based largely on those leaders' ability to get their way. But in practice, electoral politics and public debate are fully entangled. Formally elected representatives often participate in public debate, though of course the extent of this participation varies by issue. In this study, for example, few politicians figured prominently in debates about human origins or the origins of homosexuality, while many politicians figured prominently in debates about stem cell research and environmental policy. But regardless of the extent to which elected officials figure in a debate, their very participation provides a strong test of the deliberative frame. Do respondents apply the deliberative frame to politicians when they participate in the public sphere?

The answer is "yes." Respondents apply the deliberative frame to all representatives in public debate. But there is a distinct "electoral discount" for representatives seen as active in electoral politics. I use the term "electoral discount" to bring together the ways that respondents evaluated elected representatives as less legitimate, or illegitimate, across several different dimensions. While this was most widely articulated as a criticism of particular persons with recognized names, such as George W. Bush, Al Gore, or John Kerry, it was also a persistent finding in respondent evaluations of résumés, statements, and hypothetical committee appointments. Even when they recognized that elected officials might be effective and appropriate representatives in the arena of institutional politics, respondents discounted the participation of elected officials as violating deliberative preferences.

To be clear, I do not mean simply to say that respondents were dissatisfied with government in general. Respondents did express this sentiment—for example, by accusing government of doing "whatever it needs to do to appease people," referring to political debates in Congress as "a bunch of hot air," complaining about how government has "too much control" in our lives, or joking about "a [college] degree in government—I'd like to know what that would look like!" Nor were respondents simply unhappy with particular candidates who did not share their own views, though that is also common. I mean, rather, that respondents saw the motives of elected representatives as suspect (e.g., that they are corrupt), that they saw elected representatives as incapable of doing what people want them to do, and that they expected elected representatives to dissimulate about what they really think. Although this electoral discount showed up largely as criticism of particular elected representatives and their purported constituencies, the sentiment also emerged throughout the interviews in a wide variety of indictments of elected representatives.

Although I treat the electoral discount as separate for illustrative purposes, I reiterate that it is a consequence of respondent preference for deliberation in public life. What is objectionable about elected representatives is that they subvert the deliberation that respondents see as central to good debate. The reasons vary. Some politicians are seen as incapable. Others are seen as compromised. And still others are seen as simply more interested in their own careers or profits than they are in public deliberation. But whatever the reason, elected representatives fail to realize the deliberative ideal that ordinary people expect in public life. The electoral discount results from the conflict between what elected representatives do and what ordinary people think ought to be done.

Evaluation without Names

While examples abound of respondents discounting elected representatives once their names are invoked (e.g., George W. Bush), I note that before anyone even mentioned names, the electoral discount showed up as an important pattern in evaluation. Respondents negatively evaluated résumés that indicated political experience. For example, in evaluating the résumé of an elected executive involved in public debates over stem cell research, Ernest immediately raised concerns about a political background: "Currently politician . . . as soon as you say politician, that makes me think, 'Is he going to do what he believes or is he going to do what it takes to get elected?'" And Connie discounted an apparent politician as not genuinely motivated by his own opinions: "Okay. This is somebody who works for the government, and so he's been taught very well to go ahead being very noncommittal in his viewpoints. Yet obviously he communicates them very well to the public because of his background in communication . . . and he keeps his opinions to himself."

Respondents also negatively evaluated statements that "sounded" like they came from politicians. In particular, respondents invoked politicians as examples of instrumentalists who say things only to keep their careers going. Josefina, for example, evaluated a statement about global warming as "representing more of the politicians who have spent a career not supporting this and who need to back up their statements." Respondents also expressed concern about links between political and economic interests. When presented with a particularly strong declarative statement asserting global warming to be a myth, Phoebe said: "I think this represents politicians. Not all politicians, but someone who is, you know, trying to create more economic growth at the expense of the environment."

At the same time, respondents often positively evaluated statements that did not immediately suggest politicians had made them, but that actually were made by politicians. This suggests that identification as someone who is involved in electoral politics, rather than substantive disagreement over the content of the statement, prompted an evaluative discount for elected representatives. For example, although George W. Bush by name was repeatedly criticized (see below), anonymized public statements made by Bush often provoked neutral or positive responses. Responding to a statement about stem cell research and human cloning, Daniela said: "I partially agree with this statement. I don't know that I would say that I strongly oppose human cloning, but I definitely agree with the rest of the statement. . . . I think this represents a lot, I think this does represent the general American or the average American."

In selecting committees, some respondents specifically excluded politicians. Susanne, for example, refused to appoint a hypothetical committee on the stem cell research issue, indicating that it should not be a political issue at all, and expressing serious concern about introducing politicians into the process: "In my opinion, I don't think it should be a political issue, so that's a difficult thing. So we would exclude politicians, and again, to me, it's a question of education; that's not political. It becomes a political issue, and that's, to me, that is not the arena that this needs to go in."

Others excluded politicians because of characteristics they are believed to possess that disqualify them from public deliberation. Bonnie, for example, excluded "pretty much any currently active politician I can think of, because they tend not to listen." Timothy expressed a similar distaste: "I wouldn't put politicians on it. I don't think they have the brainpower, usually, or the freedom from special interests. Maybe it's not so much a matter of brainpower in every case, but they have to do something, and they have to act, and they don't have the freedom to really be careful." And Elaine discounted the involvement of professional politicians as self-serving: "They would have to sign something that says, I'm never gonna run for public office if I serve on this committee. You know, when you get these ridiculous policies that are created that nobody's ever gonna be able to follow, and they're basically created because somebody needed something to add to their résumé or something?"

When respondents selected politicians (either by category or by name) for a committee, they usually did so based on an assessment of politicians as substantively irrelevant, but useful for working with the public. Chantal, for example, thought politicians could be helpful in a bureaucratic sense: "One of them would be an appointed politician. Because I think that you definitely need someone who could explain to people what's going on, and why. Someone who can do the law and handle all those type of, those political, social, the social aspect of handling all that." Jennifer suggested that politicians provide legitimacy to the process, but clearly indicated that she could simply select the politician most favorable to her own interests: "I need a politician. Just, like, to have one on the committee just to make it seem official. A politician who is pro–gay marriage rights, and I don't know who that would be. Maybe like one of those people—the mayor of San Francisco, I think, was on the news in some of the ads or something."

I describe below many vivid examples of negative name recognition in these debates. But it is important to remember that the electoral discount, and in particular the assessment of politicians as insincere, permeated respondent evaluations even when specific names were not presented. Respondents applied the electoral discount in open discussion, in the course of evaluating anonymous résumés and statements, and in appointing hypothetical policy committees. The basic finding is that simply being seen as a participant in electoral politics marks a representative as less legitimate in public debate. For most respondents, politicians work against deliberative debate, if they work at all.

Name Recognition

Given the extent and frequency of electoral campaigns in American public life, it is not surprising that respondents had stronger responses to specific names of politicians that were presented to them, such as George W. Bush, John Kerry, John McCain, and Al Gore. But name recognition did not automatically mean evaluation in one direction or another. In many cases, respondents had no clear idea which constituencies these elected representatives might represent or what positions they might hold. Charles evaluated John Kerry in debates about environmental policy: "John Kerry, my impression of John Kerry is kind of very gray, like I don't really know that he said very much substantial and I haven't read anything by him. His campaign was a lot of rhetoric even by today's standards, which is full of rhetoric. I don't really remember anything substantial that he said."

Sometimes respondents tried to guess about a candidate's stand on issues based on what they knew of his or her identity. Yuri evaluated George W. Bush in debates about human origins: "Gosh, you know, to be honest with you I would like to say he stands for creation because, you know, he has that Christian background, but I haven't personally, like, heard him, you know, say 'This is what I'm believing' so I can't say for sure."

But beyond simply not knowing an elected representative's substantive commitments, respondents suggested that politicians were not capable of maintaining a substantive position. Respondents indicated that they could not evaluate a representative, not because they did not recognize the name, and not because they didn't know what the representative stood for, but rather because politicians are too instrumental to be associated with a consistently identifiable position or constituency. Take, for example, Ian's evaluation of John McCain: "Also a government guy. I'd need to find out a little bit more, I guess. I don't know who he represents quite yet. I don't think he does either. He's reading for the writers behind the curtain who say 'This is what you're going to be representing.' He's like 'Who do I represent, guys?'" This theme also resonated in Don's evaluation of John Kerry: "Can you tell which way the wind's blowing and I'll tell you what he stands for? Well, only based on the fact he's a Democrat that I would assume that he believes in stem cell research or the other but I mean, there's a guy that goes in so many directions. I mean, there's a man that I don't particularly like."

Respondents also evaluated elected representatives as unhelpfully beholden to a particular constituency. Most commonly, respondents associated prominent political conservatives with a disproportionately influential business or religious constituency. For example, Scott evaluated George W. Bush in debate about environmental policy: "So the President, what does he stand for in this debate? . . . I think his attitude has changed during his administration. I think that he stands for corporations, frankly. He stands for corporations and is interested in preserving the economic viability of companies." Zoe offered a similar response for debate about the origins of homosexuality: "I think he's against homosexuality, maybe not preachy, but I can't see him being approving of it. I know that he's religious. I know that's Republican and Republicans are often not too happy with the idea."

Often these strong associations were understood as overriding the elected representative's own interests. Judith, for example, claimed that "you don't keep getting elected over and over without appealing to the religious element," and Sienna thought that George W. Bush "doesn't personally believe" in an anti-environment position despite being "on the side of big business." But sometimes politicians were discounted for the opposite reason. Jennifer provided an example from debates over stem cell research in which she discounted one elected representative precisely because his political instrumentalism overrode his constituency commitments: "I recognize him. I think on this debate he is—well, at first I think he's anti–stem cell research, although I think he actually helped with some of the funding, so I'm not sure. I think he represents the fundamentalist, anti–stem cell group, although for political reasons, he might have some concessions that he's made over the years on that." Erika evaluated Bill Clinton similarly: "I think he's—I'd say that he's not gung-ho. I think he hedged his bets there. I think he was trying to cater to a lot of interests and ended up helping no one."

Finally, in one of the most explicit indicators of the electoral discount, respondents positively evaluated politicians who left (or were about to leave) office, and used them as examples to illustrate why politicians who are still involved in electoral politics should be evaluated negatively. Sterling made a more general case for involving a former president in a committee, saying that such leaders would be ideal because they "understood how government worked but had no incentives left because they're done." More specifically, both Anita and Raymond (in separate interviews) neatly illustrated this application of the electoral discount in discussions of George W. Bush and Al Gore, respectively:

> Anita: Because of his position I don't think he can just 100 percent show or say what he needs to say. But I believe, and it's just my belief, that deep down in his heart, when he's not wearing the president hat, he'll probably come out and say what he wants to say.

> Raymond: I get the sense from Al Gore, perhaps because much of his activism has to do with a nonofficial position, that it, therefore, is not bound by some of the duties he is required to perform within an official position, unlike Bill Clinton, whose concerns for the environment such as they were stated during his presidency were, perhaps, politicized, that is to say, toned down or otherwise altered due to his official station.

People in general are distrustful of government, and of elites more generally.[8] But the basic finding of the electoral discount is that respondents tended to evaluate elected officials more negatively precisely because they are part of the electoral process, which was seen to constrain their ability to act sincerely. This happens in a variety of ways. As elected officials, representatives can get discounted because they are not firmly tied to a position or constituency, either because it is not well known or, more consistently, because politicians are seen as instrumental. However, they can also get discounted because they are tied to a position or constituency, in particular when a specific constituency is seen to override their ability to act independently. In short, the electoral discount is applied to elected representatives because they fall short of the ideal of deliberative public debate.

NORMATIVE CONFLICT IN PUBLIC LIFE

Talking to ordinary Americans about religion-and-science debates yields two powerful findings. First, representatives have significant constitutive power to shape the symbolic meaning of these debates through their participation in public life. What people think that debates are about and what they think about the quality of those debates depend on which representatives are the most visible in the debates. When the most visible representatives are religion and science representatives, people describe debates as focused on religion and science. But when the most visible representatives are religion representatives and gay activists, people describe the debate as between religious people and gay people. In other words, whether or not people think that there is good debate, or that good debate is possible, hinges on their evaluations of the representatives who participate in these debates.

Second, contrary to what scholars of institutional politics would predict, ordinary persons concur with scholars of religion and science, and with many democratic theorists, that representatives should be engaged in deliberative debate. Interview respondents consistently used what I call a deliberative frame to evaluate what they see in public life and to describe what they would like to see in public life. Respondents wanted public debate over important issues to be open, inclusive, and ongoing. Along every dimension of evaluation, respondents looked for indicators that representatives were good participants in terms of realizing this ideal debate. Similarly, when given the chance to describe their ideal debate and its participants, respondents consistently identified ideal debate as deliberative, and good representatives as good public deliberators.

This fundamental disconnection between elite representatives and ordinary persons over preferences for good public debate suggests an important source of conflict that has previously gone unacknowledged in discussion of religion-and-science debates. Most research on religion and science has focused on substantive conflict, which occurs when people disagree over substantive claims about, for example, the truth of human origins or the morality of stem cell research. But the findings here suggest that we should also be focused on normative conflict, which occurs when people disagree over what counts as good or bad. Normative conflict occurs in these debates when representatives display evidence that they are not pursuing deliberative debate, as when they are trying to get their own way or advance their own cause. And this, it must be noted, is exactly what the most visible representatives of religion and science are doing in public debate.

So, what does this normative conflict mean for religion and science in public life? In theory, the point of public debate is to negotiate and manage the changing categories of social life. Representatives are the negotiators, but they are also the exemplars. Negative evaluations of representatives are also negative evaluations of what they are seen to represent. Normative conflict matters particularly because such negative evaluation can occur even when there is positive or neutral evaluation on substantive grounds. So, in theory, even scientists who agree with Richard Dawkins about evolution might end up thinking that science in public life leads to bad debate, because they disapprove specifically of Dawkins on normative grounds and because he is the exemplar who (in part) defines the category "science in public life."

If this is true, it means that we have been asking the wrong questions about religion and science in American public life. Rather than religion and science presenting a problem for public debate, public debate, and specifically the normative conflict over good debate, could present a problem for religion and science. But does this actually happen? Do these conflicting ideas about good debate actually present problems for religion and science?

In the remainder of this book I examine how normative conflicts shape "religion" and "science" in public life. To be clear, I am not claiming that normative conflicts shape what everyone thinks about religion and science generally. Obviously, ordinary persons construct their ideas about religion and science from many different sources, including accounts of their own experiences (e.g., education), interactions with friends and neighbors, and a variety of other media inputs (e.g., science fiction). However, what they think about religion and science *in public life* depends heavily on the normative assessment of the most visible religion and science representatives. This normative assessment leads to surprising limitations on the possibilities for religion and science to participate meaningfully in the American public sphere.

CHAPTER 6

Owning the Space

Religious Credibility in the Public Sphere

Ordinary Americans think that good debate means deliberative debate. But the most visible representatives in religion-and-science debates think that good debate means getting their way. As a result, the approaches that the most visible representatives take in public life conflict with the normative criteria that ordinary people use to evaluate them.

The obvious question is, Why do representatives do this? If ordinary people want something different, why do representatives act this way rather than that way? To be clear, I seek a sociological, rather than a psychological, answer to this question. I am not asking about individual motivations. Rather, I am asking why representatives participate in the public sphere at all. Even if there is some special or unique individual motivation for what they are doing, why pursue it in the public sphere?

Scholars working in the science and technology studies (STS) tradition, while not often addressing questions about the public sphere directly, nonetheless provide a helpful answer. People participate in the public sphere because it is an arena of public credibility. In Steven Epstein's influential formulation, credibility is the "capacity of claims-makers to enroll supporters behind their arguments, legitimate those arguments as authoritative knowledge, and present themselves as the sort of people who can voice the truth."[1]

People pursue credibility in a variety of settings, both private and public. But the public sphere, and in particular the portion of the public sphere that is realized in mass media, offers a unique arena of credibility.

Through mass media, the public sphere provides access to the largest possible number of supporters to be enrolled. It presents the highest-profile arena for presenting arguments and offers individual representatives a level of visibility not available in other arenas.

Throughout the STS literature, scholars tend to focus on credibility as a means of settling contests between people. Scientific controversies often involve evidence that is indeterminate or elusive. Arguments cannot always be settled with reference to agreed-upon facts or observations. So seeing scientific controversies as contests of credibility provides an explanation for how and why many controversies are resolved one way rather than another. In the classic example, controversy over Robert Boyle's air-pump experiment was settled with reference not simply to the experiment or its results but to a variety of social and political considerations that made one set of claims, and one claims-maker, more credible than the other.[2]

Given the application of the STS concept to situations of controversy, contest, and conflict, it is tempting to see debates in the public sphere as contests of credibility similar to scientific controversies, by imagining debate over, say, stem cell research as a sort of air-pump controversy unfolding on the pages of the *New York Times*. To the extent that religion and science are involved in an issue, the pervasive popular framing of conflict between religion and science reinforces this way of thinking. And credibility is actually useful for understanding how, for example, challenges to evolution in public schools have changed over time from strictly religious claims to more general secular claims about freedom of choice, exploring uncertainty, and basic fairness.[3]

But the concept of credibility is even more useful for explaining the instances when conflict does not occur. Not all attempts to gain credibility are contests between individuals. The pursuit of credibility, even in the public sphere, does not actually require engagement with an opponent. Being seen as important and as advancing your agenda can increase your legitimacy and attract supporters, even if you never defeat an opponent in single (discursive) combat. In the debates considered in this study, this is the far more common situation between religion and science. Conflict is rare. But many representatives, especially the most visible ones, are pursuing public credibility without engaging in conflict, or even engaging at all.

Thinking about representatives in the public sphere as individuals in pursuit of public credibility helps reconcile what we know about the public sphere, the relationship between religion and science in these debates, and normative conflict over good debate. Representatives participate in public life to gain a particular kind of public credibility not available elsewhere. The pursuit of such credibility, while potentially tied to credibility contests over controversial issues, does not necessarily require direct engagement with any competitor or rival in the public sphere. So it is not surprising that there is no encounter between religion and science in these debates. Yet the pursuit of public credibility by representatives in the public sphere often ends up conflicting with deliberative norms that people use to evaluate public representatives. This is especially true for the most visible representatives, whose public credibility emerges in no small part from their power to constitute what a given debate is about.

Thinking about representatives in the public sphere as individuals in pursuit of public credibility also helps explain why religion and science representatives are so unevenly distributed in these debates. Consider what a good religion-and-science debate would look like, based on what respondents suggested in interviews. A good debate would involve religion and science, but it would also involve many other areas whose representatives would bring in their own perspectives and concerns. In a good debate the most visible representatives would encounter and engage one another over an important issue of broad concern to ordinary Americans. Moreover, such representatives ideally would bring a variety of perspectives informed by their different backgrounds. For example, a good religion-and-science debate would not just include one religion and one science representative. Instead, there would be several religion representatives, perhaps including someone from the Religious Right, but also including representatives from moderate and liberal religious groups. And there would be several science representatives as well, perhaps including scientists with different or even dissenting perspectives.

In theory, this could happen. In practice, it does not. Why? Why do we not see more moderate or liberal religion representatives in the public sphere? Why do we not see many highly visible science representatives at all?

In this chapter and the following chapters I answer these questions. Surprisingly, the answers are very similar for religion and for science. We do not see those other representatives in these public debates, because they do not pursue credibility in the public sphere. Although this seems very basic, it is a striking explanation. For moderate and liberal religious figures and for scientists alike, the dominant model of credibility depends on staying out of the public sphere. Many of the reasons for religion and for science are even similar. For example, mainline religion representatives and scientists alike seek to minimize the appearance of internal dissent, present a unified front, and focus on the credibility of their institutions rather than their individual claims-making. The result is that for both fields, only some representatives pursue public credibility, and in general, those who do are acting in ways that violate deliberative preferences.

For those seeking deliberative debate, the obvious response is to simply encourage different religion and science representatives to pursue credibility in the public sphere. But the historical refusal of many possible religion and science representatives to pursue credibility in the public sphere, while consistent with models of credibility that have worked in other arenas, has reconfigured public debate and constrained the possibility of pursuing credibility in the public sphere in the future. By pursuing credibility in the public sphere using approaches incompatible with deliberative preferences, highly visible representatives have constituted religion and science in public life as markers of bad debate. This does not mean that they have changed what religion and science mean everywhere. But when people see religion and science involved in public debate, they read such involvement as contrary to their deliberative expectations.

In the remainder of this chapter and the next I explain why this phenomenon is the case for religion in public life. For the past several decades, only representatives from the Religious Right have pursued distinctively religious credibility in the public sphere. This pursuit often runs against deliberative preferences. In contrast, moderate or liberal religion representatives rarely pursue religious credibility in the public sphere. However, largely because of the success of the Religious Right in "owning the space" of religion in public life, all attempts to pursue religious credibility in the public sphere—for example, by using religious language or reasons—are now interpreted as bad debate, even when they come from moderate or liberal religion representatives.

RELIGION IN AMERICAN PUBLIC LIFE

The incontrovertible fact is that, when it comes to religion, the Religious Right dominates American public life.[4] According to the main cultural narrative, the Religious Right is an apparently unprecedented combination of theological and political conservatism with an elite political movement.[5] This union marks a sea change in American politics away from neutrality and toward the acceptance of distinctively religious language, arguments, and justifications in public debate.[6] Visible leaders such as Jerry Falwell, Pat Robertson, and James Dobson, working from well-funded organizations such as the Moral Majority, Christian Coalition, and Focus on the Family, seem to dictate the terms of debate on many contentious issues in American public life. Abortion, gay marriage, stem cell research, and even educational and environmental policy are sites of contention, not just between political parties but also among political interest groups that draw directly on conservative religious language, reasons, and arguments to support political positions. Of course American public life has always had a religious component. But although Martin Luther King, for example, could use religious language and imagery to make the case for civil rights, he also could (and did) make arguments for civil rights that did not involve religious language or reasons. What makes the Religious Right unique is that it has opened a space for moral and political argument in public life that operates solely with reference to religious authority.

There are, of course, many variations on this basic narrative. For many scholars of religion and society, the rise of the Religious Right is really the emergence of religion generally as a multifarious political dimension in American public life, whether because religion is becoming more public or because increasing pluralism demands more attention to religious differences.[7] A stronger version of this claim is that the rise of the Religious Right signals a shift in American politics from a generally benign and amenable mainline Protestant public religion to a political arena marked by deep and contentious divides over basic matters of policy that map closely onto divisions in religious belief between liberal-moderate religious groups, such as mainline Protestants and many Catholics, and conservative religious groups, such as evangelical Protestants and conservative Catholics.[8] In these accounts, it is the "Religious" part of the label that is significant. Today it is the "Religious Right," but with effort or a change in tactics or a demographic shift, it might well be the "Religious Left" tomorrow.

In a more alarmist form offered by many popular authors, the "Right" part of "Religious Right" is the most worrisome. The rise of the Religious Right in this view is the next step toward an "American theocracy" in which a once liberal democratic republic will be governed by conservative religious zealots who will force everyone to follow their restrictive moral code or use U.S. military might to force other countries to follow suit.[9] Such moves would, of course, be entirely antidemocratic and contrary to the spirit of separation between church and state.[10] Thus it is worrisome that candidates for electoral office not only must have policy positions but must also position themselves in a religious field. In this version of the narrative, when George W. Bush gives speeches not only at CPAC and the American Enterprise Institute, but also at Bob Jones University and Liberty University, it is evidence that we are one step closer to theocratic subversion of American democracy.

Clearly, these accounts diverge, most notably in their assessment of the potential problems that the rise of the Religious Right presents. But almost everyone agrees that the Religious Right currently dominates public religion. How this happened is not a source of contention, either. Most scholars agree that the Religious Right is an example of a more or less successful social movement. Like other successful social movements, the Religious Right has been highly effective at resource mobilization in support of its goals.[11] Through the prominent activity of representatives such as Falwell, Robertson, and Dobson in both specialized religious media (e.g., Focus on the Family radio, *The 700 Club* television show) and mass media outlets, the Religious Right solicits funds, defines a public moral agenda, and continually expands a common core of like-minded supporters.[12] Through affiliated political organizations (e.g., Family Research Council, Christian Coalition), the Religious Right mobilizes organized political action such as petitions, letter campaigns, and get-out-the-vote efforts for sympathetic candidates.[13] At the same time, a network of private foundations, think tanks, and faith-based business and political associations links together an "evangelical elite" of conservative Protestants who seek to replace what they see as a secular elite in military, economic, and political life with elites raised, trained, and funded within the Religious Right.[14]

I am not principally concerned here about the contingent historical circumstances that produced the Religious Right and its representatives. Obviously that story is important. And obviously, resources and organization are necessary to becoming prominent in American public life, at least in any durable fashion. But the question here is not why the Religious Right was able to mobilize resources and organizations. The question is why these resources and organizations generated one kind of public representative rather than another. What is distinctive about the Religious Right's pursuit of public credibility, compared to that of other religious groups?

OWNING THE SPACE OF PUBLIC RELIGION

So, instead of focusing on how the Religious Right became prominent, I focus on how the Religious Right continues to "own the space" of religion in American public life. By "own the space" I mean that the Religious Right, particularly through its most prominent representatives, pursues religious credibility in the public sphere by aligning the public definition of religion with the Religious Right's specific version of religion. Given the constitutive power of representatives to shape what ordinary Americans think about public debate, "owning the space" ensures that Religious Right representatives will be the only representatives defining what "religion" means in public life.

Owning the space involves distinct but overlapping activities in the public sphere. First, the Religious Right mobilizes resources to promote specific individuals as prominent representatives. This emphasis on visible representatives in the public sphere ensures that when people think of religion in public life, they think of Falwell, Robertson, or Dobson rather than, say, John Haught or Stanley Hauerwas. Second, representatives from the Religious Right use distinctively religious talk, rather than more inclusive or general secular modes of talk. The use of such language emphasizes the religious motivations of Religious Right representatives in pursuing public credibility, in contrast to moderate and liberal religion representatives who do not use distinctively religious talk. This consistent public alignment of Religious Right representatives with distinctively religious talk ensures that when people see or hear religion talk in public life, they think of the Religious Right as its only legitimate source.

Promoting Individual Representatives

The Religious Right is distinctive in promoting individual representatives in the public sphere. This promotion helps the movement "own the space" of religion by ensuring that the most visible representatives who are distinctively religious are individuals promoted by the Religious Right. This promotion has largely succeeded. The most prominent religious representatives in public debate are conservative religious figures, primarily (though not exclusively) from the American Religious Right. The Religious Right effectively mobilizes immense resources. It is arguable whether or not resource mobilization is the cause of the Religious Right's rise to prominence, particularly given the concurrent general retreat of the Protestant mainline from American public life.[15] What is important for this analysis is that conservative religious activism directs those resources primarily toward promoting particular identifiable persons as representatives in public life.

Promoting individual representatives happens through media mobilization and person-focused political activity. Most obviously, media mobilization composes a large part of Religious Right success. One key component has been direct investment in specialized religious media infrastructure (e.g., the Christian Broadcasting Network, the Trinity Broadcasting Network, National Religious Broadcasters) and programming (e.g., *The 700 Club, Focus on the Family, The Coral Ridge Hour*) that provides wide exposure for particular visible figures. Through this religious base of support, Jerry Falwell, Pat Robertson, and James Dobson have become authoritative and legitimate representatives of conservative religion for tens of millions of Americans (and many millions more worldwide) who listen to Christian radio or watch Christian television.[16]

Beyond the religious media space, these visible leaders engage in ongoing commentary and spectacle designed to draw general media attention not just to their shared moral agenda but also to themselves as the persons who represent that agenda. The latter component involves being the available religious person for journalists to cover or consult, whether for political commentary, the "religious perspective" on controversial moral issues, or radical public prophecies of danger and terror that provoke viewers to watch in anticipation of what will happen next. Religious Right representatives are so successful at this strategy that a major study of media coverage of religious figures had to remove Falwell, Robertson, and Dobson from the study sample because their dominance across all media was so complete that it made comparison pointless.[17]

Religious Right political activity also promotes individual representatives. Conservative religious movements emphasize electoral change (sometimes called "Don't change the policy—change the politician") or, more broadly, replacement of existing elites seen as hostile with elites seen as friendly to conservative religious perspectives.[18] For example, organizations like the Family Research Council offer endorsements of specific electoral candidates based on candidate compliance with a slate of positions that align with the Religious Right's common moral agenda.[19] At the same time, private networks such as The Fellowship, which puts on the National Prayer Breakfast, bring together and provide pastoral and financial support to highly placed politicians committed to linking religious beliefs to political power.[20]

Promoting particular individuals in public life may seem like something everyone does. But this is perhaps because the success of the Religious Right has naturalized such activity as normal. Liberal and moderate religious groups do not generally promote individual representatives.[21] In fact, for a variety of reasons that resist disentanglement, liberal and moderate religious groups tend to avoid direct participation in public debate entirely. As sociologist John Evans has noted, one of the key reasons is a general unwillingness to advocate positions that might aggravate or expose division within mainline denominations, resulting in an emphasis on persuasion and consensus rather than potentially divisive public advocacy. While there are issues on which liberal and moderate religious groups might be expected to have strong policy positions, these issues (e.g., poverty) are not the "culture wars" issues that drive media attention. And perhaps most important, the Protestant mainline engaged in "self-immolation after the emergence of the Christian Right," as the very idea of advocating for particular values or positions in the public sphere came to be seen as a violation of mainline Protestant values about consensus.[22]

Whatever the ultimate reason or reasons, the resulting situation is that liberal and moderate religious groups generally do not promote particular individuals in public life, even though some groups have available resources to do so.[23] For example, the Lilly Endowment controls several billion dollars (US), but distributes that money to regranting agencies, such as the Louisville Institute at the Louisville Theological Seminary, or the Lilly Fellows program at Valparaiso University, that support productive conversations among academic researchers, local church leaders, religious colleges, and denominational officers.[24] And in contrast to the Religious Right's focused efforts to install "faith in the halls of power," liberal and moderate religious political activity is conceived and executed through lobbying, either through denominational offices or through identity- or issue-driven small lobbying groups, such as Sojourners or the Religious Coalition for Reproductive Choice.[25] The main point of liberal and moderate political activity is to change the minds of the politicians who are in office, not to exchange them for politicians developed and trained within a particular religious tradition.

Unlike liberal and moderate religious groups, the Religious Right emphasizes representation in public life as a primary element in advancing a moral agenda. Thus, key actors such as Jerry Falwell, Pat Robertson, and James Dobson (among others) draw on the resources of the Religious Right to gain and maintain visibility and recognition in public life as representatives of religious groups and positions. When people encounter religious representatives in general-audience mass media, they are far more likely to encounter conservative religious figures such as Falwell, Robertson, and Dobson than they are moderate or liberal figures such as John Haught, Jim Wallis, or Richard Cizik. This is not just because conservatives have more resources, but because they use those resources to promote individual representatives in public life.

Distinctively Religious Language

Promoting individual representatives is a key component in "owning the space" of religion in public life. But this component has an obvious weakness. In theory, someone could come along and replace Robertson, Falwell, and Dobson with other religion representatives. Of course, in the current situation this would take immense resources and organization. But if owning the space depended entirely on promoting individual representatives, someone else might conceivably do it better, realigning the public version of "religion" with their own particular version and displacing the Religious Right in public life. Owning the space thus involves a second component of pursuing credibility in the public sphere, a strategy focused on using distinctively religious language in public talk.

It may seem strange to say that anyone could own the space of religious talk. After all, religious references suffuse American public life. Religious words like "God" and "blessing" recur frequently in public talk, even at the highest levels of government. For example, presidential addresses to the nation uniformly end with some variant of the phrase "God bless the United States of America." Everyone running for higher office is at least nominally religious. Presidents generally are sworn into office with their hand on a Bible.[26] Religious leaders from many denominations regularly open sessions of Congress with prayer. American money carries the motto "In God We Trust." Such religious references are fundamental to what many scholars call "civil religion."[27] They refer generically to religious concepts and symbols, but do not specify the theological content or import of those concepts and symbols.[28]

What I mean by "distinctively religious language" is that representatives of the Religious Right invoke religious reasons, profess religious motivations, and offer religious justifications in public talk, but do not provide secular, or generic, alternatives. This offers a stark contrast to moderate and liberal religious representatives who, though sometimes offering religious reasons and arguments, tend either to confine such religion talk to private settings or deploy it only in conjunction with general moral arguments that secular interlocutors can engage.[29] Put simply, Religious Right representatives tend to speak a language specific to their religious commitments, while moderate and liberal religious representatives tend to speak, if they speak at all, in a "moral Esperanto" that expresses moral commitments rather than specific religious commitments.[30]

Why this difference? The best explanation is that these different approaches to public talk reflect different basic responses to the problem of internal religious diversity. Distinctively religious language is a potential source of division. Such talk runs the risk of losing public support from those who do not share the same religious commitments. For the Religious Right, this is not actually a problem. As several historians and sociologists have noted, the history of conservative Protestantism in America is marked by public schism, division, and sectarianism that evinces a commitment to doctrine over church unity.[31] Divisive talk is business as usual. By contrast, moderate and liberal religious traditions emphasize unity in their public talk, preferring to handle internal religious diversity within the structure of the denomination or organization rather than publicizing religious differences and alienating actual and potential co-religionists.[32]

So, for Religious Right representatives, owning the space of religion in public life involves the use of distinctively religious language that cannot be mistaken for, or substituted with, the "moral Esperanto" that characterizes the public talk of moderate and liberal religious representatives. Such distinctively religious language aligns the public version of "religion" with the Religious Right. Even if, for some reason, moderate or liberal religion representatives achieved prominence in public life, it is unlikely that they would use distinctive religious talk in public life. The result is that the only representatives who are actively pursuing religious credibility in the public sphere, as distinctively religious representatives using identifiable religious language and reasons, come from the Religious Right.

RELIGION AND PUBLIC CREDIBILITY

To put this argument in terms of public credibility, the Religious Right, unlike the Religious Left, pursues religious credibility in the public sphere by promoting individual representatives who are visibly religious. By doing so, the Religious Right takes seriously the constitutive power of representatives in public life. Representatives in public debate serve a sort of cartographic function by mapping the debate for nonparticipants. Making representatives visible in public debate is key to mobilizing a supportive constituency and helps force opponents to organize a response to the policies and positions being advocated.[33] So promoting individual representatives is one key aspect of "owning the space" of American public religion.

Yet the success of such promotion is measured not only by the prominence of religious representatives in the public sphere but also by the extent to which ordinary people (whether or not they are religious or conservative) recognize prominent representatives in public life and think of one set of representatives (in this case those from the Religious Right) rather than another set (such as liberal or moderate religious leaders) as "religious." For largely contingent historical reasons, the Religious Right has become prominent in American public life as a distinctive and recognizable version of "religion." But owning the space of public religion does not come about by accident. Unlike moderate or liberal religious figures, Religious Right representatives pursue religious credibility in the public sphere. This activity populates the public sphere with visibly religious representatives who advance the Religious Right's moral agenda. The result is that when ordinary persons see a visibly religious representative in public debate, those representatives are far more likely to come from the Religious Right, such as Robertson, Dobson, and Falwell, than from other religious bases.

Ordinary Americans think that good debate is deliberative debate. But when ordinary Americans see religion representatives in debates involving religion and science, they are most likely to see persons who violate their deliberative expectations. So, given the constitutive power that representatives wield, in particular the power to establish boundaries for what is possible within a particular debate, what does it mean for religion in public life that these persons, rather than others, are the most visible religion representatives in public debate? How do ordinary people evaluate religion in these debates?

CHAPTER 7

Religion and Bad Debate

Throughout this book I emphasize that representatives exercise constitutive power simply by virtue of being visible in public debate. This cartographic power, as I refer to it, sets the boundaries of what a debate, or debates, involve. When it comes to religion in public debate, representatives of the Religious Right are the only religion representatives who explicitly pursue credibility in the public sphere. The manner of this pursuit violates deliberative expectations that ordinary Americans have of the public sphere. In theory, this normative conflict should have consequences for how ordinary Americans understand religion in public life.

But does it really? In practice, does this normative conflict emerge in evaluations of religion in the public sphere? And if so, how does it matter? To answer these questions, I analyzed how interview respondents evaluated what "religion" and "religious" mean in the religion-and-science debates in this study. I did not simply ask, "What do you think of religion in these debates?" Instead, I examined how respondents invoked religion, discussed religion, identified who and what was religious, connected religion to other ideas and concepts, and resolved apparent conflicts involving religion in their responses. What counts as religion for respondents, and what religion in public life means to them, became apparent from their responses to a variety of questions and evaluations.

For the ordinary Americans I interviewed, religion in the public sphere, no matter what the source, was commonly seen as a marker of bad debate across a variety of evaluative dimensions. Respondents understood religion in public life to violate deliberative preferences in two ways. First, prominent individual representatives from the Religious Right, whether religious figures or politicians, were recognized and evaluated negatively as public crusaders whose efforts work against good deliberative debate. Similarly, respondents were more likely to use religious identification for politicians of whom they disapproved either wholly or partly, even though most American politicians identify as religious. In contrast, ordinary persons suggested as ideal representatives persons seen as open-minded and willing to engage in considered, deliberative debate, such as respected local ministers, friends, or neighbors.

Second, and more broadly, the Religious Right's association with distinctively religious language prompted negative evaluation of any religion talk as contrary to good debate. Because of the Religious Right's success in "owning the space" of public religion, respondents expected that religion talk, whatever the source, indicated opposition to deliberative debate. When respondents evaluated typical statements and résumés stripped of identifying information, they identified religious language of any kind, even when uttered by moderate or liberal religious figures, as inhibiting rather than contributing to good debate. This normative conflict held across respondents despite substantive agreement or disagreement with the particular claims that representatives made in these debates.

In two separate ways, the normative conflict between the Religious Right's pursuit of religious credibility and the preferences of ordinary persons for good debate ends up defining religion in public life as contrary to good debate. On one path, individual representatives are evaluated as "public crusaders" more interested in advancing a moral agenda than participating in deliberative debate. On the other path, ordinary persons evaluate public religious language and reasons as contrary to norms of deliberative debate. The result is that in public religion-and-science debates, no matter which path is followed to the conclusion, "religion" means "bad debate."

EVALUATING INDIVIDUAL REPRESENTATIVES

Obviously, Religious Right representatives are prominent in religion-and-science debates. But visibility does not guarantee that ordinary persons recognize the various figures in American public debate. Nor does it guarantee that ordinary persons will evaluate such figures favorably if they do recognize them. Gaining visibility in public life is not in itself

TABLE 5 PERCENTAGE OF RESPONDENTS WHO
RECOGNIZED SELECTED RELIGION REPRESENTATIVES

George W. Bush	100
Bill Clinton	100
Pope John Paul II	100
Al Gore	100
Arnold Schwarzenegger	100
John Kerry	98
Mitt Romney	96
Jerry Falwell	90
Pat Robertson	78
James Dobson	60
Bill Frist	34
Sam Brownback	20

sufficient for "owning the space." In fact, respondents did not always recognize these persons, nor did they always have an idea of who in particular might represent religion in public life.

Table 5 reports the percentage of respondents who recognized selected prominent representatives who had made a religious claim in at least one debate under consideration.[1] Successful politicians certainly appear to be more recognized than others, but recognition is not automatically connected to visibility in public debates. For example, Arnold Schwarzenegger's name recognition is more likely attributable to his many years as a successful actor in blockbuster Hollywood movies than to his career as the elected governor of California. Similarly, recognition can occur based on inhabiting a recognized office rather than individual promotion. For example, the late Pope John Paul II served as the supreme pontiff of the Catholic Church for more than twenty-six years. Even if most people do not recognize him by his birth name (Karol Wojtyla), most people know there is a pope and understand that the pope is a church leader. So while Pope John Paul II is a significant religious leader with 100 percent recognition, probably anyone with the title "pope" will have high recognition as the leader of the Catholic Church.

The other three religion representatives in table 5 vary considerably in terms of recognition. Falwell, while neither a successful politician nor otherwise famous (e.g., not a former actor), nonetheless has high recognition, with nine out of ten respondents recognizing him correctly as a conservative religious figure. Pat Robertson has substantially less recognition, with about three out of four respondents recognizing his name.

James Dobson was only recognized by about three out of five respondents. Despite their success at becoming prominent representatives in the public debates I have identified here, recognition of these Religious Right figures was far from universal. They were more widely recognized than many others, to be sure, but such recognition was far from guaranteed.[2]

More interesting than the top-level recognition percentages are the ways in which respondents recognized representatives, and how they evaluated such representatives when they recognized them. The general finding is that respondents consistently linked "religion" with "conservative." This happened in three ways. First, when respondents recognized Religious Right representatives as religious, they negatively evaluated such representatives as "conservative" public crusaders. Second, respondents recognized only conservative politicians as religious, even though almost all American politicians are nominally religious. Third, when respondents suggested ideal representatives for good debate, they named persons who either are not religious or do not use religious language in public life. In short, there was no link between "religion" and "liberal" or "moderate" when it comes to representatives. Only the "conservative" members of the Religious Right and their apparent associates were recognized (and evaluated negatively) as religious representatives.

Recognizing Religious Representatives

Clearly, not all prominent representatives were recognized equally. But when prominent religious representatives were recognized by name, they were recognized as conservative. For example, respondents either recognized Pat Robertson as a conservative religious figure or did not recognize him at all. There are no instances of someone thinking that Pat Robertson is a liberal or moderate religious leader. The same is true for Jerry Falwell and James Dobson.

Such recognition as conservative tended to be immediate. For example, Lydia quickly pegged Jerry Falwell: "Superconservative. Just so 'hell fire and damnation.' He's Jonathan Edwards." Jennifer had a similar evaluation of Falwell as conservative: "I think he's an evangelical preacher, right. So he would be the Republican right wing." Respondents also consistently grouped religious conservatives together and saw them as largely interchangeable, as, for example, in Timothy's evaluation of Jerry Falwell followed by Pat Robertson:

Timothy: I've never heard him speak explicitly about this, but I'm sure he's on the more right-wing side of the debate that—maybe, and extremely so.

Interviewer: [listing next name] Pat Robertson.

Timothy: Ditto.

Similarly, Ernest identified common ground between Falwell and Dobson, placing them at one extreme of a left-right continuum:

Interviewer. James Dobson.

Ernest: Yeah, he's way off to the right. And that's the Focus on the Family guy, right?

Interviewer: Jerry Falwell.

Ernest: He's probably his best friend—he's got to be way over to the right also.

Such recognition of Religious Right figures was generally accompanied by disapproval. Recognition was rarely based on positive evaluations. I note that this was as true for evangelical Protestant respondents as it was for others. Being evangelical did not predict approval or disapproval of religious conservatives. Falwell, Robertson, and Dobson in particular were evaluated as exemplars of what not to do or be in public life. When asked about Pat Robertson, Daniela provided an especially memorable, though not atypical, example:

Oh, God, he's even worse [than Jerry Falwell]. Pat Robertson is one of the most frightening men, I think, in the United States. Have you ever seen *The 700 Club*? We wound up watching this show by accident, because I was like, "Oh, it's a news show. Let's see what's going on in the world, right?" And so we started, and I have never been so offended in my life. I mean this was right, I think, when we were first about to invade Iraq, right? And, I mean, his view was like let's go kill all these God damned Muslims, and it scared the hell out of me. I was like, how does someone like this get on television? I mean [with reference to environmental issues], Pat Robertson would say not only should [you] drive your SUV, but you should try to hit a couple Muslims on the way.

However, respondents did not generally use "conservative" to mean strictly theologically or politically conservative. Recognition did not map neatly onto respondents' own religious commitments. Table 6 reports some interesting variations in recognition for Falwell, Robertson, and Dobson across major religious categories. Falwell's recognition

TABLE 6 PERCENTAGE OF RESPONDENTS WHO RECOGNIZED SELECTED
RELIGIOUS CONSERVATIVES, BY RELIGIOUS CATEGORY

	Mainline	Evangelical	Catholic	Other/None
Jerry Falwell	91	95	83	87
Pat Robertson	100	82	75	62
James Dobson	64	95	33	33

is fairly consistent across respondents, regardless of their religious identification.[3] James Dobson's recognition among evangelicals (conservative Protestants) is almost universal, but drops off significantly for mainline Protestants and even more for Catholics and Other/Nones.[4] And Pat
Robertson seems to be better recognized by the persons in the dominant
religious traditions (in the United States) than by Other/None persons.

Even among evangelical Protestant respondents, who might be
expected to know all about these figures, there was not consistent recognition of, or knowledge of, the Falwells and Dobsons of the world.
Persons from other religious groups varied greatly in the extent to which
they recognized the most prominent religious representatives in public
debate. (This is true in both directions, as more mainline Protestants
than conservative Protestants recognized Pat Robertson.)

So recognition of religion representatives as "conservative" was not
simply disagreement based on substantive similarities or differences. The
term "conservative" also implied that these religion representatives are
working against good debate. Specifically, the descriptor "conservative"
marked religious public crusaders seeking to impose their moral agenda
on others. For example, when I first brought up the issue of the origins
of homosexuality, Arthur, a mainline Protestant, gloomily predicted that
Jerry Falwell would eventually show up in our discussion, since Falwell
is "just always being the advocate of, you know, family matters and all
of that." And in Raymond's opinion, such representatives are not even
capable of such debate: "I have to say that for guys like Falwell—and by
'guys like Falwell' I mean those who are sort of public and frequently
televised with their evangelical preachings and so on—I have a boundless
degree of cynicism regarding anything that comes out of their mouth. So
even if he were to say things pertaining to environmental management,
protection, sustainability, I would not trust it any further than I could
throw the guy, but I haven't heard him say anything about that."

There were a few exceptions to the negative evaluation of Religious
Right figures. Nicole, a Catholic, "likes the way [Jerry Falwell] talks"

and said that he has "some valid points." Felix, a fundamentalist, thought that both Falwell and Robertson are "good, sound fundamentalists" whose "thinking is from the biblical standpoint." And sometimes good intentions counted for something, even if respondents disapproved of the representative in other ways. For example, Teresa, a Catholic, said that she thinks James Dobson is "a good man and a loving man, but I think he's definitely very traditional in his view of marriage and family." But by and large, respondents tended to recognize the names of Falwell, Robertson, and Dobson in particular as religious conservatives who exemplify what is most disagreeable about religion in public life.

Only Conservative Politicians Are Religious

Another important pattern is that respondents of all religious backgrounds recognized only conservative politicians as "religious." In the American political context, almost everyone running for higher elected office is nominally religious. For example, George W. Bush is United Methodist. John Kerry is Roman Catholic. Bill Clinton is Baptist. Al Gore is (or perhaps was) Baptist.[5] Mitt Romney is Mormon. Sam Brownback converted from United Methodism to Roman Catholicism while in office. There is a wide range of possible religious identifications for politicians in public life, and everyone running for higher office could be identified legitimately as religious.[6] Yet it was conservative politicians who were recognized as "religious."[7] For example, Damien, an evangelical Protestant, offered this evaluation of George W. Bush: "The—yeah. I guess just—and I don't know that so much of what people paint on him, you know, but I would say he represents the conservative right. The religious conservative."

Identification of politically conservative representatives as "religious" was not simply meant to indicate position on a left-right continuum. Respondents linked "religious" and "conservative" to indicate a particular kind of politician who remains committed to a position and is not open to others. "Religious" shared with "conservative" the implication that these are bad representatives because they work against good debate. For example, Charles discussed George W. Bush's position on the origins of homosexuality:

> I do recognize him. My impression of him is that while he probably wouldn't go gay bashing, he probably wouldn't directly associate with homosexuals either, or knowingly anyway. And if he did, it might be for a photo op, but I don't imagine that he's inviting many members of PFLAG over to the

Crawford ranch. I think it's because his view of people is so archaic because it's based on, like, such a fundamentalist view of religion. It's so rooted in that, that he doesn't deviate from that at all, do you know what I mean?

Similarly, Anita, an evangelical Protestant, thought that Mitt Romney opposed stem cell research "because of his religious background," as did Summer, a Catholic, who pointed to Romney's "religious beliefs and his conservatism." Even Crystal, a mainline Protestant who claimed to be "kind of ignorant of his religious background" and thought that Romney's "business kind of persona as being more dominant anyway," nonetheless considered Romney's religious background as something possibly relevant, even if she ultimately rejected it as causal. And Don said: "Well, I mean, I know Mitt Romney is a Mormon and I know that Mormons don't believe in—I don't know where they stand in stem cell research. I haven't ever asked the kids that, but I would think that they don't believe in abortion."

While not every respondent described politicians in religious terms, sometimes referring instead to their economic interests or alliances with corporations, or to their personal ambitions, the important pattern to note here is that when respondents did consider religious affiliations and motivations to be important, it was almost always in their descriptions of conservative politicians such as Bush, Romney, Frist, and Brownback. Such use of "religious" indicates not only political affiliation but also a negative evaluation of these politicians as bad representatives in public life.

What is almost entirely missing from interviews is recognition of nonconservatives as "religious." This is striking. Take, for example, John Kerry, who is known to be Catholic and even had confrontations with various Catholic leaders over his positions on abortion and stem cell research, notably prompting at least one prominent leader to call for his excommunication. Yet despite being given the opportunity to evaluate Kerry and discuss his position on stem cell research and the environment, respondents almost universally either did not know his position or assumed that as a Democrat he supported stem cell research and was also pro-environment. Put another way, his political identity as a Democrat was the only salient characteristic. The fact that he is Catholic did not come up in most interviews at all, even among interviews with Catholic respondents. The single exception occurred in an interview with Laura, an evangelical Protestant, who nonetheless discounted Kerry's religion as a factor:

Well, I think that John Kerry is Catholic. I know he's from the East Coast. I used to live in Boston. I know that he is a Democrat, and I know that he is liberal-minded, and so if I had to stereotype by putting those different types of factors all together, I would probably guess that he would be on the scientists' side. It's not to say that he isn't religious, because Catholicism, completely valid religion—I just don't think that he would put that at the forefront when dealing with an issue. I think he would keep religion as something personal and private, and that he would mostly be focusing on the environmental issue as something that affects everybody and kind of just leave the religious stuff out of it.

Similarly, despite many opportunities to discuss Bill Clinton and Al Gore, respondents simply did not bring up religion as salient for these representatives, nor did they identify them as "religious." With the one exception in Laura's interview, it is conservative politicians who are "religious."

Ideal Representatives Are Not Conservative

The existence of moderate or liberal religion representatives is not only an empty (or unrecognized) space in current religion-and-science debates. It also seemed to penetrate to respondent imagination of possible debates. Part of the interview schedule included soliciting suggestions for possible ideal participants in each of these debates. Granted, it is sometimes difficult for people to produce any specific name. But when respondents suggested good representatives who would produce good deliberative debate, they rarely suggested public religious conservatives. Respondents sometimes suggested liberal or moderate "religious" figures who were personal acquaintances (e.g., pastors, friends). They also suggested nonconservative (along, say, political dimensions) public figures who were not clearly identified as "religious." Most commonly, though, they described the religion representative that they would like to see, but for whom there was no obvious public exemplar.

Respondents often suggested religious figures whom they knew personally, whether or not they agreed with them substantively. As before, respondents wanted good debate, and they understood conservative religion representatives in public life to be inimical to good debate. Respondents thus had to look to their personal lives and connections to find examples of good religion representatives for ideal debate on religion-and-science issues. Vicki suggested one of her former spiritual mentors: "One of my [mentors] who is gay and went through leaving the Methodist church because he could no longer be a pastor there, given the circumstances, and joined the Episcopal church, but he is not serving in a pastoral position there. I just can't bring any of the Focus on the Family guys in. I just can't."

This selection of private rather than public figures happened even when respondents were themselves religious conservatives in the theological sense. Damien, an evangelical Protestant, suggested his pastor for debates on the origins of homosexuality because of his pastor's willingness to deliberate rather than just put forward his own point of view. Even though Damien is "conservative" in the religious sense, his ideal representative was someone from private, not public, life:

> I think I would put my pastor in there. I'd put him in there because I think he's absolutely willing to engage in the talk and also like—also be like—not seek to punish or to treat homosexuals as outcasts or anything by any means. I think there's a certain sense of whatever, it doesn't matter there's everyone—everyone is equally fallen, everyone needs God, so it's not to—there's no sense of condemnation or anything like that, and I think—to me that's a really important thing.

Similarly, Morgane, an evangelical Protestant, suggested the president of a local conservative faith-based ministry as a good representative, precisely because, in Morgane's view, she would be able to engage without forcing a favorable outcome. This ability was important on issues in which uncertainty drives debate, as Morgane demonstrated: "I would have her, because she recognizes that on very difficult issues there are not going to be—there may never be an answer—and so we're going to debate it in prayer and trust that God is wise and in control. I just think that's the life perspective that I have on some difficult things that I can't wrap my brain around."

Respondents sometimes suggested as ideal representatives leading religious figures who do not generally participate in public debates. Lydia, for example, suggested the Dalai Lama, the spiritual leader of Tibetan Buddhism, because he would "straighten out" the other religious representatives who Lydia sees as closed-minded: "I'd put the Dalai Lama. (Laughter) Well, it's just because it's like, your tendency is to pick people out of your political viewpoint, so you start laughing because you gotta really now like, get more global here and you gotta be more open-minded. So I would pick the Dalai Lama because he'd straighten everybody out." Put another way, the Dalai Lama is a safe choice because he is not distinctively religious. People know that he is Buddhist, but beyond that he does not participate in contentious public debate.

While few other respondents named specific figures as Lydia did, they did offer descriptions of ideal representatives. In most cases, these descriptions sketched an ideal representative who might be religious, but who would be committed to open debate. Sometimes this showed up as a commitment to ecumenism. Connie, for example, suggested something like the leader of the World Council of Churches: "I don't know what the correct title is, but the, I know there is a, and correct me if I'm wrong, there is somebody who represents both the Christian and the Jewish religions. There's somebody that heads that up. So, yeah, I would want somebody who has the diversity of, of that."

More specific to religion-and-science debates, respondents sometimes described ideal representatives as religious elites who would be open not only to other religious points of view but to scientific views that could inform the discussion. For example, on the issue of human origins, Shannon, an evangelical Protestant, suggested that he wanted a theologian: "someone who—someone fairly conservative but not conservative to the point where they think that science doesn't have a right to exist apart from religion. They're willing to give equal footing to both. Even if they just don't necessarily—they maybe don't necessarily have to believe in evolution or not, they just have to believe that religion and science can coexist and do their own thing, see distinctions between them."

In evaluation of individual representatives in public religion-and-science debates, respondents linked "religion" and "conservative." When respondents successfully recognized individual religion representatives, they recognized them as conservative. Similarly, respondents recognized many prominent politicians, but only conservative politicians were recognized as "religious" and evaluated in terms of how their commitments to their positions resist deliberative participation in public debate. Conversely, given the chance to offer names or descriptions of ideal representatives in public debate, respondents either referred to people whom they knew in private life, or described ideal religious representatives as persons capable of moving beyond their religious commitments, either through ecumenism or through more general openness to potentially conflicting perspectives.

The success of the Religious Right in promoting individual representatives appears to have a strong constitutive effect that links "religious" to "conservative" in the public sphere. For respondents, this triggered a negative evaluation of religious representatives, as conservative religious representatives (e.g., from the Religious Right) were seen as working against good debate through their public crusade approach. The result was that only those religious persons who violated deliberative expectations in the public sphere were seen as distinctively religious. But the constitutive effect extended to the imagination of future good debate as well. Respondents had difficulty imagining any moderate or liberal religious figure who would pursue credibility in the public sphere. Taken by itself, this finding suggests that promoting individual representatives from moderate or liberal religious groups might be a simple (though not easy) solution to achieving good debate. But is this really the case?

EVALUATING PUBLIC RELIGION

Certainly the prominence of Religious Right representatives might explain the link between "religious" and "conservative" in evaluation of specific individual representatives. However, in interview exercises that did not depend on naming specific individuals, respondents still displayed a strong tendency to read religious indicators, such as denominational affiliation on résumés or "God talk" in statements, as markers of bad debate. Respondents saw the use of religious language as counterproductive to public debate and therefore undesirable.[8] Recourse to religion or religious language was seen as closed-minded and contrary to norms of public debate as open, ongoing, and engaged in by people in principle willing to change their minds.

Respondents linked "religion" to bad debate in three ways. First, they negatively evaluated religion indicators because religion is seen to work against good deliberative debate. Second, respondents understood religion talk to be what conservative religious representatives do. This evaluation of religion talk as conservative even extended to use of moral language more generally. Third, respondents categorized religion talk as conservative even when it (really) came from liberal or moderate religious figures, or they rejected such talk as not distinctively religious. Even without the touchstone of individual Religious Right representatives to guide evaluation, ordinary persons understood "religion" as contrary to good debate.

Religious Markers Indicate Opposition to Good Debate

Consistently, respondents from a range of religious backgrounds evaluated the use of religious language in statements (e.g., "God") or religious attributes in anonymous résumés (e.g., "Christian") as useful indicators of closed-mindedness, contrariness, and other forms of opposition to good debate. In general, respondents displayed a preference for deliberation that recourse to religion, either as an attribute of persons or an attribute of language, is seen to violate. For example, Elaine understood a statement about environmental harm being an offense against God to indicate harsh extremism: "[reading statement aloud] 'To harm this world by environmental degradation is an offense against God.' Um, I think this is pretty harsh. This is someone, again, an environmentalist, and I can see, this is an aside, but I can see someone with this attitude being very like you know, throwing rocks at whaling ship kind of things."

With regard to the role of religion in public life, most respondents were Rawlsian in practice. By "Rawlsian" I mean that, like philosopher John Rawls, ordinary respondents understood public debate to be an arena where religion has no legitimate place. In normative terms, religion should remain private, since it is a source of conflict over prior commitments rather than a universally shared basis for deliberation.[9] Of course, respondents did not explicitly describe themselves as Rawlsian. But they consistently evaluated the use of religion in public life to be inimical to good debate. While religion might inform one's opinion, it should not ground public talk or arguments.

So when religion did appear, either as an attribute of persons or language, it was evaluated as contrary to good public debate. For example, Holly evaluated a religious affiliation on a résumé as indicating involvement in public crusade: "Just the background. Just the basic background and his religious affiliation, and being a founder of a Christian university. I mean I would definitely think that obviously since he's ... found[ed] a Christian university, he feels as though his morals and values are so important that he needs to impose that on somebody else."

Respondents did not often distinguish between various forms of religion. Most did not understand the theological significance of particular denominational affiliations. For example, on the anonymized résumé for a representative affiliated with the Church of the Nazarene, respondents tended to say that they had no idea what that meant. But that did not prevent negative evaluation. To the contrary, respondents tended to treat any religious language or affiliation as indicating some form of public crusade. Ian, for example, was not bothered by his lack of theological knowledge. When he saw something that indicated religion, he immediately reacted with revulsion and said, "I don't know why, but even any religion, any time I see evangelical, I just scream, like I hate being pushed for anything. I just scream internally." Likewise Vicki indicated that religion talk indicates unreasonable commitment to a particular viewpoint: "I think it's true that there are people who are so caught up in defending the notion that there is a Loving God who created everything that they're afraid of what any other form of understanding would open them up to."

In some cases, respondents recognized that they were mobilizing a negative stereotype of "religion." Whether religious or not, sometimes respondents said things like "I shouldn't say this" or "This is probably just a stereotype, but . . ." when evaluating apparent religious attributes or language. For example, Zoe responded to an anonymized statement by Jerry Falwell by saying, "Well, my first reaction is that this person's a nut. Most of the time, I keep that information to myself."

But as respondents described debates in response to open-ended questions (e.g., "Who do you think is debating this issue?"), respondents often described "religion" as the reactionary "side" in a bad public debate. On one side of the issue—whether environmental policy, human origins, origins of homosexuality, or stem cell research—is a complex mix of actors and interests, while on the other side are religious conservatives (or the Religious Right, or whatever). One side uses religious language, while the other does not. Sienna typified this approach. When asked to describe who was arguing in debates over origins of homosexuality, she said: "Mostly, it is like the religious-conservative side versus, I mean, versus the gay community; but there's also people who aren't in the gay community who agree with them. So more the liberal, social liberals."

Crystal, a mainline Protestant, discussed how being a religious conservative might disqualify a person from participating in public debate over the origins of homosexuality. Without being exposed to people who do not talk in the same way, it is difficult for someone to move beyond religion talk to engage productively:

> I really think that this debate is frequently between people who haven't looked at the other side. Much more so than the stem cell research one. I think that, I think that the people who fall on the Far Right, stereotypically Right, conservative Christian side really don't have any friends that are gay, and I think that that's certainly, I mean I think there's, there's a real lack of exposure and that bringing people with these very multifaceted different perspectives into a room together kind of I think does allow for, for kind of a—I think it would allow for more progress. I mean I think that that's just sort of exposure to all of the different aspects of it does sort of move this issue forward, and I think that's kind of the trend, and that's, hopefully that's the trend that we're kind of as a society moving into.

For Sienna, Crystal, and many other respondents, religion meant stubborn opposition. There were many instances in the interviews when "liberals," "scientists," "the educated," "the intelligent," and so forth were part of a wide array of people joining forces on one side of the issue, while the other side consisted of the "conservatives" and "religious" people who were single-minded, uncomplicated, and united in opposition based on religious language and arguments. Even if, as Crystal noted, such opposition is grounded in ignorance rather than ill will, it is still contrary to the deliberative norms of good debate.

Only Religious Conservatives Use Religion Talk in Public

One of the most persistent notions among respondents is that only religious conservatives use religion talk in public. In several instances, a description of a representative as "founder of a Christian university," for example, or even any indication of involvement in politics, meant that they were seen as conservative. For example, Yuri, an evangelical Protestant, said this when looking at a résumé: "Hmm, host of a Christian news and talk program; that scares me because a lot of times Christian news and talk programs could be way, way conservative or just very, very, just off." Similarly, Dwight understood religious broadcasting to be the purview of religious conservatives:[10] "Okay, leading religious broadcasting company. I'm not really sure. I mean I can guess. Actually, I can guess who it might be, but I am not absolutely sure at all who it is, so I don't know. That's tough. The time frame, his age and the time frame makes me think he might be relatively fundamentalist, well, Christian in this case, in terms of his approach to taking the literal word of the Bible, but it's hard to say for sure. It's the leading religious broadcasting company that gets me."

Sometimes a respondent who shared a religious affiliation with an (anonymous) representative would nonetheless identify it as conservative, precisely because that affiliation is mobilized in public debate. For example, in evaluating a résumé of a psychologist participating in debates over the origins of homosexuality, Sienna immediately pegged him as "a religious conservative" because of his affiliation with a Catholic psychology clinic. As Sienna is herself Catholic, I asked what that meant specifically to her. She replied, "I guess we mostly all tend to— everyone thinks we're all very conservative. So you would just say that they all are conservative." For Sienna, while Catholicism in private could be varied and complicated, anyone emphasizing their Catholicism in public was probably conservative.

Such evaluation was not restricted to pure religion talk. Respondents also understood public talk about morals more generally to be the purview of religious conservatives. Such moral talk was seen as raising unresolvable problems that get in the way of reasonable debate. Josefina (an atheist) said that a declarative statement that we shouldn't talk about the "global warming controversy" because it "shifts the emphasis away from the great moral issues of our time" must have come from (in her terms) the "conservative religious right." When I asked her to explain, she said, "Just that somebody's concerned about the moral issues of our time; the integrity of marriage and teaching of sexual abstinence are definitely conservative religious morals."

In the more expansive version of this association between "religious" and moral issues, several respondents evaluated mention of moral issues as indicating several objectionable dimensions of religious life at once. Judith, for example, barely suppressed her outrage in evaluating the same statement about the "great moral issues of our time": "Good grief! Bible belt, Bible thumper, uneducated or middling educated. Not to say never; they've taken a couple of classes someplace in a night school, I suppose. They live in the town they grew up in. Go to church, think Bush is the greatest guy that's ever been around. Will [Mike Huckabee] run? Gotta vote for him, waiting for him to be in office. This is just—[expressing exasperation] they've actually brought integrity of marriage into the debate of the environment."

And to reinforce the link between public religion and conservative religion, when respondents expressed ambiguity or uncertainty about various "religious" indicators, the complicating factor or confounding exemplar usually came from their private lives, rather than from examples of liberal or moderate religion in public life. For example, Barry, an atheist, showed such thinking when evaluating the résumé of a participant in debates over homosexuality, despite his initial association of "religious" with "conservative": "They're associated with the Presbyterian Medical Center. In my experience religion fosters a more conservative attitude towards the gay community, but I'm not going to assume that, because I've had a lot of friends myself who are very religious yet very open to the gay movement."

For respondents evaluating statements from religion-and-science debates, religion talk was something that only conservatives do in public. Using religion talk in public was the mark of the Religious Right, which was negatively evaluated as contrary to good debate. So was talk about moral issues, which was seen as an extension of religion talk that conservatives use to confound good debate over important issues. Even when there was ambiguity or uncertainty over religion talk, it was because respondents referred to counterexamples from their private lives. If religion talk was public, it was probably working against good debate.

Solving the Riddle of Nonconservative Public Religion Talk

Yet liberal and moderate religious representatives, though not prominent in public life, occasionally use religion talk. When respondents encountered religion talk that was obviously not conservative, it presented a conundrum. Respondents resolved this conundrum in two ways. First, they found ways to describe such use of religious language as somehow not distinctively religious. Second, they evaluated such use of religious language as conservative, even though it came from liberal or moderate religious figures.

In the first instance, religion talk was not treated as religion talk, but evaluated as something else neither distinctively religious nor necessarily conservative. Such talk "could be anything." For example, when evaluating the statement "To harm this world by environmental degradation is an offense against God," Amanda, a mainline Protestant, said: "I would say this is one of those rare cases where you have a religious yet liberal-leaning person, but I could be wrong, and I know that even the Catholic Church, they put out new sins all the time, and you can get updated lists, and I know that environmental harm is even there as being sinful now. So it could be anybody; I'm having a hard time saying for sure, but I do agree with it for sure."

Solomon evaluated the same statement by pointing to religion talk as a common language for communicating unusually powerful emotional experience. Anyone sufficiently moved might use religion talk in this way. An apparently religious statement could be made by "somebody who was religiously, some religious-based opinion, or could be from somebody who isn't necessarily a religious person but came from a very deep sense of a heart-felt statement, if you will. A heart-felt statement that you would hear when, again, something of the magnitude of a hurricane, or 9/11 would happen, and even those who had never said the word 'God' would say the word 'God.'"

In Ken's evaluation of the same statement ("To harm this world by environmental degradation is an offense against God"), religion talk not obviously conservative might instead be a kind of translation from one kind of language into another. Moderates, liberals, or even the nonreligious might use religion talk in order to argue their point in public: "This is a hard one, for me at least, 'cause it could come from a Christian with very strong environmental views. It could come from an environmentalist who has no religious—any religious beliefs who wants to use the Bible as evidence for why the environmental case is so important. I'd have hard time—I have a hard time really pegging—or not pegging, but even generalizing where that might—someone might say this statement."

The second way whereby respondents resolved the apparent conundrum of nonconservative religion talk was simply to evaluate it as conservative and contrary to good debate. In these cases, respondents saw religious references as conservative even when the statements (really) came from liberal or moderate sources. So, for example, when John Haught, a Roman Catholic who supports evolution, said that beneath all the arguments of Intelligent Design advocates "there lies a deeply human and passionately religious concern about whether the universe resides in the bosom of a loving, caring God or is instead perched over an abyss of ultimate meaninglessness," he became a public crusader to Holly, who evaluated his (anonymized) statement as conservative: "I don't agree with this statement at all. I think this person is more emphatic Christian based and I just don't agree . . . [He] represents the more affluent Christians that are emphatic and think that only their viewpoint is correct."

Richard Cizik's use of religious language to discuss the environment ("To harm this world by environmental degradation is an offense against God") also prompted evaluation as conservative, even though this is an issue on which Cizik, a former vice president of governmental affairs for the National Association of Evangelicals, deviates sharply from the Religious Right.[11] Sterling, for example, evaluated the statement as though it came from a religious extremist, even though he agreed with the substance of the claim: "Yeah, this would have been made by probably an evangelical, who was not so much an environmental extremist, but more evangelical Bible-believing person would be my opinion on this. And I would agree with this statement." Penny similarly evaluated Cizik's statement, objecting even to his use of religion talk to make a point in public debate as unreasonable and appealing to emotional intimidation: "And I don't—I mean, that's such a—such a powerful statement. And yet we do it every day, so it's like if I'm constantly degrading the environment by just being present, and yet God still loves me because God doesn't make any junk, then I don't know. That's very—it's a very shaming statement. It's a very shame- and fear-based [thing] to say.

In some cases in which liberal or moderate figures used religion talk, respondents evaluated such talk as not distinctively religious. Although religion words were used (e.g., "God"), respondents understood the use of these words to be conducive to good debate. Because it is not distinctively religious, such talk can serve either as a language of expression or translation even for those who are not themselves religious. However, in other cases in which liberal or moderate religious figures used religion talk, respondents evaluated such talk as conservative and contrary to good debate, against the intentions of the representatives who used such talk.

PUBLIC RELIGION AND GOOD DEBATE

In general, respondents understood public religion to be contrary to good debate. This happened in two ways. First, respondents negatively evaluated individual representatives who were seen as "conservative" in public life. When respondents recognized Religious Right representatives as religious, they negatively evaluated such persons as public crusaders intent on advancing a moral agenda. Respondents also recognized conservative politicians, but not other politicians, as religious. As with the religion representatives, political representatives evaluated as "religious" were seen to be advancing a particular moral agenda through politics. In both cases respondents used "religious" to mark representatives who were seen as engaging in public crusade and therefore as opposed to good debate. Reinforcing the link between "religion" and "public crusade" in this sense, respondents suggested as alternatives ideal representatives who were either not religious or not engaged in public life.

Second, respondents negatively evaluated religious attributes and language in public life, even when they shared religious commitments with the representative being evaluated. Respondents were de facto Rawlsians who understood religion in public life to be unfavorable to good debate. In evaluating résumés and statements, respondents evaluated religious markers as indications of closed-mindedness and unwillingness to consider alternative perspectives and conclusions. Further, respondents understood religion talk in public life as something that only conservatives engage in, and only as part of advancing a moral agenda. While respondents pointed to examples of friends, family members, neighbors, and others in their local social networks that complicated their evaluation process, they generally understood the realm of public religion talk as the purview of conservatives. They even evaluated religion talk from liberal or moderate representatives either as not distinctively religious or, more commonly, as conservative regardless of its actual source.

The Religious Right has succeeded in "owning the space" of religion in American public life. The pursuit of religious credibility in the public sphere has, in this sense, worked. But from a normative perspective this success has resulted in constituting religion in public life as contrary to good debate. Respondents mobilized a normative preference for deliberative debate that conservative religion was seen to violate. Yet to ordinary persons, it is only conservative religion that operates in public life, in the form either of individual religion representatives or of religious arguments and reasons.

The result is that ordinary persons understand religion in public life as opposed to good debate. The Religious Right not only owns the space but, in doing so, has also exercised the cartographic power of representation to define what counts as the space of "religion" in the public sphere. The boundaries are set, and they appear to be durable, as they are reproduced even within the imaginations of respondents from a variety of religious backgrounds.

CHAPTER 8

Faceless Science

Scientific Credibility in the Public Sphere

One of the most striking features of the religion-and-science debates examined in this study is the lack of prominent scientists across debates in public life. While several representatives make claims based on scientific authority, few of these representatives are actual scientists. And when scientists appear, they tend to be confined to one issue. This is strange. The public sphere provides, particularly through mass media, an important arena for pursuing credibility. And as many scholars of science have shown, the pursuit of credibility is central to the scientific enterprise. Yet the most prominent representatives pursuing scientific credibility and making claims based on scientific authority are not actual practitioners of science.

So where are the scientists? Why are scientists not more visible in the public sphere? Many people think they should be. For example, a popular book called *Unscientific America,* by best-selling authors Christopher Mooney and Sheril Kirshenbaum, argues that we are unable to deal properly with many current problems because of general scientific illiteracy. According to the book's authors, a chief reason for this illiteracy is that science loses out in public debates because its apparent opponents, in particular American religious conservatives, are simply better than scientists at gaining and keeping the attention of ordinary Americans. Despite the rise of many new media efforts (e.g., blogs) dedicated to popularizing science, Mooney and Kirshenbaum claim, "the bloggers cannot save us" and what we really need is "Renaissance scientists" who can "tell stories" and "appeal to the interests of broader audiences."[1] Or, in other words, what science needs is its own version of the Religious Right, in the form of a few visible science representatives who will carry the banner for science in the public sphere, no matter what the issue or concern.

In this and the following chapter, I use findings from media analysis and interview data to explain scientific participation in the public sphere. Like most scholars in science and technology studies (STS), I start from the position that science is a multidimensional cultural institution whose existence and authority depend on maintaining credibility in public life.[2] What counts as science, scientists, or scientific authority does not derive simply from fact or truth claims, or from a clearly demarcated set of rules for producing the knowledge that drives such claims (e.g., "the scientific method"), but from the apparatus of credibility that surrounds such claims.[3] Many different actors—including (but not limited to) scientists in the lab, social activists, university administrators, corporate accountants, government regulators, school boards, lawyers, and judges—engage in "boundary work," the "strategic practical action" that negotiates the particular boundaries of science in a given place and time.[4]

STS scholars have shown repeatedly that the dominant model of scientific credibility involves scientists avoiding the public sphere. This model of scientific credibility is supported by a public narrative that defines credible scientists as dedicated seekers of knowledge who manage an uncertain enterprise by being consistently virtuous.[5] Pursuing individual credibility in the public sphere is a signal that the virtuous scientist has been corrupted by (the pursuit of) money, fame, or power, rather than pursuing scientific truth. So active scientist participation in the public sphere is undesirable and even fatal to scientific credibility.

Thinking about the public sphere as an arena of credibility helps clarify what is at stake. Efforts to mobilize some scientific version of the Religious Right, or to recruit a new Carl Sagan, are not just efforts to introduce new science representatives into the public sphere. They are efforts to replace a model of scientific credibility that avoids the public sphere with one that intervenes in the public sphere. As the example of the Religious Right shows, such an approach can succeed in terms of gaining visibility in the public sphere. But, as the Religious Right example also shows, such visibility does not automatically translate into approval by ordinary persons evaluating representatives in public debate.

For science, as for religion, efforts to establish credibility in the public sphere often run afoul of deliberative preferences for good debate.

In interviews, I found consistently that ordinary persons negatively evaluated science representatives in public life. This negative evaluation was not due to opposition to science or "antiscience" attitudes. Contrary to what scholars in the "epistemological conflict" tradition would claim, almost all respondents expressed support for science, despite various religious commitments, even when its process or products violated their moral preferences.

Rather, the negative evaluation was due to general support for the model of scientific credibility that imagines scientists as credible in part because they do not seek public attention or attempt to intervene in public debate. This "faceless" model of public credibility, drawing on historically resonant notions of virtuous scientists and promulgated through science journalism and a complicit public education system, generates widespread public support for science in the abstract.[6] But the process that successfully generates "faceless" public credibility for science also reinforces the notion that good debate does not have scientists involved.

SCIENCE IN AMERICAN PUBLIC LIFE

In contrast to the case of religion, in which the Religious Right clearly dominates American public life, it is actually difficult to say what science representatives are. Who represents science? The obvious answer is "scientists." But as previous chapters report, prominent scientists in public life are rare. Lonnie Thompson, an Ohio State University–affiliated climatologist, is among the top ten in environmental policy debate. Michael Behe, a Lehigh University–affiliated biochemist, and the late Stephen Jay Gould, a Harvard and NYU–affiliated paleontologist and evolutionary biologist, each show up prominently in human origins debate. And Dean Hamer, a U.S. National Cancer Institute–affiliated geneticist, shows up among the top ten representatives in debates over the origins of homosexuality. In each case, when scientists show up prominently, they do so only in a single debate. In the religion-and-science debates in this study, no scientists show up across debates consistently. And even this limited sort of prominence is unusual. Certainly many different scientists show up in general-audience mass media articles, but they tend to do so as local authorities for individual news stories rather than as prominent representatives across debates. Many scientists are mentioned once, but few are mentioned often.

But we know from "science communication" literature that science in public life is not limited to the activities of scientists.[7] While there are a few scientists who actively seek prominence in public life (e.g., the late Carl Sagan), science in public life involves much more than the simple "scientist tells world" model. Many different actors play a part in producing science beyond the academy, laboratory, or field site. For example, specialized magazines such as *Popular Science* and *MAKE,* or television shows such as *Mythbusters* and *It's Effin' Science,* communicate and frame science facts, methods, and findings for a broad audience of interested persons. Movies, comic books, and thriller novels laud scientific achievement and stimulate popular imagination about science and technology.[8] Science journalists write stories for general-audience mass media newspapers that summarize the results of scientific findings and "translate" these findings for a popular audience.[9] Science museums organize collections and exhibitions that show particular aspects of scientific discovery and invention, often in idiosyncratic ways that bring together many different kinds of social worlds and link science to other domains of social life.[10] And of course many public figures draw, or at least attempt to draw, on the authority of science in order to bolster their claims in public life. Science in public life is not limited to scientists with a public profile.

Yet even with a more generous definition of science representatives as "persons who draw on scientific authority in public life," there are few prominent science representatives in these debates. Most are affiliated directly with a research institution (e.g., Michael Behe, Julia Parrish). Some are also scientists who write (or wrote) for a popular audience, such as Stephen Jay Gould and Richard Dawkins. And some are persons active in public life who advance their agenda by calling on scientific authority, whether they are themselves scientists (e.g., Behe) or not (e.g., Gore). Many different science representatives show up, and for many different reasons. But unlike the situation for religion, no obvious set of representatives persists across debates. Science in the public sphere is not obviously tied to a coherent set of practitioners. Science does not have the equivalent of the Religious Right.

According to ordinary Americans, good debate is supposed to include a variety of contributors. Good debates involving science should involve, at a minimum, some prominent scientists who can contribute to public deliberation. So, as with the religion representatives in the previous chapter, this strange distribution presents an obvious question. Where are the highly visible science representatives? And, perhaps even more important, why are the most highly visible science representatives across debates not actually scientists (e.g., Al Gore)?

Avoiding Public Debate

The answer is deceptively simple. Scientists are doing other things instead. Like members of the Religious Left, scientists are not prominent in the public sphere, because they generally do not seek prominence in that sphere. While scientists communicate with mass media elites to varying extents, it is highly unusual to seek prominence in the public sphere. This phenomenon is widely noted in a variety of literatures, from history of science to science communication, and even in many popular books. Everyone basically agrees that scientists generally do not seek prominence in public life.

But not everyone agrees on why this happens. Sociologist Robert Merton, for example, famously attributed this reticence to internal scientific norms (e.g., "disinterestedness") that mark the scientific profession as a distinct approach to knowledge production.[11] Like Merton, social historian Steven Shapin points to characteristics of the scientific profession. But unlike Merton, who identifies enduring and essential values, Shapin attributes avoidance of public prominence to a shift over time from thinking about science as personal genius to viewing it as impersonal method.[12] Communication scholars, meanwhile, regularly suggest that it is not reticence, but a lack of competence, that restricts scientists' prominence in public life.[13] For example, scientists tend to focus on the accuracy of particular factual points in communication, which sometimes derails the communication process.[14]

The interesting thing about these (and many other similar) explanations is that they are not exclusive: they could all be true. Certainly there is evidence to support each of them. Each academic approach (history, sociology, communication) finds the same thing and explains the finding in terms of its disciplinary conventions. However, these disciplinary descriptions of the phenomenon are not actually different. These observations are consistent because they are all practical implications of a more fundamental explanation. Each describes one aspect of an underlying model of scientific credibility that depends on separating the credibility of science as an institution from that of any particular scientist.

As many STS scholars have observed, the public credibility of science is problematically linked to the inherent uncertainty of the scientific enterprise. Certainty engenders confidence, but science is an uncertain business.[15] Cases that work in the lab do not always travel successfully to the field, or even to other labs.[16] Requirements and regulatory constraints change expectations and structure possibilities.[17] Technical equipment fails, or never quite works as expected.[18] These circumstances produce uncertainty not only in the process of science but also in the results. While there are undoubted scientific successes, there are also many failures and many unfulfilled promises.

The challenge of credibility is to take an uncertain enterprise and render it trustworthy. Science needs resources, and getting these resources depends on being seen as something worth supporting. The obvious response to this challenge is to minimize (the appearance of) uncertainty and to focus on significant successful results that vindicate science in the face of uncertainty. Certainly scientists attempt to minimize (the appearance of) uncertainty through various work-arounds— for example, by writing lab reports that leave out failures and dead ends.[19] But this is not a robust solution. After all, work-arounds can fail, too.[20] And to the extent that credibility is linked to the kinds of material successes that occur infrequently, such as developing a cure for polio or achieving human spaceflight, every failure to achieve something equally impressive (e.g., flying cars, cures for cancer or HIV/AIDS or Alzheimer's) reduces the public credibility of science.

Credibility Narratives in the Public Sphere

Because it cannot reliably depend on other kinds of evidence for building credibility, the public pursuit of scientific credibility relies on the power of narrative. Narrative, as I use the term here (following Jerome Bruner), is a "version of reality whose acceptability is governed by convention . . . rather than by empirical verification and logical requiredness" and "whose intention is to initiate and guide a search for meanings among a spectrum of possible meanings."[21] By organizing information into accounts such as "stories, excuses, myths, reasons for doing and not doing," narrative provides a sense of time and order, as well as a normative sense of what is good and bad about the contents of those accounts.[22]

In contrast to factual statements such as "Plutonium is radioactive" or "Humans and apes share a common ancestor" or even "Scientists are cool," narrative offers stories such as "Brave scientist Reed Richards exposed himself to dangerous radiation, but now, as Mister Fantastic, he fights evil and saves the world" or "A loving and merciful God created the universe six thousand years ago for His pleasure."[23] Narrative communicates how information fits into a broader cultural landscape, why anyone should care, and even how you should feel about it.

Communicating facts is useful, and easy to test on surveys. But, as cognitive scientists have demonstrated, people do not learn meaning simply by learning facts. They learn meaning by locating knowledge in the context of other symbols and meanings that they have already acquired.[24] Narrative engages meaning and significance. So narrative is important for credibility because it conveys information not just about what is to be believed but also about who is to be believed and why.

Building credibility through narrative means telling stories that establish and reinforce the notion of scientists as virtuous inhabitants of a credible profession. For example, basic science textbooks often tell a story about the measurement of stellar magnitude (the brightness of stars) as a continuous journey of scientific progress through two thousand years of recorded history.[25] The point of the story is not really that the actual daily practices of today's astronomers resemble what Ptolemy did two thousand years ago. Empirically, they do not. Nor is the point that Ptolemy and (for example) the astronomy professor at the local community college are making equally significant contributions to human knowledge. A quick check verifies that they are not. Rather, the point of the story is that current astronomers are credible precisely because they constitute one of those kinds of people who successfully did amazing things in the past. Such "credibility narratives" move uncertainty from a source of weakness to a source of strength. As the story goes, precisely because science is inherently uncertain, it requires a special kind of person to deal directly with that uncertainty and produce reliable knowledge. Credibility narratives emphasize the virtues of scientists as trustworthy and moral judges of knowledge and inquiry in the face of uncertainty. This approach shifts the source of credibility from questions of truth, accuracy, or track record to questions about who is to be believed and why.[26]

But this does not mean simply promoting individual representatives, as in the case of the Religious Right in public life. Instead, credibility narratives define the scientific profession as a vocation that attracts a particular sort of person who can be trusted precisely because their virtues and moral commitments equip them to produce reliable scientific knowledge despite the uncertainty of science's processes or practices. Scientists are credible because they are a particular kind of person, not because they are necessarily more able to minimize uncertainty in practice or consistently produce successful results.[27]

In the public sphere, credibility narratives about science are often perpetuated through mass media journalism. Journalists perpetuate credibility narratives because they fit narrative conventions of popular media. They make good stories. Of course, as the definition indicates, narrative power is governed by convention.[28] Not any story will do. Stories about scientists cannot merely be stories about people who do mundane technical work in laboratories, even if that is (often) empirically the case.[29] Instead, compelling stories about scientists instantiate appealing and accessible cultural tropes. For example, popular writing portrays scientists as detectives, providing an "interpretive repertoire" for understanding the otherwise boring aspects of inductive reasoning as exciting crime-solving.[30] Likewise, journalists leverage local, regional, or patriotic elements to portray scientists as the embodiment of national or ethnic ideals.[31]

Scholars of science communication and public understanding of science often point to such reliance on narrative conventions as a problem for science communication. Scientific findings are not simply conveyed, but transformed, by the media, a process that has been termed medialization.[32] An extensive literature on "framing" raises concerns about differences between what scientists actually find in their research and what various media actors say about them.[33] While scientists are regularly in contact with media actors, and report that they are interested in communicating science to the public, empirically it seems that media actors are in control of credibility narratives, even though many science communication scholars seem to think that scientists should be in control.[34]

But what seems a problem for science communication is actually a direct consequence of pursuing public credibility through narrative, rather than by seeking public prominence for particular scientists. The obvious drawback of credibility narratives is that you cannot tell them about yourself. As Steven Shapin has observed in tensions over "entrepreneurial science," part of the virtue in the scientific profession resides precisely in not doing such things.[35] Presenting one's own narrative is seen as self-serving or, more generally, as something that scientists just don't do.

Scientists themselves typically see the pursuit of individual public credibility as problematic rather than beneficial. The model of faceless public credibility is so ingrained in the scientific profession that scientists police each other's attempts at public outreach. For example, while Carl Sagan's outreach efforts through his books and the *Cosmos* television series were successful in reaching a large popular audience, his increasing prominence in the public sphere corresponded directly to decreasing approval and respect from other scientists.[36] Likewise, Stephen Jay Gould has been the target of criticism from other biologists and journalists who have portrayed his public outreach as compensation for his failure to persuade other scientists of his scientific arguments about evolution.[37] In qualitative studies of science outreach, scientists regularly cite such "informal sanctions" as reasons to avoid public outreach activities altogether.[38]

Of course, scientists can engage in public outreach that does not emphasize their own individual credibility, by promoting science rather than individual scientists. But even indirect efforts are often seen as problematic. For example, scientists occasionally act as scientific consultants on movie projects to check for scientific accuracy, suggest speculative scenarios, or just make a set look like a laboratory.[39] Such work would seem beneficial for science. People like movies. And any individual benefit would accrue to fictional scientists, like the virologists in *Outbreak,* the geneticists in *Jurassic Park,* or the astronomers in *Contact.* But even these cases attract criticism from other scientists. For example, in a review published in the *New York Review of Books,* Stephen Jay Gould criticized the science consultants on *Jurassic Park* for presenting one view of evolutionary biology as authoritative, thereby making one group of real-life scientists more credible to the broader dinosaur-loving public.[40]

So scientists do not pursue public credibility by directly seeking prominence in the public sphere. Instead, the public credibility of science is maintained by other actors who produce and reproduce credibility narratives. This practice places the control of such narratives into the hands of other people, such as journalists, science teachers, and popular authors of various fiction and nonfiction genres, some of whom are prominent in public life but are not themselves scientists. But it maintains the central image of the scientist as a virtuous inhabitant of an uncertain profession, whose virtue in part depends on avoiding public life in favor of concentrating on producing true knowledge.

THE MYTH OF RELIGIOUS "ANTISCIENCE"

The pursuit of the public credibility of science, rather than the public credibility of scientists, presents a basic methodological problem for understanding how people evaluate individual science representatives. To the extent that such pursuit succeeds, it shifts the locus of evaluation from individual science representatives to science in general. So it is possible that positive or negative evaluation of science representatives in public life simply reflects the extent to which respondents positively or negatively evaluate science in general, rather than science representatives in particular.

This is a particular challenge for a study in which most respondents, like most Americans, are religious. In scholarly and popular literature alike, there is a pervasive claim that religion makes ordinary persons "antiscience" in various ways. From this perspective, religious beliefs and commitments inhibit support for science. In some versions, the reason for this inhibition is that religious truth claims and scientific truth claims conflict (e.g., over human origins) and this conflict contributes to "antiscience" attitudes.[41] In other versions, the reason is that religious persons have moral objections that surface with regard to science.[42] And in a less direct version of the argument, religious persons are less educated (or less able to be educated), and therefore less exposed to the scientific knowledge that would compel support.[43]

The religious "antiscience" claim is one attempt to resolve an apparent paradox in findings about support for science in U.S. society. On one hand, major surveys such as the General Social Survey and the National Science Board Science and Engineering Indicators consistently find that people express general support for science and scientific research. As the National Science Board recently noted, "Overall, Americans remain strong believers in the benefits of S&T even while seeing potential risks. Surveys since at least 1979 show that roughly 7 in 10 Americans see the effects of scientific research as more positive than negative for society."[44] Yet, on the other hand, ordinary persons regularly express resistance or opposition to science as it is currently practiced, prompting the accusation from scholars and popular authors that ordinary persons are often "antiscience."[45] This "antiscience" position takes the form of limiting funding to certain scientific research programs, pushing for changes in science curriculum to include (for example) Intelligent Design, and expressing skepticism about scientific findings such as climate change.[46]

Explaining the paradox fully is well beyond the scope of this book.[47] But we can address the proposed explanation based on the notion of religion inhibiting support for science. On its face this explanation seems improbable in the U.S. case, since approximately 80 percent of Americans are religious in some form, and surely some of them are also among the 90 percent of Americans who show support for science in national surveys.[48] Of course, religious commitments vary and could therefore vary in their support for science. For example, some studies indicate that conservative Protestants in particular are less likely to support science.[49] But if religious backgrounds and commitments do inhibit support for science, this effect could easily outweigh the effects of normative conflict over good debate. So it is important to address this possibility.

Figuring out whether religion inhibits support for science among respondents is not straightforward. To the extent that underlying commitments have power, it is because people invoke them in particular ways for particular reasons. Asking "what" questions, such as "Do you support science?" or "Do you believe in evolution?" fails to, on one hand, specify what is at stake and, on the other hand, expose the reasoning behind respondent answers. To get at the "how" and "why" aspects of this problem—that is, to get at the reasoning processes and not just the outcomes—I asked respondents to respond to the following scenario about a (fictional) proposed ten-year moratorium on basic scientific research:

> Let's say someone proposed a ten-year-long moratorium[50] on basic scientific research. Their reasons are (1) we need to assess our current data, (2) we need to get consensus on policy positions resulting from research findings, and (3) we need to think about the moral or ethical implications of science. Would you support such a plan?

Given the provocative nature of the scenario, I expected first that respondents would actually respond rather than deflect, and second that the responses would help clarify the conditions under which they would support a moratorium (if at all). Because there are many available discursive resources for talking about scientific research, I anticipated a wide range of responses. Respondents might seek clarification at an issue level, rather than answering the general question. They might suggest that the deliberative process is working and that intervention is unnecessary. They might take a principled stand about freedom that has little to do with substantive scientific content of research. They might see moratoria as interfering with scientific progress. Or, given the religious distribution of the interview sample, they might use religious language or express specific forms of opposition or support grounded in religious commitments.

In almost every case, however, respondents opposed moratoria for reasons that aligned with support for ongoing scientific research. This support held even when respondents were faced with objections that aligned with their own opinions and beliefs about moral or ethical issues. When confronted with arguments or contrary evidence that undermined their initial reasons, respondents moved among multiple reasons as required to maintain their position of support for ongoing scientific research. The bottom line is that respondents maintained a commitment to ongoing research that exceeded their commitment to any single objection, reason, or justification, whether from religious commitments or from any other source.

Initial Responses Opposed Moratorium

Out of sixty-two respondents, sixty immediately rejected the moratorium as initially proposed. The most common reaction to the scenario as presented was surprise that anyone would want to limit science, despite the respondent having been primed with reasons why such limitation might be helpful. Susanne and Bonnie (in separate interviews) showed indignance and disbelief:

> Susanne: To stop all scientific research just to catch our breath is absurd. . . . I just cannot imagine stopping research. I mean, that's like saying, "Everybody turn off your brain for a little while."

> Bonnie: It's such a fundamental "no" that I'm having trouble putting the "why" into words. Who knows what we would miss during those ten years? Who knows what we could have discovered that would have saved lives that were lost in those ten years? Why would we ever want to stop learning?

Most respondents were more measured in their responses, but still did not support limitations on science as initially proposed. The most common reason for rejecting the proposal was an expressed connection between scientific research and human progress, such that limiting science might even be harmful to society. Solomon, for example, offered a typical explanation for why we should not limit science, even for good reasons: "At first, again this is an interesting question. As you started to ask the question, I thought, Gee, it makes sense; let's stop there and assess what we have. But I think that we are in a day and age in which there are so many possibilities, so many exciting things being discovered now as we speak and being studied that I would not want that stopped. I think we would regress instead of move forward."

Charles echoed Solomon's concerns about progress: "I wouldn't support that because I think that that would really, I mean, obviously that would set so many things back a decade. Think about how many things have been discovered in the last decade, how many important things have been discovered and looked at and researched. . . . I mean imagine going into 2000, but only having the technology of 1990. I mean, the world would look so different." And for Josefina, limiting scientific research would get in the way of solving important problems: "I think we should keep doing [scientific research] because, I mean, there's other countries that are in need of aid and that in those ten years we can, we can help them, which is why we're having environmental issues right now, right?"

Put another way, most respondents linked opposition to a moratorium to reasons based on support for scientific research, not on objections to the act (based either on principle or characteristics of the act itself) or to the scenario as presented. The core point here is that respondents overwhelmingly saw a moratorium as an impediment to ongoing scientific research, which they saw as desirable for many different reasons. While the commitments to particular reasons differed in the initial responses, the commitment to ongoing scientific research held across respondents. This is consistent with higher-level survey results (cited above) that indicate a general support for science.

Mobility of Reasons Resists Moral Concerns

After the first several interviews, it became clear that the specific content of responses was less interesting than the tactics that respondents used when they were challenged. In almost all cases, respondents continued to oppose a moratorium on scientific research. What is more interesting is that respondents invoked and then moved among multiple reasons, values, and narratives in order to find ways to continue their support for science, even when faced with possible dilemmas posed by the follow-up questions. Take, for example, Holly's mobilization of her personal experience when I proposed an alternative one-year break from scientific research: "No, not even. Never. Because why, why take a cure from somebody, you know? My, my grandfather had a heart attack and he had arteriosclerosis, and they came up with a cure the next year. He died in 1969, and in 1970 they came out with something that would clear out the arteries. You know had that been available to him, he would have been alive still." For Holly, scientific benefits are tangible, and her assessment of science reflected the alignment of scientific benefits (in this case a medical cure) with her own personal experiential concerns about the value of human life and health.

Other respondents mobilized more abstract reasons to continue in the face of moral concerns. Lydia, a lifelong performer and teacher, discussed why she thought science ought not to be limited: "Because it's the creative process. I'm an artist, and science is still the creative process. In the questioning, the constant questioning. The constant problem-solving. The constant data collecting. Something new is revealed. Don't cut off the pipeline. You do not know . . . So you just have to be courageous in the face of 'don't know.'"

Given the scenario's explicit discussion of moral objections, one of the more interesting responses to challenge occurred when respondents did not directly address moral or ethical issues, then when pressed on this point, offered different ways that moral concerns either did not or should not matter to evaluating science. Initially, Susanne did not engage the objection about moral or ethical issues, focusing instead on how moratoria would limit the growth of human knowledge (see "absurd" quote above). When pressed on the possibility that scientific research has moral or ethical implications, she confidently replied, "If education is done correctly, there won't be a moral or ethical issue, and if there is, it can be solved." A similar response came from Damien, a high school chemistry teacher. When pressed about limiting science for moral or ethical reasons, he also detached the scientific process from moral accountability:

A: I think that the cool thing about science is, so much of it isn't through our efforts. Like meaning, I think, the vast majority of science discoveries are purely accidental. . . . I think in terms of the real discoveries in science, you know, like—people just do stuff and then something goes wrong and that's a huge discovery all of the sudden. So I'm—because of the scientific process I would say let science continue.

Q: Even if there's something bad that comes out of that?

A: Even if there's something bad that comes out of it, yes.

Another common tactic was for respondents to begin by suggesting that moratoria would limit progress, then when pressed on this point, to respond by saying that even if it would not, that you could not, or should not, stop science anyway. For Zoe, debates should be avoided precisely because they might lead to limitations on science. When I pushed her on the possible moral concerns raised by those who might oppose science, she replied:

A: . . . I know that's a tough one, but . . .

Q: Why is it tough?

A: Because then somebody might say "Why not stop?" Cuz, you know, it's just depending on which side of the debate you're on.

Both Ian and Grace (in separate interviews) recognized that moral and ethical concerns are important, but provided reasons that a moratorium could not happen anyway. After I pressed Ian on whether or not a scientist should have to think about moral or ethical implications, he replied:

A: They never have. That's not in their nature generally. I shouldn't generalize about people, but yeah, that's not generally in their nature. They want to know how something works at all costs. We could talk about the atomic bomb, that the atomic energy thing was not meant to be a bad thing at first, but anything that has the potential to become a weapon becomes one regardless.

Q: So science is going to go on regardless [of any restrictions]?

A: Yeah; well, it will. It would be like Prohibition. If somebody's really a scientist, he isn't going to listen to rules like that anyway. . . . So you can't stop science now.

Grace offered a more sweeping version of this argument, employing a broad definition of science to defend her position that moral and ethical concerns could not be addressed: "Well, science is everywhere; you can't stop it. I mean, you can't—you eat food, that's science. I mean, you have babies, that's science. You have, you know, everything is science. You cannot stop science; I mean, it just happens. Bad people and good people doing science are going to happen no matter what. You can't stop it."

Perhaps the most striking outcome of this mobility of reasons was that some respondents expressed agreement with moral and ethical concerns to the extent of offering reasons why scientific research might be stopped, then, when faced with the prospect of limiting research based on those reasons, immediately suggested that they should be disregarded so that research could continue:

Q: What's a good reason to stop [doing scientific research]?

A: Things that injure people. I think that the sanctity of life is really important, and I think that any time that that might be compromised, that's a good place to stop.

Q: But don't you think that we should stop and figure that out first? We should wait until it happens and then stop it?

A: Sometimes you just have to, sometimes you don't; sometimes people have differing opinions on things, and so you just—I don't know, I still think you should go forward.

Respondents mobilized many different explanations and reasons, but they did so to support science, offering examples of how scientific research should continue despite expressed concerns. They also discounted and dismissed moral or ethical concerns about science as valid reasons to limit science. Finally, multiple respondents found ways to exempt scientific research from moral considerations, even if that meant overriding the moral concerns they themselves had expressed.

Underlying Commitment to Ongoing Research

The finding that there is an underlying commitment to ongoing scientific research (rather than just opposition to the use of moratoria) was further reinforced by the few cases in which respondents were open to the use of a moratorium. Erika rejected the initial proposal, but offered a five-year moratorium as a counterproposal. While she acknowledged that we might lose out on something coming out of everyday lab work, she recognized the importance of the concerns in the proposal. Yet even this concern had limits. When asked why five years would be OK but ten years wouldn't, she cited concerns over losing an educational generation of future scientists: "Well because I think—well, I don't think five years is long enough to examine all that's there, but I think after five years you have a whole new group of students coming out of schools, and they're gonna want to research things and they'll probably have lots of really good ideas." Even after expressing sympathy for moral and ethical concerns, Erika's support for a moratorium depended on the future ability to do more science. And she added immediately thereafter, "I don't think there should be a moratorium on invention," signaling that even her support for a moratorium may not actually have been intended to stop research.

In a similar vein, when pressed for a shorter time limit, Bernard made his commitment to ongoing science part of his support for a shorter moratorium: "To take a deep breath and step back, and make sure the research was better directed, better funded, better understood, better outcomes, make decisions on the ethics and moral side of it in that shorter period of time, yeah, I could support a couple years."

And Dwight emphasized that the only legitimate reason to limit research would be that available resources are scarce: "I would not

146 | Faceless Science

support [a moratorium] as an overarching policy statement, any period of time basically. If, during the debate about where resources are allocated, and we're short of resources or there's just nobody really interested in doing it or something like that, then, yes, I can see that happening and would support [a moratorium] to that extent."

Only a few respondents were willing to use any version of a moratorium, even when continually pressed with reasons to do so. Other than the two respondents discussed below, none supported the original proposal. And even though some respondents agreed that a shorter moratorium on scientific research might be acceptable, their reasons did not reflect concern, moral or otherwise, about science. Rather, the proposed limits depended on commitments to continued scientific research.

The Exceptions

Two respondents, however, had no qualms or hesitation about a ten-year moratorium as initially proposed, and did not immediately offer reasons to support science. When presented with the scenario, Felix immediately responded, "Sure. I would support that." Norma similarly replied, "Yeah, it sounds reasonable to me." From a sampling perspective, what distinguishes Felix and Norma is that they are fundamentalist Protestants. Here, for example, is Felix's rationale for supporting a moratorium:

> Well, like I indicated, I think society has gone off from a wrong foundation that we have now a society that doesn't accept that there is a God creator. Without that as the base, all of the decisions following that I feel are all wrong. So any moral or policy issues would have serious implications for me. Red flags as I see them, because I think all of the debates, all of the issues, are flowing from the initial concept that there is no God creator.

On its face, this finding seems to support the largely discredited idea that there is epistemological conflict between religion and science. But true fundamentalist Protestants in the United States are a small religious minority, probably less than 10 percent of the overall population.[51] These anomalous cases illustrate by contrast an interesting feature of the responses to the moratorium scenario. Throughout the sample, religious respondents (including all other evangelicals and conservative Protestants) consistently mobilized reasons and arguments to support science. And some respondents explicitly drew on religious commitments to support, rather than oppose, scientific research. For Phoebe, science should continue without limitations because we will work out the right things to do over time: "I just think it's funny because, you know, God gives us free will and we as humans will take things as far as we can. We've got this new thing, like stem cell research; we want to see how far we can go with it. I can't tell you where that will be, but I think that God gives us free will, and then it just takes us a long time to learn, you know, but we do eventually."

Likewise, Meg saw scientific research as a part of what we are supposed to be doing: "I just cannot imagine living in a world where you weren't exploring, where you weren't questioning, where you weren't learning. You'd almost be going back into the Dark Ages. It would be like a ban on living. I think God gave us the inquisitiveness that we have. We just have to be careful how we use it."

Instead of illustrating how religion interferes with support for science, the two exceptions seem by contrast to show how aligned the other sixty respondents were in their support for science, despite having a wide range of religious commitments. Put another way, unwavering support for science bound together evangelical Protestants, Catholics, mainline Protestants, other religious believers, spiritual-but-not-religious, and nonreligious Americans in the interview sample. What distinguished Felix and Norma, then, was not specifically that they are religious, but that they totally rejected the assumptions that were shared by the sixty other respondents.

The key here is to see that Felix's answer is not just a reference to God or religious beliefs, but rather a fundamental critique of modernity as something that has "gone off from a wrong foundation." For some scholars of religion it is precisely this critique of modernity that defines fundamentalism, rather than any particular religious commitment (hence there can also be Islamic fundamentalists, Hindu fundamentalists, and so forth).[52] As the exceptions in this study, Felix and Norma illuminate how very uncommon it is to oppose science, and how such opposition is not grounded simply in religious commitments, but rather in a fundamental critique of the entire apparatus of modernity, of which science is a primary product. Ultimately, even Norma acknowledged that science will probably continue: "I think everybody is just out there to find answers and we don't want to stop, and, you know, we're pursuing to find answers and maybe we can't even find the answers, but we don't want to stop, because there is always the possibility that you'll find the answer."

With the exception of two genuine fundamentalists in this study, religion or religious commitments did not usefully predict support for, or inclination to limit, science. Rather, respondents displayed an extraordinary faith in science. This faith and confidence in science trumped differences in religion. Likewise, the reasons offered by religious persons were not distinct from those offered by nonreligious, or differently religious, persons in the sample. For example, no matter what their background or experience might indicate, respondents did not understand moral or ethical concerns as legitimate reasons to support a moratorium. To the contrary, they mobilized multiple reasons and values to justify ongoing scientific research, even when confronted with arguments suggesting that these values may be in conflict with science. Whether religious or not, and despite significant heterogeneity of religious characteristics, respondents basically drew on the same default responses, provided the same reasons, and resorted to the same strategy of switching among reasons as necessary to support their conclusions. The religious "antiscience" claim simply does not hold up.

Perhaps more important, these findings show that ordinary persons distinguish between the credibility of science and the credibility of its practitioners. Positive and negative evaluation of scientists, and of science representatives more generally, do not simply reflect religious (or other) objections to science. This is, of course, consistent with a variety of other findings in sociology indicating a distinction between opposition to science and opposition to, for example, the apparent moral orientation of scientists.[53] But it is important to know as we consider how normative conflict over good debate intersects with science in American public life.

SCIENCE AND PUBLIC CREDIBILITY

In American public life, science representatives are not seeking to "own the space" of science. Scientists actually seem more like the Religious Left in their avoidance of the public sphere. This is not to say that science representatives never show up. But science in the public sphere is not quite like religion in the public sphere. No equivalent of the Religious Right exists for science. Even with an expanded definition of science representative as a "person who draws on scientific authority in public life," few science representatives are prominent, and it is rare for a science representative to feature in more than one debate. In terms of achieving prominence in public life, individual science representatives are not very successful. Historical cases suggest that this approach has successfully insulated the institutional credibility of science from the (highly variable) credibility of individual practitioners. Science is credible in part because its inhabitants do not attempt to become prominent in the public sphere. But by defining credible scientists as persons whose virtue resides partly in avoiding public life, this approach reinforces the expectation that scientists are simply not contributors to public debate. So while science representatives might draw on scientific authority, the presence of a scientist in public debate is grounds for suspicion.

What are the implications for the deliberative debate that ordinary Americans are seeking? The case of the Religious Left shows that possibilities for deliberative debate are fully entangled with normative conflict in the public sphere. A shift toward deliberative debate involving religion—that is, toward inclusion of Religious Left representatives as visible participants in these debates—runs afoul of the definition of "religion" in public life that the dominant Religious Right has constituted in public sphere debates. In a sense, the Religious Left, simply by being religious, is mistaken for a contributor to bad debate, rather than to good debate. Even if members of the Religious Left changed course and started pursuing religious credibility in the public sphere, the norms of the public sphere would limit their participation.

In contrast, a shift toward deliberative debate involving science—that is, toward inclusion of scientists and additional science representatives as visible participants in these debates—runs afoul of the very model of public credibility that makes science a respected source of credible knowledge. The dominant model of scientific credibility, in theory, prevents deliberative debate from occurring. But is deliberative debate simply a matter of changing internal scientific practice and getting scientists more involved in the public sphere, as science communication scholars suggest? Or, as is the case with the Religious Left, do the norms of the public sphere limit the ways by which science can participate in public life?

CHAPTER 9

Science and Bad Debate

Are deliberative expectations entangled with scientific credibility? Do ordinary persons link scientists to bad debate? To answer these questions, I analyzed how interview respondents evaluated what "science" and "scientific" meant in the religion-and-science debates discussed in this study. As with religion, I did not simply ask, "What do you think of science in these debates?" Instead, I examined how respondents invoked science and scientists, identified who and what was scientific, connected science to other ideas and concepts, and resolved apparent conflicts involving science and scientists in their responses.

If deliberative expectations are entangled with scientific credibility, what we should see is that ordinary persons negatively evaluate scientists who show up in debates in this study. However, this negative evaluation should not reflect a general disapproval of science, since the public credibility of science depends on public narrative rather than on individual scientists. We should also see that ordinary persons apply deliberative preferences to science representatives in distinctive ways. Of course, when science representatives violate deliberative preferences in other ways (e.g., through politics), this should be negatively evaluated regardless of scientific status. But we should also see negative evaluation of scientists simply for participating in public life at all.

Throughout interviews and across issues, this exact combination of positive evaluations of science and negative evaluations of scientists in public life appeared consistently. Science in the public sphere is respected in the abstract, as an institution worth supporting even under circumstances that may violate substantive religious or moral preferences. However, this support for science did not translate into approval of scientists in public life. For the respondents in this study, the presence of scientists in public life indicated bad debate.

Respondents understood scientists in public life to violate deliberative preferences in two ways. First, ordinary persons understood scientists to be virtuous, in part because they do not participate in public debate. Respondents understood such participation to be inappropriate. While ordinary persons recognized scientific expertise as important, they tended to conceive of "scientist" in terms of a role with interchangeable inhabitants rather than in terms of individual distinction or prominence. Even when respondents thought that scientific advice was necessary for debate, they rarely named an individual scientist and simply described a category of participant (e.g., "biologist" or "scientist"). On the rare occasions when science representatives did show up in public debate, respondents either evaluated them in terms that distinguished scientists from nonscientists (e.g., Al Gore as politician) or negatively evaluated them as scientists who were inappropriately involved in politics. From the perspective of ordinary persons, the proper role of scientists is to be faceless inhabitants of science as an institution.

Second, respondents negatively evaluated the use of scientific authority to settle debate. They strongly preferred science to inform debate in various ways, but in practice they often saw science as a conversation stopper that violated deliberative expectations. This was a problem particularly when some science representatives were seen as leveraging their scientific authority to attack other, more deliberative participants. Notably this was true whether or not respondents actually agreed with the substantive claims or argument of the attacker. On the rare occasions when respondents named an individual scientist as an ideal participant in public debate, the suggestion was invariably a scientist who takes a deliberative and open-minded stance toward alternative sources of authority. To the extent that science representatives draw on scientific authority to limit good debate, ordinary persons thought science should be faceless.

EVALUATING PUBLIC SCIENCE AS PARTICIPATION

Nobody knows Lonnie Thompson. As table 7 reports, nobody knows Dean Hamer, either. Every respondent recognized Charles Darwin, Al

TABLE 7   PERCENTAGE OF RESPONDENTS
WHO RECOGNIZED SELECTED SCIENCE
REPRESENTATIVES

Charles Darwin	100
Al Gore	100
Arnold Schwarzenegger	100
Galileo Galilei	98
Stephen Jay Gould	33
Michael Behe	13
Joseph Nicolosi	2
Eugenie Scott	2
Dean Hamer	0
Lonnie Thompson	0

Gore, and Arnold Schwarzenegger, and only one did not recognize Galileo Galilei. But after those figures are named, recognition of prominent science representatives drops off sharply. Science representatives rarely emerged as prominent representatives in these debates. But as table 7 shows, those who showed up prominently in the four debates in this study were largely unrecognized. Most often recognized were dead scientists and live politicians who drew on scientific authority to make claims (primarily about climate change). Least often recognized were living scientists in various current debates.

To be clear, this lack of recognition was not due to special ignorance of mass media, or of science issues specifically, among respondents. Almost 70 percent of respondents had "studied scientific subjects" in some form, usually in high school or college. About one in four respondents (26 percent) claimed to read about, or watch media specifically related to, science issues (including science fiction). Most respondents followed the news in some form, whether through cable news shows, nightly television news, magazines, or Internet news sources. So respondents in this sample were not obviously less informed, educated, or interested than other U.S. citizens, either generally or specifically with regard to science issues. Certainly they had few problems recognizing many other prominent individual representatives (as reported in chapter 7).

Table 7 illuminates a key challenge to understanding how ordinary persons evaluate science in public life. Unlike religion representatives, prominent and distinctive science representatives are few in number. In what follows, I consider respondent evaluations of prominent science representatives where possible. But such data are not generally available, so many of the supporting data in this section rely on other kinds of evaluations from interviews. For example, respondents viewed and evaluated résumés with scientific indicators, and viewed and evaluated statements that science representatives made in public. These résumés and statements came from a range of representatives, not just the most prominent. Respondents also regularly suggested and discussed science representatives for their ideal committees for the various debates. Much of the evaluation of science in public life that I report below comes from what respondents would like to see from scientists in public life as described in their responses to the committee questions. In short, the evidence reflects the objective conditions of science representatives in public debate. There simply are not many opportunities to encounter or recognize representatives who are not already prominent for reasons disconnected from science.

By the same token, the recognition data in table 7 does not indicate why, for example, Lonnie Thompson went unrecognized, even though he may be a science representative as I have defined it and as journalists have presented him. In the case of the Religious Right, respondents could say how and why they know about Jerry Falwell, for example, or Pat Robertson, as by indicating that they read a book or saw an episode of *The 700 Club*. But asking a respondent, "Why don't you recognize Lonnie Thompson?" was neither productive nor helpful. After realizing that simply getting a series of "no" answers to the recognition question wasn't actually telling much about why, I started following up that question with a joke about how I would rename my project "No One Knows Lonnie Thompson."[1] This technique often generated further reflection from respondents about why they might not recognize someone in a particular debate. Elaine's response ultimately proved to be the key to unlocking the question of why no one knows Lonnie Thompson: "Then, he's probably like somebody who really knows what he's talking about (laughing). If I had to guess, since it's not a name that I recognize, it's probably somebody who like knows facts, and knows both sides of the issue, and has information to back up his statements, and isn't looking to get elected for something."

Elaine's musings about why no one knows Lonnie Thompson capture a neat distinction among science representatives between scientists in public life and participants in public debate. This distinction showed up across all aspects of evaluation from respondents. Most respondents held highly favorable views of science and its value to society. This favorable "default setting" extended partly to cover scientists. Throughout interviews, scientists appeared as respected and valued contributors, particularly on committees to discuss and decide policy issues.

But respondents consistently defined this role in specific, circum-scribed terms that precluded broader participation in public debate. Sci-entists were seen as an important source of expertise who could be informative in an advisory capacity on issues in which such expertise is seen as relevant. But scientists were not considered general experts whose usefulness increases through broader participation. Scientists were even considered interchangeable in the sense that any appropriate scientist could act in a specific advisory capacity. Yet respondents considered sci-entists as only one kind among many possible legitimate contributors. Finally, scientists were seen as potentially informative and useful science representatives because of what they are not: self-interested or, more broadly, political. Affiliation or other indications of economic or politi-cal interests were seen as corrupting and disqualifying in public life. In sum, the specific normative expectations of scientists in public life meant that participation in public debate beyond the presumed role constraints resulted in negative evaluation of such representatives.

No matter what the context of evaluation, respondents left no doubt that scientific expertise was important. For example, 85 percent of respondents suggested some variant of "scientist" as an important con-tributor for at least one committee. Vicki's thoughts on her stem cell research committee capture much of the reasoning that other respond-ents used to bring scientists into public debate:

> I would like some people doing stem cell research, scientist[s] or doctors doing stem cell research. I would like ethicists, very important to sort of be able to keep on track how far is too far against the gene or with the cloning types of things, but should there be a limit to some of what is possible? And I think so. There would be ethical questions [that] become very, very impor-tant and I guess I would make that a religious/ethicist . . . I guess besides the research part of—yep, let's say its two scientists, one of whom is also medi-cal, although they're probably both medical. It's always good to have healthy debate within the scientific community. And then I'd like to see somebody from the medical community who is actually involved in the practical, inter-acting with the Pete's patients and interacting with Alzheimer's patients—you know, that kind of physician. And I'd like to see an activist from within the Parkinson's or the Alzheimer's community, you know, a Michael J. Fox type, whether it's him, specifically or not; I don't know if he's the best candi-date, but someone who is struggling with one of these diseases and kind of can bring the perspective of why it would be valid to be able to pursue stem cell research and apply those things.

For Vicki, as for most other respondents, scientific contributions to public debate were important. Whenever respondents did not select some variant of "scientist," it was usually because they did not think of scientific expertise as relevant to the issue, not because they thought scientists have nothing to contribute. That scientists were considered key contributors is thus probably unsurprising in discussions of public debates defined in terms of religion-and-science involvement.

But Vicki's response also captured some key elements of other respondent answers. First, respondents tended to conceive of "scientist" as a role with interchangeable inhabitants rather than in terms of individual distinction or prominence. Only 33 percent of respondents ever suggested a specific scientist by name. Even when respondents thought that scientific advice was necessary for debate, they rarely named an individual scientist and simply described a category of participant (e.g., "biologist" or "scientist"). In these cases, any scientist (who met the basic criteria) would do. For example, Miley offered a typical response to the committee question for human origins debate: "Okay, well, I don't know specific people, but I don't know. I'm not even really sure. I'd probably try to have it as even as possible, maybe two religious people; I'm not exactly sure who. Two scientists, scientific people that have studied evolution and have all the evidence for it; then, maybe one kind of neutral—not so much neutral, but who could get facts from both."

Second, "scientist" did not mean "universally useful expert on all topics." While scientists are interchangeable to some extent, they were considered to be subject matter experts rather than sources of final authority. Vicki's answer quoted above may indicate "scientist," but she further specified a particular kind relevant to that debate because of expertise in stem cell research and medical intervention. Similarly, respondents did not just pick "scientist" for every debate. Miley's answer above indicates that her generic scientists must have studied evolution. Likewise, Crystal resembled Vicki in indicating that stem cell debate needs stem cell researchers and experts: "So, if embryonic little persons could talk, I would put one on the committee. I would put leading research scientists that can speak to all the different parameters that, you know, how do they treat stem cells and different things like that. I would put, probably put a leading theologian who could kind of talk to the ethical issues. I would put somebody on the medical side of things who deals with the diseases and things that are impacted by research."

Third, Vicki's response showed that scientists are an important source of expertise, but not the only source. For Vicki, scientists contributed one kind of practical expertise among many on the issue of stem cell research, with other contributors including ethicists, practitioners, and even patients or patient activists.[2] Crystal's statement above similarly indicated that many participants are legitimate contributors, not only scientists.

However, respondents consistently indicated that scientists are expert contributors among many others, not just the messengers for a particular viewpoint in a standardized debate. Discussions of committees, statements, and résumés often pivoted on distinctions between legitimate contributors of scientific perspectives and others, such as politicians, who might provide a similar non-expert perspective. For example, Sienna, in her selection of a committee on human origins, distinguished scientists as a category of expert on relevant subject matter, rather than on politics or religion: "Okay, I could probably do that. I would do like, you know, leading scientists, I guess, evolutionary scientists. Probably, you know, a couple religious people, one maybe. Jeez, I don't know. I don't know if I'd wanna put politicians in there or not. Probably not. Yeah, I don't know. I guess I'd just say a little—like people from both sides of the debate who are experts."

Likewise, given a statement from Al Gore that used scientific language to discuss global warming, Holly said that the statement obviously did not come from a scientist, because it is too "dumbed down": "Well, yeah, I agree with this statement. I, I think that there's a little bit of lacking of science. It's basically dumbed down, as well, about how global warming works. . . . I don't believe that this person represents a scientific community at all, because it's so dumbed down. But this person definitely has read what's out there."

Respondents rarely suggested scientists by name when discussing participation in public debate. Given the limitations of the data, it is impossible to say definitively whether respondents did not suggest scientists by name because they did not know of any scientists, or because they did not think that any given scientist mattered more than any other. What is clear is that ordinary persons thought that "scientists" were important for informing debate. Notably this was not because scientists are universally useful contributors. Rather, respondents saw scientific experts as constrained participants among a range of stakeholders.

At the same time, respondents carefully circumscribed the role of expert scientists, especially in debates that included non-experts who might also make claims based on scientific authority. Whether choosing representatives on a committee or evaluating résumés and statements, respondents defined the proper role of a scientist in part by defining inappropriate behavior and inappropriate representatives. Consistent with the expectation that scientists are virtuous inhabitants of a credible profession, respondents pointed out motivations that disqualify persons from public debate, such as self-interest or political gain. It is not enough simply to be an expert scientist. A science representative must also conform to expectations about why and how he or she is participating in public life.

On a few occasions, respondents expressed anti-intellectual sentiments that seemed simple condemnation of scientists. Meg, for example, evaluated an anonymized version of Richard Dawkins's résumé as that of an "intellectual who thinks he probably knows it all, and probably liked to have everybody else think he knows it all, too." This was obviously a personal judgment about "know-it-alls." But it was also an evaluation of probable motives for participating in public life. For Meg, this scientist appeared to be someone who would be participating for selfish reasons, namely, to effectively show off his knowledge rather than inform good debate.

Such negative evaluation of apparent or potential self-interest showed up consistently. Like Meg, many respondents remarked on possible indications that participants were in debate for their own purposes. For example, Pamela, for her ideal debate over stem cell research, "would like people who are able to digest and understand scientific evidence and studies, and the whole overall topic." Expertise is important. At the same time, Pamela "would eliminate anybody who has any chance to profit, or have personal gain as a result of whatever it is that the committee goes through, or decisions that they make, or laws they come up with, or whatever." While expertise is important, it does not supplant or override questionable motives for participation, particularly self-interest.

But though respondents consistently evaluated self-interest negatively as a motive for participation, their expectations about self-interest and other questionable motives clearly varied depending on the (potential) participant. For example, when I asked Don whether or not he recognized Arnold Schwarzenegger by name, Don indicated suspicion of Schwarzenegger's motives. Even so, Don did not evaluate him negatively:

> Don: I think he's an environmentalist and I think he's going to make money on it with his windmill farms.
>
> Q: Do you think that's why he's an environmentalist?
>
> Don: I don't know but whether it's just occurred to his convictions and he's willing to put his money where his mouth is.

Respondents expected politics in debates involving science. And where there is politics, there are politicians. Ordinary persons consistently discounted politicians as self-interested, instrumental, and inimical to good debate. But like Don (quoted above), respondents expected politicians to be this way. In fact, they were surprised when politicians were not entirely self-interested. Timothy called Gore "a crusader" who "represents the most concerned elements about the environment." Penny said that Schwarzenegger is "surprisingly pro-environment" given "how he got his start in politics." In these cases respondents already applied the electoral discount.

The more interesting point is that respondents often shaped their evaluations of science representatives differently based on whether they saw such representatives as scientists or as politicians. On the rare occasions when science representatives did show up in public debate, respondents sometimes evaluated them in terms that distinguished scientists from politicians, or negatively evaluated them as scientists who were inappropriately involved in politics. Respondents expected scientists not to be "political." Arienne, for example, distinguished between the résumé of a state official in charge of ecology, whom she called a "politician," and the résumé of an academic zoologist, who "is going to represent the nonpolitical agenda, or the people who want to save the earth." For Arienne, this distinction was a difference between legitimate and illegitimate contributors to public debate.

But having already applied the electoral discount, respondents generally did not make this distinction to pile further rebuke on politicians. Rather, respondents distinguished between science and politics in order to separate legitimate and illegitimate modes of participation for scientists in public life. For example, I showed Ken the statement "I just don't see how we can turn our backs on [stem cell research]. We have lost so much time already. I just really can't bear to lose any more." Ken immediately showed a negative reaction and identified the statement as coming from "a kind of scientist with a political agenda or just a politician, 'cause it's making a very emotional plea" that is not informative but rather "seems to be forcing other people to agree with them." For Ken this political mode was an illegitimate mode for a scientist. Any scientist who engaged in politics in this way must have a political agenda.

The distinction between legitimate and illegitimate modes of participation is important because, for respondents, politics corrupts science. In some cases this showed up as a personal corruption in which politics limits what a representative can and cannot say or do, even though such representatives might be substantively aligned with scientists on an issue such as climate change. For example, when I asked Arthur about Arnold Schwarzenegger, he remarked that Schwarzenegger is "a Republican, so he definitely, I think, is beholden to small government and corporate interests," but that "it is good that California has been taking the lead in some environmental policy like those extrastringent emission standards." For Arthur, Schwarzenegger's achievement of passing California emissions standards was an unusual exception to an otherwise predictable corruption of science for political gain.

In other cases respondents thought that politics corrupted science at the institutional level. Specifically, political involvement in the institutions of science made affiliation with those institutions suspect. Leo, for example, indicated that ordinarily he would think that an NSF-affiliated scientist would advocate positions based on scientific consensus. However, in looking at the employment history on one scientist's résumé, he said that "it might be kind of a toss-up on this one because I know that the Bush administration staffed the NSF with people who didn't believe in man-centered climate change or even that it was occurring." For Leo, political involvement in scientific institutions such as the NSF changed the calculus for evaluating a scientist's participation in such institutions. Similarly, Oscar indicated that scientists participate in stem cell debates for their own financial and political gain. When I pressed him on this, he replied that scientists might not be entirely after the money and that "maybe their driving force is true; they want to do the advancement of science and you know . . ." He quickly added, "But I think it's all driven by money. If they were doing it for free, I don't think they'd be so enthusiastic about it." For Oscar, even if scientists were not always personally motivated by political or financial gain to participate in public life, their institutional position made their science inseparable from those concerns.

For respondents in this study, politicians were not just subject to the electoral discount, though that was certainly a consistent finding. In addition, politics transformed science by corrupting its inhabitants and institutions, changing science from an independent source of knowledge to an instrument of power. Of course, respondents expected that politicians would use "science talk" just to get their way, whether or not they believed in the scientific claims themselves. For example, Laura described Bill Clinton as "gifted with rhetoric" and said that if "he were like Al Gore and he were speaking about the importance of stopping global warming," he could get everyone on his side, because "he could play up religious stuff in one venue, and play up scientific stuff in another venue." But the more important point is that, while politics may be a legitimate (if objectionable) mode of participation for politicians, it is an illegitimate mode of participation for scientists in public life.

Scientists were acceptable participants in public life as long as they were informative and largely interchangeable. Respondents tended not to suggest individuals, either because examples were not plentiful or prominent, or simply because it is not generally easy to remember names of representatives. So respondents described an interchangeable category of "scientist" or, more specifically, "biologist" or "stem cell researcher." "Interchangeable" here is not used in disregard of areas of expertise. A physicist was not a relevant expert for debate over stem cell research. Rather, scientists were interchangeable in the sense of "faceless." There was rarely a preference for a specific science representative. Rather, science representatives were, and should be, generic scientists who informed debate as one (or more) representatives in an array of relevant stakeholders. At the same time, they were seen as potentially informative and useful science representatives precisely because they were not self-interested or, more broadly, political. Indicators of such corrupting influences were consistently evaluated negatively by respondents.

EVALUATING PUBLIC SCIENCE AS DELIBERATION

Of course some scientists do appear in public life. Sometimes credibility narratives populate public debate with exemplars, and sometimes scientists break the rules. While science representatives rarely achieve prominence, they do occasionally show up, even if the overall impact is much less than that of the Religious Right either within or across issue debates. Likewise, while most respondents treated scientists as faceless when they suggested ideal participants in public debate, a small minority of respondents nevertheless suggested a specific science representative at some point.[3]

In all of these cases, however, respondents evaluated and suggested scientists based on deliberative norms. They reiterated their deliberative expectations by suggesting science representatives who not only were informed experts in a given field but also were open-minded participants who recognized the multisided nature of public debate and were willing to listen to a wide range of other participants. Ideal science representatives are deliberative. But actual participation by specific scientists in these debates was seen to be nondeliberative and therefore in conflict with the deliberative expectations that ordinary people hold. In deliberative terms, scientists who actually showed up in religion-and-science debates fell well short of expectations. Sometimes this was because they are obviously uncivil and aggressive. But a more subtle objection from respondents was that scientists in public life are innately more likely to be nondeliberative, as experts tend to use expertise to limit or end debate rather than inform a broad conversation.

Evaluating Individual Scientists

As respondents tended to suggest categories of ideal participants rather than names, it is not surprising that few scientists ever showed up as ideal participants in public debate by name. However, on those few occasions when respondents named individual scientists for a committee, they did so with reference to deliberative norms. Respondents recommended individual scientists who (they believed) take a deliberative and open-minded stance toward other debate participants and other sources of information. Likewise, respondents recommended excluding individual scientists who do not.

Individual scientists who did show up as positive suggestions were uniformly scientists who appeared deliberative. Damien, for example, said simply that he "feels comfortable" picking Michael Behe for a committee on human origins because Behe is a "sort of moderate who listens to both ends" and hadn't been "completely discounted [by] one end or the other end." Walter struggled a bit to name the "NIH director during the time of the human genome" who had "written books about things like intelligent design," but after I suggested "Francis Collins?" continued with "Yeah, yeah. Collins . . . somebody who was at least open to discussing both the scientific and religious aspects of this debate."[4] So individual scientists were not entirely absent from interviews, but those who showed up were ones who had demonstrated a willingness to be deliberative.

Even so, respondents indicated that such scientists were exceptional, either because they were willing to go against what might be scientific consensus, or because they were uniquely insightful examples of what scientists are. For example, Phoebe chose "the guy who invented the atom bomb, Oppenheimer," because "after the bomb was used and he realized what his science had done and the impact it had and would he have done it again and he's not sure he would have, and I think that kind of insight is what is needed." Similarly, Max, who earlier in the interview had remarked on the scope and openness of Michio Kaku's book *Parallel Worlds,* suggested Kaku on multiple committees because "he's phenomenal . . . the modern-day Carl Sagan" and "he would be able to help lead and say 'Hey, listen, we gotta think about this. We gotta think about that.'" For Phoebe and Max, these individual scientists would make good contributors because they were uniquely conscious of a wide range of concerns.

Not all individual scientist suggestions were positive. When I asked Kyle to suggest an ideal committee on human origins, he expressed a preference for deliberative participants, then ran into problems when trying to suggest an individual scientist capable of such deliberation. He started to name specific examples but stopped and said, "I don't know if I'd want the more outspoken evolution[-supporting] critics. I mean, I'm sure that Richard Dawkins is a good scientist, but I don't know if I'd want him involved in that debate." When I pressed Kyle to say why not, he replied, "Just from what I've read of him, his treatment of religion and religions, and just his spirit I think is a bit unfair, even though he might be an excellent scientist."

Kyle's suggestion to exclude Dawkins was a specific instance of a more general disapproval among respondents of anyone appearing to leverage their scientific authority to attack other participants. Perhaps no single representative exemplified this problem better than Richard Dawkins. While respondents varied in their assessment of his (anonymized) résumé, many evaluated it positively. Connie, for example, noted that the résumé indicated "atheist" as religious affiliation, and says that in debates over human origins a person with that résumé would "be kind of neutral" and "gray in his thinking" in a positive way. Connie didn't "think he would come out and specifically sit back and say I'm, I'm for it because of my religious affiliation." Instead, Connie indicated that he is informed and educated enough to "give a very good argument on both sides." In terms of his résumé, Dawkins seemed an ideal expert for informing public debate.

Yet when faced with what Dawkins actually said, respondents consistently identified Dawkins as "harsh," "arrogant," "overstated," "strident," "acerbic," "rude," and "angry." Like many other respondents, Connie strongly and negatively evaluated what he said about people who do not believe in evolution: "I totally disagree with this statement. This is definitely the kind of statement you would see someone who is a nonbeliever and who thinks he's right." This negative evaluation of Dawkins's statements occurred even when respondents otherwise agreed with the substance or truth claims in those statements. For example, I showed Charles the same statement that Connie read (in a separate interview). Charles immediately responded, "I agree with it . . . evolution does make a lot of sense." But he nevertheless denounced the statement as "a little harsh, a little judgmental" and "a really far leaning extreme point of view" that "doesn't really allow for different points of view." By being aggressive in public life—in this case calling people who do not believe in evolution "ignorant, stupid, or insane"—Dawkins moved from the legitimate role of an informed participant in public life to the illegitimate role of a scientist who uses his scientific credibility in nondeliberative ways, whether to attack others or to end debate.[5]

In contrast to Dawkins's attacking statement, nonattacking statements by scientists were evaluated positively. A statement from Dean Hamer, one of the few prominent science representatives in the study, suggests that sexuality is not simply genetic and that "clearly there is a lot more than just genes going on," which is "the same for every human behavior." Respondents consistently evaluated this statement positively. Samuel, for example, described the person who made the statement as "someone that's sort of in the middle, isn't picking sides, wants to understand more and just try to provide other options to come up with a conclusion versus being on one side or the other"; in other words, a representative who can be deliberative.

However, it is Dawkins's language, rather than Hamer's language, that was seen to exemplify the participation of actual scientists in public life. Even respondents who were themselves scientists made this claim. Daniela, a biotech researcher, discussed her frustrations with Dawkins and other scientists as she thought out loud about what she might do to change debate:

> Yeah, I think, again, trying to educate my fellow scientists into not galvanizing this debate too much, and not demonizing. I think that the scientific community, we have shot ourselves in the foot in the way that we have framed this debate, and the way that we have made these people out to be ignorant and to be stupid. And what winds up happening is a lot of general Americans get clumped into that, where they really don't belong, right? Just because it becomes—and this is a problem with all of America today right now. It's us versus them. And we need to stop doing that. And if you're not one of us, you're one of them. If you're not so sure we should be cloning humans, then you're some crazy religious zealot.

Though less often encountered in these interviews, individual scientists did show up. When scientists were suggested for committees or evaluated positively, it was usually because they were seen as deliberative, even if such deliberative tendencies were considered unusual or exceptional. But individual scientists seen as leveraging scientific credibility to attack other representatives were consistently evaluated in strongly negative terms. Such behavior violated normative expectations, not only of representatives in general but specifically of scientists in public life. This conflict creates a particular kind of bind for scientists in public life who attempt to defend science or engage in various forms of public boundary work. When representatives draw on scientific credibility to attack other people in public life, they violate deliberative norms. In this sense, public boundary work is highly risky. While it may have some benefits for the credibility of science as an institution, any particular scientist engaging in such activities runs afoul of normative expectations.

Expertise as Limitation

These findings indicate that there is a highly constrained role for scientists in public life that must simultaneously be informative and deliberative. In theory, respondents are not opposed to scientists in public life altogether. Of course, sometimes scientists violated normative expectations by attacking other representatives in public life, as described above. But a larger problem is that, for many respondents, there was something about science as a site of knowledge production that made it especially difficult for its inhabitants to meet respondents' normative expectations. Although respondents showed a strong preference for science to inform debate in various ways, in practice they often saw science as a conversation stopper that violated deliberative expectations when brought into public life by scientists.

Across interviews, respondents expressed deep concern about commitment to prior positions for those entering public life. They saw scientists as entering public debate with preconceived positions and commitments that limit the scope of debate. Such commitment is characteristic of scientists; it is not characteristic of deliberative representatives. While Bernard, for example, was not one of the more loquacious respondents in this study, he nevertheless provided an important insight on this point. In selecting a committee on environmental policy, Bernard wanted to "make sure the scientific community was represented." But he clarified that the representative should be "an open-minded communicative scientist" and not "one with positions." Bernard's response neatly illustrated both the narrow range of acceptable participation by scientists in public life and the concerns that ordinary persons have. For Bernard, "a scientist is all right" as long as that scientist does not have "positions."

Perhaps unsurprisingly, given the substantive topics under discussion in interviews, one of the most common "positions" that generated concern from respondents was a committed opposition to religion. This might at first seem to belie the findings in the previous chapter about religious support for science. Note, however, that the distinction I am describing is not about science, but about opposition to religion. Even though religious and nonreligious persons alike supported science, they saw any explicit opposition to religion as undesirable, not because it was scientific, but because it violated deliberative norms.

Respondents consistently expressed concern that scientists, especially from an academic setting, might participate in debate in nondeliberative ways precisely because religion was somehow involved. Summer, for example, in discussing who might be included or excluded from a committee on human origins, described herself as "not somebody to be out in front and confrontation" but thought it important to "remind people that it's possible to be faithful and scientific," because "there's a pretty significant arrogance out there with even people in academia often towards anything that smacks of religion." And Chantal, while saying that debate over human origins was "not, like, the biggest thing in the world," nonetheless thought that "it's important that there is at least a debate going on, and that the academic world doesn't just shut out different ideas."

For Bonnie, like many other respondents, the ability to listen was an important requirement for deliberative participation. Although she wanted "people with a strong scientific background," she required that they "have shown a pattern of being able to listen respectfully without necessarily being swayed unreasonably." And like many others, Bonnie pinpointed hostility to religion as a possible source of contention. "At least one or two" of her scientist participants "should probably have some kind of religious background, because it helps with listening respectfully to people who also have a religious background." However, her overriding concern was about deliberation rather than just hostility to religion. A religious background was not "an absolute requirement if they've clearly demonstrated an ability to listen and understand what's important to the people they are listening to." What was bothersome to respondents about the prior commitment was that it would interfere with deliberation, not specifically that the commitment went against religious beliefs or positions.

Nonreligious respondents also raised the potential issue of scientific anti-religion commitments. Jennifer added theologians and her own mother to one committee in order to provide examples of "some of the openness to the background of people who do have religious beliefs" for "professors and teachers that would be normally teaching from a really structured 'if you don't believe evolution, you're stupid' kind of standpoint." As a strong supporter of science, Jennifer thought that such openness was necessary so that scientists "can present scientific ideas in a way that does not belittle people who do hold religious beliefs" and, beyond public debate, "so they can have students in their classroom who are not feeling threatened by their exposure to scientific ideas." Again, while Jennifer expressed a qualm in terms of religion, the motivating concern focused on the ability to deliberate effectively and thereby contribute usefully to public debate without alienating other participants.

A few respondents indicated that scientific expertise entails holding positions that make good debate impossible. Larry, for example, had just finished telling me about a book he had read recently by Karl Giberson titled *Saving Darwin: How to Be a Christian and Believe in Evolution*. When he described his understanding of the debate, he expressed concern about anyone, especially scientists, entering debate with too much commitment to one particular position. While he acknowledged that "people in all forms of religion" might also present a problem, he emphasized that "there's just a lot of people in the scientific community [who] are convinced of their convictions and beliefs." Larry also pointed out that "there's a lot of people," scientific or not, "on both sides that are more vocal and wanting to influence and change people on the other side."

Similarly, Teresa expressed concern about nondeliberative tactics that inevitably result when prior commitments encounter an otherwise deliberative space. Teresa thought that "the whole global warming thing is really overblown," because "as a scientist" she doesn't "see that it's supported by scientific evidence." Her concern was not only that (other) scientists were somehow wrong, but also that the prior commitment might preclude useful approaches to solutions that everyone would support. As she put it, "Whether there's global warming or not, being more careful with our resources and having less pollution and all of us doing our part in that is certainly a good thing to do." Pushing people to make changes through what she called "scare tactics," then, reflects a prior commitment that not only subverts good debate but might actually be counterproductive in achieving useful solutions.[6]

Perhaps the strongest reactions came in response to my request to evaluate a statement by Arnold Schwarzenegger that "the debate is over" and that since the science is settled, we should proceed to mitigate climate change. Like many other respondents, Teresa "pretty much disagree[d] with the whole thing" and said that, based on a "lot of reading" that she had done, "a large body of scientists" think that climate change is "a normal shift" that is not caused by human activity. Note, however, that Teresa was consistent in her approach. The Schwarzenegger statement effectively validated her concerns about closing debate by claiming scientific authority. In this Teresa was hardly alone. Josefina, for example, also had a strong reaction to the Schwarzenegger statement because "they start out saying, I say the debate is over, [but] I don't think the debate should be over." Like Teresa, Josefina was not "one hundred percent absolutely convinced that we're destroying the earth and that global warming isn't part of a natural cycle." But also like Teresa, Josefina objected more to the closing of debate than to the specific truth claim. She continued by saying "there are things we can change, but whether it will change global warming or not, it's still good for the environment; it still should be looked at."

Whether considered as individuals or as faceless inhabitants of a scientific occupation, science representatives were often evaluated negatively. In some cases, such as that of Richard Dawkins, this was simply because the representatives who showed up and talked in public were saying things that are unkind or uncivil. Such attacks are obviously not deliberative. But respondents also indicated a deeper concern that scientists, as experts, are especially susceptible to nondeliberative activity. Respondents valued expert information in debates, but they worried that too much commitment to prior positions subverts more than it benefits good debate. While this concern showed up often as a specific concern about anti-religion commitments, different kinds of evaluation nonetheless reinforced the finding that the underlying concern was actually about any kind of prior commitment. For respondents in this study, any attempt to use expertise to close or limit debate, even if it came from an expert source, violated normative expectations about deliberative participation in good debate.

PUBLIC SCIENCE AND GOOD DEBATE

In general, respondents evaluated science representatives in public life in a manner entirely consistent with the model of scientific credibility that links the credibility of science as an institution to the avoidance of public sphere prominence by individual scientists. First, respondents expressed widespread and persistent support for science as an institution, even when it might otherwise violate their substantive religious or moral preferences. While they may have disapproved of scientists in the public sphere, they saw science generally as credible. In expressing this approval, they reached for the very reasons and stories (e.g., national progress) that are part and parcel of the public narrative of scientific credibility perpetuated in mass media.

Second, ordinary persons imagined scientists in public life to be largely anonymous rather than individually distinctive. Anonymity in this case did not indicate a lack of importance. Ordinary persons recognized that scientists, as subject matter experts, have much to contribute to public debate. But there was a clear and consistent conception of "scientist" as a role with interchangeable inhabitants. Respondents described their ideal participants in anonymous terms. More important, they distinguished between science and politics. On one side of this distinction, science is anonymous and informative. On the other side, politics is what happens when individuals try to get their way in public however possible (e.g., through an emotional appeal or selective use of science talk). Respondents expressed concern that politics, as an individual activity designed to seek public attention for one's own purposes, corrupts science. The result is that one side of the distinction contains many possible science representatives (more broadly defined) who are actually considered "politicians." On the other side are the only proper science representatives, the "faceless" inhabitants of science as an institution, who are so virtuously anonymous that they cannot be charged with self-interest or with seeking political gain.

Third, ordinary persons expressed dissatisfaction with actual scientists participating in actual debate, as they were seen to subvert good debate. Respondents preferred the anonymous informing expert over the actual individual scientists whom they encountered. Part of this dissatisfaction resided in the obvious violation of deliberative expectations by representatives who attacked other representatives or otherwise behaved in ways inconsistent with good deliberative debate. In these cases ordinary persons would rather have someone else speaking for science in public life. But part of this dissatisfaction also resided in the concern that scientists might be inherently incapable of participating in public life without subverting good debate. The ideal of a deliberative scientist might be unachievable precisely because scientists, as experts, import strong commitments that override any commitment to good debate. Such prior commitments (e.g., anti-religious sentiments) were seen as limiting the possibility for good debate and negating any potential benefit of having expert informants. Respondents preferred no involvement by scientists to bad involvement that subverted good debate.

The evidence from respondent interviews suggests that the pursuit of scientific credibility is fully entangled with the deliberative norms of the public sphere. Certainly scientists generally do not seek prominence in public life, as they see such activities as inconsistent with the credibility of science as an institution. What the interview data show is that ordinary persons see things the same way. However, as with the case of the Religious Left, this understanding of scientific credibility is expressed in terms of good debate and deliberative expectations. Also as with the Religious Left, it seems that the possibilities for science to participate in the public sphere in the future depend not only on the flexibility of institutional conventions or practices, but also ultimately on a fundamental reorientation toward what ordinary persons want to see in public debate.

CHAPTER 10

The Future of Religion and Science in American Public Life

The pivotal finding of this book is that it is not conflict between religion and science that limits possibilities for good debate in the public sphere, but conflict over good debate that limits the possibilities for religion and science to be involved in the public sphere. The most consistent finding across all interviews, debates, and dimensions of evaluation is that ordinary persons want deliberative debate. Scholars also agree that deliberative debate is an important requirement for a vibrant, peaceful, and just democratic society. But representatives, those elite persons who are supposed to be deliberating, often participate in debate for reasons that have little to do with deliberation.

Deliberative debate seems desirable both theoretically and democratically. But achieving it involves aligning very different versions of good debate in public life. So, what is to be done? For religion and science representatives, is it possible to align the pursuit of credibility and the desire for deliberative debate? And how might the rest of us, whether scholars, ordinary Americans, or both, move forward knowing what we know now?

RELIGIOUS CREDIBILITY AND GOOD DEBATE

Millions of Americans draw on religion as a source of strength, guidance, and moral direction. Religion should, in theory, be a rich and diverse resource in a deliberative public sphere. But this is simply not what happens. For largely contingent historical reasons, the Religious Right succeeded in gaining religious credibility in the public sphere. But the manner in which it has pursued such credibility also virtually guarantees that no credible religious alternative can emerge. Historically the Religious Left has not sought religious credibility in the public sphere. Now, it is possible that its members no longer have the option. In the current American context, religion as a category of public life is fully marked as contrary to good debate.

How might things be otherwise? Is it possible to restore religion as a useful resource in public life? Can religion be part of good debate in the future? As it stands, normative conflict provides an additional barrier to future good debate involving religion. But there are at least two possible responses suggested by scholarly literature and by ordinary persons who want debate to be different. One possible response is to exchange bad representatives for good representatives. The other is to abandon public life altogether and instead cultivate deliberative talk over important issues in private life and in local contexts rather than through public debate.

Different Representatives

First and most obviously, one way to restore religion in public life would be to exchange representatives who work against deliberative debate with representatives committed to public deliberation. Certainly there is an opportunity for a changing of the guard, as indicated by the death of Jerry Falwell and the retirement of James Dobson from Focus on the Family's leadership. The possibility exists for different representatives to step up.

But this is unlikely to occur. Liberals and moderates pursue religious credibility outside the public sphere. They do not have sufficient resources to promote individual representatives in public life in addition to their other efforts. It is simply too difficult for such organizations to change, particularly as the denominational structures of liberal and moderate religions resist major reconfiguration. By contrast, the Religious Right's loose affiliation of decentralized organizations more easily reconfigures to adapt to changing circumstances. But even if liberal or moderate religious groups could reconfigure, they would be at a disadvantage, as they would have to overcome the incumbent advantage of the Religious Right. Where the Religious Right needs only to plug in another conservative representative, liberal and moderate religious groups would have to start from scratch in promoting individual representatives.

A more subtle problem indicated in interview responses is that even if a different representative showed up in public life fully intending to deliberate, any use of religion talk in public would be evaluated either as not distinctively religious or as conservative. Even in the few examples offered in this study, liberal and moderate religious figures who used religion talk were not understood to be different from, on one hand, secular figures or, on the other hand, Religious Right figures. So, in the unlikely event that liberal and moderate religious groups could successfully establish individual representatives, they would still have to overcome the challenge of being seen as conservative or as not distinctively religious by ordinary persons whose understanding of "religion" in the public sphere has been shaped by the Religious Right. Successful liberal or moderate representation depends on completely redefining religious credibility in the public sphere and establishing new connections to liberal and moderate versions of "religion," not just providing an alternative representative in public life.

The most likely possibility for exchanging representatives is to switch out existing representatives for new Religious Right representatives who are less obviously opposed to deliberative debate. A newer generation of conservative religious representatives, such as Rick Warren and Joel Hunter, certainly appear to be kinder and gentler than their predecessors. But it is not at all clear that these new-generation representatives are actually committed to public deliberation. As political scientist Jon Shields reports, while many of these younger conservative representatives seem less threatening to deliberative debate, they are no less committed to advocating an agenda than their predecessors.[1] They engage in dialogue and sometimes use nonreligious language, but they do so to assist in a public crusade rather than to productively engage possible alternatives.

Yet the success of the Religious Right in establishing itself as opposed to deliberative debate may also have poisoned the well for more deliberative Religious Right alternatives. Ordinary persons accustomed to public religion talk as a signal of bad debate are less susceptible to distraction from cosmetic changes in religion representatives. Religious scholars sympathetic to the Religious Right might argue that increasing participation in public life is an important improvement over nonparticipation, but ordinary persons retain the commitment to deliberation that these new Religious Right representatives lack. It is unlikely that ordinary persons will see new Religious Right representatives as committed to good deliberative debate, even if they seem to be kinder and gentler in public life.

Promote Personal Engagement

One cause for hope is that ordinary persons currently have rich, diverse, and considerate attitudes toward other ordinary persons, even if they do not have these attitudes toward public religion representatives. Respondents often talked about discussing issues with friends who had substantively different opinions on issues. Such talk draws on personal connections and mutual respect that stabilize debate and allow conflicting ideas to engage productively. In this context, religion talk is a vital part of expressing personal experience and can be usefully deployed without a commitment to conversion or advancing a moral agenda.

So, given that the wide range of personal religious experience is effectively reduced in public life to one narrow element of conservative religion, another answer to restoring good debate might simply be to abandon public life. Liberal and moderate religious groups already do this. The "quiet hand of God" approach is arguably a way to pursue religious credibility in arenas of credibility outside the mass media public sphere.[2] For example, mainline Protestants and many Roman Catholics work through institutions whose purpose is to improve local communities and the welfare of individual persons rather than trying to "own the space" of public religion. So, instead of going on *The 700 Club* and railing against stem cell research as a new kind of abortion, mainline Protestants might, for example, host a moderated community discussion on stem cell research at a local church. Such an approach is less glamorous and often less politically effective than owning the space of public religion, but it is geared toward different ends, ones more compatible with deliberative debate.

But abandoning public life for more private or personal engagement may run afoul of two separate but equally challenging problems. The first is that sometimes public life is the only place where intervention is possible. Rapid technological changes, shifts in the balance of political power, or significant current events (for example, the 9/11 attacks) might generate public debate that would benefit from religious contribution. Without a presence in public life, liberal and moderate religious groups would be disadvantaged, both temporally and logistically, in contributing to these debates. Of course, such contribution might be marginalized or read as conservative in any event, but abandoning public life means abandoning even the possibility of intervening at the level of broad public debate. This could pose a serious problem, particularly if the public debate concerns policy that would directly affect liberal or moderate religion. For example, curriculum changes that emphasize America's conservative religious heritage might be difficult to oppose, even though they immediately threaten the religious credibility of liberal or moderate American religion.

The second problem is that there is very little barrier to entry for religious conservatives to take the same tack as their liberal and moderate counterparts have. In addition to its extensive national presence through overarching umbrella organizations like the NAE, the Religious Right involves several conservative religious denominations that have local congregations, access to local communities, and church facilities. Very little prevents the Religious Right from simply adding the "quiet hand of God" to its arsenal. In fact, as Jon Shields favorably notes in *The Democratic Virtues of the Christian Right,* the Religious Right is doing this right now by training activists to engage in both structured and informal conversations with, for example, college students on the issue of abortion. For Shields, this additional engagement cultivates "democratic virtues" by getting people participating in talk about important issues rather than developing apathy toward them.[3] Yet Shields also recognizes that such efforts are not fully deliberative, as they do not include a commitment to openness to other perspectives. What Shields describes is a strategy for the Religious Right to "own the space" of private talk, not just public talk. So there are no guarantees that abandoning public life will yield any particular advantage in private life when it comes to religion talk.

Prospects for Religion

The basic problem for public debate involving religion is that there is an asymmetrical burden on those opposed to deliberative debate and those who seek to promote it. It is theoretically possible for some person or organization to mobilize sufficient resources and promote their own competing religion representatives in public life. While this is unlikely given the Religious Right's resource base, it is at least a faint possibility to replace "public crusaders" with religion representatives who want good debate. However, even if this unlikely replacement should occur, the second point of conflict would remain a problem. If all religion talk is associated with public crusade, even if it comes from moderate or liberal religious representatives, then replacing representatives will not necessarily change how ordinary persons evaluate religion talk.[4]

Future good debate does not (only) depend on different representatives or on refocusing efforts at a more effective level of intervention. It depends on redefining the connection between "religion" in public life and ordinary persons in terms of shared preferences for good, deliberative debate. The Religious Right does not have this burden. It is easier to maintain the status quo than to completely overhaul how people think about religion in the public sphere. So, rather than trying to "own the space" of public life, perhaps the most promising strategy for liberal and moderate religion is to develop ways to express distinctively religious positions without using the kind of distinctively religious language that marks bad debate.[5]

SCIENTIFIC CREDIBILITY AND GOOD DEBATE

Millions of Americans look to science for progress, whether economic or national or, even more broadly, as a fundamental basis for human flourishing. Science should, in theory, be a key informative resource in a deliberative public sphere. But building credibility for science as an institution has made the public sphere nearly untenable for individual science representatives. In the current American context, the actual representation of science by science representatives usually indicates bad debate.

How might things be otherwise? Is it possible for science representatives to participate as resources in public life? Can science be part of good debate in the future? I can envision three possible scenarios for the future. First, science can basically continue its pursuit of a conservative strategy in which concerns about good debate continue to be disregarded in favor of maintaining the credibility of science by maintaining its institutional boundaries in their current form. Second, scientists can exactly meet the normative expectations of ordinary people by participating in public life as expert informants who engage in productive discussion and debate. Third, scientists can withdraw from public life altogether and focus instead on research and dissemination of findings either through scientific publication or through government or corporate applications of scientific research.

A Conservative Approach

I describe the first scenario as conservative because it involves a total commitment to preserve science by destroying all possible competition or direct challenges. Again, since science has no armies, by "destroying"

I mean "removing from any possibility of claiming scientific legitimacy." This scenario is basically what is happening now in American public life. For example, when various forms of creationism or Intelligent Design attempt to claim scientific credibility or otherwise challenge science in public life, a variety of actors attack pretenders as "pseudoscience" in a range of public and institutional settings by, for example, testifying before school boards, publishing opinion pieces in print and electronic fora, and participating as expert witnesses in courtrooms.[6]

There are two strong reasons to continue this strategy. The first is that conservative impulses are easy to defend, as many people have interests in preserving science in its current institutional incarnation. Scientists want to be employed and have grants to support their work. Science educators want to have a standard reference version of science that can be taught repeatedly and consistently. Corporations want access to technology transfer arrangements. Governments want to be seen as more scientific, and therefore more advanced, than other governments. Even activists and reformers have an interest in the institutional structure of science remaining largely consistent, as reform or activism efforts can be concentrated without having to deal with unpredictable responses. In short, many actors are motivated to keep things more or less the way they are now.

The second reason to continue is that the strategy is working, and has been working for decades in the U.S. context. Whether as a core participant in the design of public school curricula or as a core contributor to American military supremacy, science is so tightly woven into the fabric of American institutions that to challenge science's institutional legitimacy is an almost unthinkable proposition.[7] Creationists, for example, have made no inroads whatsoever in the legal arena since the 1950s and, in fact, have consistently been forced to retool for new institutional environments in which their potential share of scientific credibility decreases substantially with every encounter.[8] What is striking is that even though these legal challenges are technically about religion in public life, in almost every instance most of the legal arguments distinguish particularly between science and nonscience. Short of promulgating a "right to science" in the U.S. Constitution, it is difficult to see how much stronger an institutional position science could have. From such a position, and with a history of success (at least since World War II), continuing the conservative strategy makes sense.

But there are also serious risks to this strategy that are obscured by science's current institutional configuration. One risk is that conceding authority in public life actually reduces the ability of key scientific actors to control their own destiny.[9] Allowing the courts to define "science" in Intelligent Design cases works because the court's definition of science aligns with the definition that favors academic scientists. But allowing other actors and institutions to defend science means that if any significant institutional reconfiguration occurs, science might well be dispossessed. That an institutional reconfiguration could be fatal to science in its current form is the concern that drives claims about, for example, "the Republican war on science."[10] It is not that science is in direct danger, but that its legitimacy depends almost entirely on a superior institutional position that is not guaranteed for the future.

Another risk, one uniquely identified in this study, is that the conservative approach defeats challengers only at the cost of some public credibility. Ordinary persons who otherwise support science see such activity as entirely contrary to the good debate that they expect from representatives in public life. But a conservative approach by definition emphasizes preservation and must proceed with such preservation even if there are other undesirable effects. Without a more subtle approach to challengers, science in public life continually runs the risk of overstepping its limits and prompting ordinary persons to produce the institutional change that offers the greatest threat to science in its current form. So while this approach works currently, if it fails, it will fail spectacularly.

Advisory Role

A second possible scenario involves reconfiguring science in public life to meet the expectations of ordinary persons for good debate. At minimum, this would mean engaging in discussion and debate without attacking fellow scientists or other participants. While it might be as simple as persuading current participants to change their ways, a more likely approach is to exchange current representatives for different representatives who meet expectations. Such a scenario is largely consistent with several similar suggestions (though of smaller scope) throughout recent literature in the public understanding of science and science communication.[11]

There are three potential problems with this approach. The first is practical. Scientists who can do this successfully simply may not be available.[12] Ordinary persons may be correct that scientists are more accustomed to defending prior commitments than engaging in deliberative debate. But if such participants are not currently available, future participants could be trained to participate in deliberative debate as a key part of scientific education. The ideal result would be that a fully educated and trained scientist would also be fully prepared to participate as an expert informant among a range of informants without attempting to impose closure on debate or otherwise subverting debate.

The second problem is a challenge for scientists and other actors who benefit from the current institutional configuration of science in American society. Deliberative participation would require conceding that good policy results from the whole polity, not from scientists (or their deputies) telling everyone the scientific way to do things. For those who see public debate as an opportunity to advance their agenda and get their way, participation in deliberative debate might be viewed as a loss of scientific credibility, since not getting their way would likely be construed as losing authority. Such actors might also be concerned that science would be seen as less valuable if it were distributed as part of an array of authorities rather than unified as a dispositive authority in its own right. But whatever the specific concern, there are obviously few motivations for scientists and related actors to concede their current authority, no matter how good the reasons.

A final problem is that it might be good to be informative and advisory, but that leaves open a question about the distribution of such information and advice. To whom might advice be given? The problem here is that two ideal requirements of scientists in public life actually conflict in practice. While respondents consistently indicated that they did not want science in public life to be political, the unpalatable truth is that giving advice in the American context is an inherently political activity. Science already risks accusations of corruption by politics because of its close ties with the apparatus of state power, most notably the military. Even if scientists are prepared to be deliberative, and even if they are willing to be deliberative at the cost of their superior institutional position, they likely would still run afoul of the discount applied to representatives who are, in various ways, political actors.[13]

Promote Personal Engagement

A third scenario involves abandoning public life altogether. While this would not achieve the ultimate goal of scientists productively participating as informed experts in deliberative debate, it would not violate normative expectations, either. Such an approach would probably reinforce the already entrenched notion that scientists are virtuous, in part because they are too busy doing science to participate in public life.

Such a withdrawal sounds extreme. But there are two reasonable ways it might occur. First, instead of attempting to intervene in public debates more broadly, scientists could cultivate deliberative talk over important issues in private life and in local contexts (e.g., educational settings) rather than in public debate. In effect, scientists could take ownership of credibility narratives by telling and discussing scientific stories in these contexts. This would be a useful contribution without incurring the various penalties associated with being (apparently) non-deliberative scientists in public life. Such a strategy might even build credibility for science in a more useful and sustainable way not linked to current institutional configurations.

The problem with this particular way of withdrawing from public life is that it also abandons defense mechanisms. Since no central authority manages science in public life, there is nothing to stop any particular representative from gaining an advantage in public life by claiming scientific authority. While any representative who did this might be discounted or disregarded for any number of reasons, such a move is not easily countered at any level of engagement that does not directly confront the (potential) challenger.

A second reasonable way the withdrawal might occur is to stop using narrative to say that science is credible and instead focus on evidence of success or failure. For example, instead of teaching about significant scientific heroes and discoveries, science educators might highlight the substantive contributions of science and its success or failure in achieving what scientists have claimed it will achieve. In many respects this is already a requirement of science in its relationships to other institutions. The military requires that its bombs actually work, for example, and projects that fail enough times (e.g., particle beam weapon research) are discontinued. This would simply be a continuation of the accountability approach to science more broadly.

But the major risk is that once science leaves public life, no one will miss it. To the extent that the centrality of science to social progress depends on narrative rather than objective circumstances, abandoning narrative in favor of results means a decline in institutional authority. There have already been instances of scientists questioning whether the narrative account of science should really be driving educational policy.[14] Abandoning narrative would mean recalibrating the institutional authority of science to match its practical contributions. Such recalibration is not guaranteed to benefit science or its practitioners.

Prospects for Science

The basic problem for public debate involving science is that scientific credibility currently depends on strategies that make personal intervention in public life by scientists or other science representatives untenable. The basic problem for science is that meeting the deliberative expectations of ordinary Americans would likely produce a decline in scientific credibility. The result is that the conservative approach is likely to continue, as is the assessment of scientists in public life as subverting good debate.

The possibilities for deliberative debate depend on science in public life building its credibility through other means, such as delivering consistently clear and beneficial results and communicating those benefits effectively, or telling its own stories in less public settings. But even if one of the friendlier scenarios above is seen as desirable, the problem remains that science is a distributed institution with few clear leaders and no obvious center of power. The more difficult question may not be what science can do, but who can do it?

MOVING FORWARD

Representatives clearly have some challenges ahead. But what about the rest of us? Whether we are scholars, ordinary people, or both at the same time, we seem to want the same thing. All of us are seeking good debate. So, moving forward, what might we do differently? How can things be otherwise? To conclude the book, I consider three specific versions of these questions. First, if the way we currently study religion and science is inadequate, how might we do better? Second, if the way we currently study American public life is inadequate, how might we do better? Third and finally, if American public debate is currently bad, how can it be made good?

Studying Religion and Science

Religion and science are not inevitably in conflict, as scholarly and popular literature sometimes suggests. But even the more nuanced versions of science-and-religion scholarship rely on assumptions about the causal powers of religion and science, either as essential modes of thinking or as influential institutions, that find support only when other kinds of thinking or other influential institutions are sidelined in analysis. Yet, as this book has shown, the importance of religion and science is highly variable within broader social processes. Religion and science do not always actually matter, even if they are present. Sometimes debates are seen as between religion and science (or religion versus science), but sometimes they are not. To the extent that most current scholarship assumes that religion and science will always matter, most current scholarship on "science and religion" is wrong.

Studying religion and science as institutional participants in larger social processes reopens productive paths of inquiry that the essentialist causal approach forecloses. Religion and science no doubt display distinct institutional features in American public life. But many of these features are actually a product of specific contingent patterns of participation in public life rather than essential features inevitably imported into public debate. What most scholars cite as cases of religion-and-science conflicts are actually tiny subsets of a much broader conflict over norms of public debate, in which religion and science are players but not always even the stars of the show. Indeed, depending on how normative conflict unfolds, so-called religion-and-science debates might actually be *about* something else entirely.

So one way that we might do better is to discard the assumption that extremely rare encounters between religion and science representatives are a good model for understanding all of the other kinds of public debates involving religion and science. Instead, we can study religion and science as two among many participants in the social process of working out issues through public talk. Instead of studying only science and religion as important participants, we can consider whether or not, and how, religion or science become seen as important within public debate. Likewise, instead of asking questions about whether religion or science failed or succeeded in public life (e.g., whether enough people believe in evolution), we might ask how debate produced a particular version of religion or science that gained traction in public life.

I recognize that the current academic organization of subfields in some ways precludes this approach. Sociologists of religion are called sociologists of religion because they start by looking for religion and moving outward from that point, for example. But what I suggest is a shift away from assuming that religion (or science) will inevitably matter, even if there is a history of scholarship that suggests that it will. Instead, scholars should select a variety of cases in which religion and science should matter, or might matter, then focus first on whether or not they do. This would mean, for example, shifting from thinking about religiosity as a gradient of influence on scientific support (as in many survey-based studies of religion and science) to thinking about religiosity as something that might or might not matter when people consider science.

If there is only one principle to carry forward into future scholarship on religion and science, it is that nothing about religion and science is automatic. Distinct institutional features are the product of social processes. Sometimes these features are hard-won. Other times they are imposed. Still other times they are accidental. But no matter what our future methodological or substantive approaches to studying religion and science, we must acknowledge that public life produces religion and science as categories that ordinary persons use to organize their conceptual and social worlds. They can be produced differently.

Studying Public Talk

For scholars of public life, this book makes future research more complicated. Public debate is multidimensional and cannot simply be reduced to the substantive dimension of a given issue. This means that current approaches focusing on epistemological differences in substantive positions ("polarization"), the truth or falsity of a given position ("misinformation"), or the delivery of information ("messaging" or "framing") are probably inadequate. While such studies may usefully predict how public opinion surveys will turn out, or even how elites will act within specific institutional settings (e.g., Congress), they cannot account for the normative dimension of debate. Looking only to the substantive dimension of debate for explanations of why debate fails is at best incomplete, and at worst misleading. Even correct findings might be correct for the wrong reasons.

But taking the normative dimension into account may resolve two related problems that scholars of public debate face. The first problem is that the dominant model of how persons operate does not accord with the complexity of actual human persons. Current approaches to studying public debate portray most members of the public as deficient or defective in various ways. Emphasizing messaging, framing, truth, and so forth is another way of saying that when people do not do what scholars expect, it is because those people are dumb, misinformed, easily swayed, or ignorant. Even criticism of institutions (e.g., based on "media bias") essentially claims that ordinary persons are putty in the hands of smart people who manipulate them. When the only explanation you have is based on the substantive dimension of debate, every bad debate looks like knowledge deficiency. Taking the normative dimension of debate into account restores a more realistic model of persons as complicated, multidimensional, and variably capable or interested for reasons that are not reducible to how much they know about, for example, the funding practices of embryonic stem cell research.

Taking the normative dimension of debate into account may also solve a second problem. It is difficult to dispute that the vast majority of knowledge produced to influence public debate has basically no effect. Scholars who study and attempt to influence public debate are routinely ignored by elites and ordinary persons alike. The current solution to this problem is to continually generate and throw even more knowledge at public debate (in the form of papers, commentary, editorials, books, and the like) in the hope that something will happen this time. But the findings in this book suggest a different strategy. Instead of assuming that all debates are about epistemological claims, scholars should begin by considering the normative dimension of the particular debate in which they are interested, and structure any intervention in public debate to minimize normative conflict. If ordinary people prioritize good debate, it is probably more useful to design interventions that align with these preferences, rather than, say, only reiterating the truth of a particular epistemological claim.

But to take the normative dimension of public debate into account, we have to find out what those normative preferences are. We have to find out what the ordinary people who inhabit democratic society actually want, not just what theorists want them to do. This will not always be easy. There are practical ways to engage the normative dimensions of debate through interviews and archival research. Probably there are also ways to construct survey questions that take the normative dimension into account, though I have not tried to do this within the scope of this book. But if much of our effort is effectively wasted on failed attempts to influence debate through epistemological intervention, it is certainly worth trying to incorporate the normative dimension of debate into our attempts. We might well find that things turn out differently.

Seeking Good Debate

As it stands, public debates in which religion and science are involved are simply not very good on any account. The basic engagement that precedes deliberation does not even happen. Representatives participate in public debate for a variety of reasons, only some of which are compatible with deliberative debate. There are problems not only of substantive conflict but also of normative conflict. And the structure of public debate, whether good or not, shapes future possibilities for institutions to participate in the public sphere. If this book is taken only as a snapshot of the state of current public debate in America, the outlook might seem negative.

I think that our shared commitment to deliberative debate provides cause for hope. Obviously, we will not always agree substantively on issues that matter. But we can develop and foster ways of engagement that take normative as well as substantive conflicts into account. At a minimum this will require reimagining competence in public talk as a matter of listening and engaging other perspectives rather than ignoring or simply talking past them. At more local levels, this can be achieved by discussing what is at stake and what the expectations are for debate before substantive discussion occurs, on the model of anarchist direct action meetings or Quaker meetings. More broadly, institutions that participate in public life, such as religion and science, can promote these deliberative competencies among future representatives, for example, through required communication courses in universities and seminaries.

Of course, this all assumes that, given the opportunity, we will actually encounter and engage one another. But it is probably unreasonable to expect people to engage one another in deliberative debate about everything all the time. On many issues, we simply do not share interests, concerns, or level of commitment. We often talk past one another, or talk about the same thing in different ways that confuse and confound our discussions. Participation in public life is difficult, time-consuming, and just plain hard work. Even if we all want deliberative debate, as a practical matter it is not always possible. Trying to pursue deliberative debate on every issue all the time is likely to lead to frustration.

So, moving forward, how do we know when the pursuit of deliberative debate will be worth our limited attention and resources? Here, I think, is where conflict in public life offers particular reason for hope. This may sound strange. I opened the book by talking about conflict as a problem for public debate. But in a public sphere where engagement of any sort is uncommon, conflict in public life is a useful signal that there is something worth engaging over. Whether it is over substantive or normative dimensions of debate, conflict demonstrates that fellow citizens are willing to spend their time and effort contesting something that is important to them.[15] And conflict shows that we can encounter and engage each other in the public sphere over issues that matter. That is a promising starting point for those seeking good debate.

But even bad debate is better than nothing. Really the most striking thing about American public debate is that it exists at all. Throughout this book I identify many reasons why debate should break down and even, logically, why debate might grind to a halt or devolve into straightforward power struggle. But by and large this does not happen. Certainly I have suggested many reasons to be concerned, even critically so, with the state of debate in American public life. But the fact that public debate exists, that people can talk in public over issues that matter without resorting to personal violence, provides hope. Even if future debate cannot be made good, it can always be made better.

Methodological Appendix

ISSUE SELECTION

To find issues likely to provoke the public engagement between representatives of religion and science that most scholars of religion and science talk about, I worked from the premise that public conversations between representatives of religion and science were unlikely to occur if there were no claims at stake. So I started by looking for issues in which some participants make claims based on religious authority and some participants make claims based on scientific authority. Even this minimal approach excludes a variety of possible issues that involve something about religion or science, but are unlikely to produce religion-and-science debates because religion or science makes no public claim. For example, there are no significant religious claims about scientific or technical issues such as aerodynamics, and there are no significant scientific claims about religious issues such as veneration of saints.[1]

To maximize the chance of finding sustained public debates, I eliminated some issues that met the minimum criteria but that did not have significant public policy implications. For example, the bodily resurrection of Jesus is an issue concerning which some participants make claims based on religious authority (e.g., the Bible says that Jesus reanimated after three days in the tomb) and other participants make claims based on scientific authority (e.g., it is medically impossible to reanimate a body after three days). But there are essentially no public policy implications stemming from the bodily resurrection of Jesus, so I did not expect that issue to generate sustained public debate.

I also eliminated issues confined to a very small group of persons. For example, some members of the Church of Jesus Christ of Latter-day Saints claim that Native Americans are a "remnant of the House of Israel" descended from the Tribe of Manasseh through the Mormon prophet Lehi, whereas geneticists claim that there is no scientific evidence that the populations are linked.[2] Since this is an issue confined to one part of a religious denomination that, as a whole, constitutes less than 2 percent of the U.S. population, I did not expect this issue to generate sustained public debate.

After eliminating many issues in which religion-and-science debate was unlikely to exist, I selected four issues surrounding which I would expect to see sustained public conversation between representatives of religion and science in mass media. These four issues were human origins, stem cell research, environmental policy, and the origins of homosexuality. Each debate involves participants making claims based on religious authority and participants making claims based on scientific authority. Each debate also involves stakes not just for one particular group, but for a variety of different groups for different reasons. And each debate has broad policy implications at local and national levels.

TEXT ANALYSIS

The process of retrieving and analyzing textual data for this project depended on a combination of manual and automatic processes. For technical purposes, I defined "debate" as the collection of articles on a given religion-and-science issue contained in a sample from mass media. For example, "stem cell research debate" refers to all articles retrieved based on keywords associated with stem cell research. An "article" is the whole body of text contained in a newspaper article. News articles, news commentary, and opinion pieces counted as articles, while book reviews and letters to the editor did not count as articles. I did not limit articles based on word count.

To create the data set for this study, I used a combination of keyword searches and (for debates that resist keyword search) categorical searches to retrieve a set of articles about each issue from the Lexis-Nexis Major US Newspapers database, which contains the full text of articles from approximately thirty of the highest-circulation papers in the United States. Obviously there are many other possibilities for source data, such as local town newspapers, alternative press papers and magazines, and new media sources. But even with these alternatives available in the public sphere, newspapers still provide the "master forum" of American mass media.[3]

To ensure that the data set included the parts of debate in which someone makes claims based on religious authority and someone makes claims based on scientific authority, each issue required slightly different search and retrieval criteria. For example, environmental policy search results had either to be classified as "about" religion OR science, in addition to having the keywords "climate change" or "global warming." This combination requirement also helped exclude more general articles about, say, the "environment" in which teachers operate. Similarly, for debate over the origins of homosexuality, a more general search for "gay" or "sexuality" would bring in many articles that did not involve either religion or science, so I chose keywords that reflected arguments about the origins of homosexuality from scientists and from religious groups in order to retrieve a more focused set of results.

For each issue, I initially sought to extract all relevant newspaper articles that had been published within the previous ten years. But because of limited computational resources, the system would crash if the sample was too large. In the case of environmental policy and stem cell research, the ten-year window yielded samples that were too large to process successfully. Rather than try to pick and choose which aspects or subsamples of debate should be included, for those debates I simply constrained the size of the data sample by going back five years rather than ten. This still provided enormous amounts of data for those debates.

I used the following keyword/category combinations and date ranges to retrieve the articles for this study from the Lexis-Nexis Major US Newspapers database:

- Environmental Policy: "global warming" or "climate change," must have major categories either "religion" or "ecology/environmental science," 2002–2007
- Origins of Homosexuality: "gay gene" or "ex-gay" or "reparative therapy," 1997–2007
- Stem Cell Research: "stem cell," 2002–2007
- Human Origins: "creation*" or "intelligent design," 1997–2007

I manually reviewed and corrected the search results. I deleted articles that were artifacts of the search engine (e.g., matching "openly gay Gene Robinson" to "gay gene"), contained only a reference to some other article (e.g. "her last article was about the gay gene"), or were otherwise technically correct but irrelevant to the substantive debate (e.g., a photo essay with matching caption text but no article text). I also deleted duplicate articles that appeared in the same paper (e.g., morning and afternoon editions, or national and local editions in the same city), but did not eliminate multiple instances of wire service articles as long as those articles had physically appeared in different papers.

IDENTIFYING AND RANKING REPRESENTATIVES

I establish at the beginning of this book that everyone who appears in public debate in mass media is a "representative." To identify and rank representatives across all of the debates in this study, I used a computational linguistics technique called named entity recognition (NER). In NER, entities such as places, persons, dates, organizations, and so forth are not predefined in lists as search terms, but are identified by semantic and/or grammatical rules as they appear in unstructured data. Unlike a traditional information retrieval method, in which one might search a document for "Focus on the Family," NER allows one to search a document for all named entities without knowing the names or titles of such entities before the search begins.

I analyzed the data set of newspaper articles for each debate using GATE, which is a free and open-source computational linguistics platform, and the ANNIE (A Nearly New Information Extraction) plugin for named entity recognition and extraction.[4] ANNIE applies NER and adds contextual annotations to the original data set files. These annotations are additional tags embedded around named entities. For example, the identified personal name "Jerry

Falwell" would be saved as "<PERSON>Jerry Falwell</PERSON>." A custom Perl script processed the annotated file, extracted the tagged entities, and wrote a formatted text file for import into a PostgreSQL database. From there I used structured query language (SQL) to construct views and queries for analyzing the article and entity information.

I created views and queries to rank representatives by visibility within each debate as well as across all debates. After testing different ways of ranking representatives, I found that the measure most consistent with my research design is the number of articles in which a person is mentioned. The best alternative is total mentions, but it is possible that one feature article may contain dozens of references to a person, while being the only article ever written about that person. I think of articles as opportunities for readers to become aware of a representative. Many mentions in one article do not provide any visibility if a reader never sees the article, and are therefore misleading as a measure of visibility for representatives across a debate. Across debate as a whole, the most important component of visibility is that there are many opportunities for a reader to become aware of a representative.

I also created views and queries to look at the co-occurrence of representatives and organizations within the same article, to help contextualize how and why representatives showed up in these debates. In addition to providing information about who tends to show up in the same articles together, this query also made it possible to correct for co-mention of synonymous but differently named entities. For example, if an article uses the term "American Civil Liberties Union" once in the article and "ACLU" for the rest of the article, these are treated as separate entities with one article mention each. But since they co-occur in articles, and this is traceable through the query, I could disentangle the entities and correct any ranking counts accordingly.

Because a lot of actual language use does not follow rules, named entity recognition is not perfect. At many different steps in the process I had to intervene to correct, update, and improve the process using my human cognitive skills; for example, by adding complex organizational names to a list of known entities. But NER is very good. I started this process by doing an entirely manual analysis of one debate (approximately three hundred articles), then doing a computational analysis of the same data set and comparing the results. The results were very similar, and when some of the ambiguous entities were disambiguated manually, the resulting ranking of entities was nearly identical to that generated by the entirely manual process, even though it was generated in less than one-twentieth of the time.

MAPPING TOPICS

The debate maps that I created for chapters 2 and 3 draw on a combination of computational linguistics techniques for "topic discovery" and an admittedly subjective translation of raw results in order to communicate the topical structure of public talk in the debates under study. For a human analyst looking at a sample of documents, qualitative discourse analysis usually involves identifying meaningful concepts, themes, or conversations, coding texts using these concepts and themes, then aggregating the resulting coding data to look for broader patterns in discourse. By contrast, computational topic discovery looks for textual patterns first, then presents those patterns (called "topics") to the analyst for qualitative identification and interpretation.[5]

For topic discovery I used a technique called Latent Dirichlet Allocation (LDA).[6] Given a text corpus, LDA calculates topics as a probability distribution over words. Topics are latent patterns in the corpus, rather than direct similarities between documents, or simple clusters or co-occurrence of words. In the LDA model, topics contain words, and a document may contain multiple topics. So, for example, an LDA analysis of scientific abstracts might find one topic that contains the words "genetic embryo somatic dna" and another that contains the words "viral allograft antigen lupus." LDA could also calculate the probability that "viral" will be associated with "viral allograft antigen lupus," the probability that this topic will show up in any document, and the exact mixture of topics in any given document. But it would be up to the analyst to interpret the first topic as *reproductive genetics* and the second topic as *immunology*.

The relationships between words, topics, and documents that LDA identifies are remarkably similar to the relationships that a human would identify in the same data.[7] So an advantage of LDA is that it accurately identifies important qualitative differences over a much larger set of data, and in a much shorter time frame, than a human analyst. Even more important, however, is that because it is a quantitative (if probabilistic) method, the relationships among topics and across documents that it identifies are precisely measured, rather than simply associated. This allows types of analysis simply not possible for human analysts. For example, LDA can plot the relative significance of a topic to discourse by looking at the relationships among topics and how closely they are related to each other and to the corpus as a whole.

I analyzed the four debate corpora using the Topic Modeling Toolbox, a MATLAB toolbox for doing LDA analysis.[8] The toolbox, which is free for scientific use, contains all of the functions necessary to create the debate maps in this book, including topic discovery, probability ranking, and calculation of document and topic relationships. The toolbox allows several parameters and hyperparameters to be set by the user, including how many topics should be discovered, how many iterations should be attempted to model the topics, and the cutoff for low-probability topics. There are ways to maximize the probable fit of a model mathematically, but this does not guarantee that the result will be comprehensible to people. LDA still requires a human analyst to make judgments about levels of abstraction and the coherence of qualitatively different topics. So for these settings I relied on conventions in the most current literature, then adjusted the level of abstraction until the topics were clear and coherent to human comprehension.

In raw output form, "topics" show up simply as collections of words identified by a designator (e.g., T_82) and accompanied by probability information (e.g., 0.03). LDA requires the human analyst to interpret the topics that it identifies in each corpus. For each debate, I have interpreted each topic and given it what I judge to be an accurate topic name that describes the subject of its contents (e.g., "Left Behind Series" or "Human Genetic Evolution"). While I have made every effort to select appropriate topic names, it is possible that another person might come up with different names for these topics.

To create the final debate maps, I used the toolbox to calculate symmetrized KL distance between probabilities of topics over documents, then created a spatial arrangement of substantive topics using multidimensional scaling. To reduce visual clutter, I removed the lowest-probability and the nonsubstantive topics from the visualization.[9] The resulting debate maps are visual translations of the data generated by topic discovery into human-readable and informative maps that expose the topical structure of debate without swamping the reader with raw data. Inevitably there are some subjective elements in this translation. However, I judge the ability to analyze massive data sets for qualitative differences as more important than, on one hand, only reporting raw data or, on the other, executing a far more limited analysis using more conventional qualitative discourse analysis methods.[10]

BIOGRAPHICAL AND ARCHIVAL RESEARCH

In chapter 4 I address the question of what representatives think counts as good debate. The ideal way to approach this research question would be to sit down and personally interview every representative in every debate directly, with follow-up questions and plenty of time for discussing the nuances of each representative's approach. For two major reasons, this is not possible. First, it is physically impossible to interview the thousands of representatives who appear in these debates. Second, even taking a sample of these representatives, it is unreasonable to expect that a sociologist could gain access to, for example, George W. Bush, Laura Schlessinger, Pat Robertson, and Richard Dawkins, to interview them in the first place.[11] So I did not attempt to answer this question by interviewing elite representatives directly.

Instead I drew on a variety of secondary sources to answer the question. I began by creating a purposive sample of the representatives who showed up in the computational analysis. I stratified the sample by visibility (number of articles in which the representative was mentioned) and affiliation (science, religion, other). I established cutoff points for low, medium, and high visibility in each debate, relative to the overall distribution. I then randomly selected representatives in each category until I returned, at minimum, one religion representative, one science representative, and at least one other representative who was neither a science nor a religion representative, from each level of visibility.

Because representatives are not evenly distributed across debates, I took several corrective measures to ensure fair coverage for the analysis. If a given representative was no longer living (or had not been alive in recent memory), I selected a different representative from the same category and level of visibility. If a representative in one debate had already appeared in another debate, I selected an additional representative from the same category and level of visibility. If either religion or science representatives were not available in the same level of prominence (e.g., no highly prominent science representative), I selected the same category but from a lower level of visibility. And in cases in which the distribution of top representatives included multiple obvious nonreligion and nonscience representatives in different areas (e.g., politics, media), I selected additional representatives to ensure coverage of these other areas.

Constructing the sample in this way takes more care and judgment than a simple random sample. However, it is necessary because the distribution of religion and science representatives in these debates is not precisely comparable. Religion representatives tend to be relatively few in number, but more visible. For example, a few members of the Religious Right are highly visible in several debates. By contrast, science representatives tend to be relatively more numerous, but less visible. For example, each newspaper story about a new discovery in genetics tends to quote a scientist in the study, or a local college professor, rather than a single national figure. A random sample would entangle (potential) differences between religion and science representatives with (potential) differences in high- and low-visibility representatives. The purposive sample, in contrast to a random sample, guarantees inclusion of science and religion representatives of similar visibility.

In practice, this selection method resulted in a sample that included the top religion and science representatives in each debate, even if such representatives were not necessarily in the top ten for a given debate, supplemented with similarly prominent representatives in other areas. The resulting sample included forty-three representatives from four debates. Some are prominent across debates, some only in one.

For each representative in the sample, I constructed a biographical profile that included a variety of data, including personal characteristics, samples of public speech or writing, and, where available, biographical profiles, human-interest articles, and media interviews. Of course the amount of available data varied by person. For example, I found many more sources of data about Jerry Falwell than about John Haught, and many more sources of data about George W. Bush than about Christine Gregoire. This material was also used to construct the anonymized résumés and anonymized quotes used in interviews with ordinary respondents (see below).

In addition to constructing the biographical profiles, I also analyzed the discursive material for each representative to see what kinds of qualitative patterns emerged in the public talk of these figures. Most of these sources are transcripts or videos of interviews conducted by others with prominent (or not-so-prominent) representatives. In these texts I looked at how representatives described their own approaches to public debate. The intent was to identify what representatives thought public debate ought to be. I looked at how each selected representative talked about what she or he did in public life, looking in particular for indications of how a normative vision motivated the person's participation. From that analysis I derived the broad categorical distinction between "public crusade" and "elevating the conversation" reported in chapter 4.

INTERVIEWS

The bulk of the data cited or quoted in support of what ordinary people think comes from sixty-two one-on-one, face-to-face interviews that I conducted between April 2008 and April 2009. The only universal restrictions on respondent selection were that subjects had to be at least eighteen years old and could not be a public media figure. All interviews were confidential, so all respondent names in this book are pseudonyms, and any personally identifying details have been edited from responses.

The interview itself consisted of five stages for each debate (see full interview schedule below). First, I asked open-ended questions about a given debate (named generically, e.g., "stem cell research debate") such as "What is this debate about?" and "Who do you think is debating?" Second, I presented a sample of anonymous résumés (one at a time) and asked whom each person represents in that debate, and why the respondent thought so. Third, I presented a sample of quotes (one at a time) and asked whom the respondent thought the person who made that statement represents, and why he or she thought so. Fourth, I went through the top ten names mentioned in each debate and asked whom respondents thought each person represented in that debate, and why. Finally, I asked them to select their ideal committee for making decisions related to that debate.

I repeated this sequence for each debate as time and respondent availability permitted. Each stage represents a different dimension of evaluation: preexisting knowledge of the debate (open-ended), evaluation based on identity (résumés), evaluation based on interests (statements), evaluation based on recognition and association (top ten list), and finally, what qualities of representatives are most important (committee selection). I note that because respondents might understand different questions in different ways, despite interviewer guidance, the findings reported throughout the book do not depend solely on one dimension or interpretation of one question (e.g., not just the committee question), but hold across several different dimensions of evaluation.

I digitally recorded every interview and hired professional transcribers to create interview transcripts from those recordings. I reviewed each transcript and corrected the few misunderstandings or errors with reference to the original recordings. Sixty-two interviews yielded approximately 2,500 pages of transcribed text, or approximately forty pages per interview. In each interview I also took extensive notes about qualitative features of responses to provide a basis for a later coding scheme.[12] After all interviews were complete, I followed generally accepted practices of axial and open coding to manually analyze each interview transcript. I initially identified important concepts and themes in the interview data, drawing on my interview notes as a guide to create a preliminary coding structure. When a new theme emerged in analysis, I updated the preliminary coding structure and reviewed prior interviews as necessary.

Sample Description

I used a purposive sampling strategy designed to maximize range rather than achieve statistical representativeness.[13] Given the religion-and-science content of these debates, I set explicit recruitment targets using a two-dimensional matrix of religious affiliation and occupation. I purposively sought and enforced heterogeneity in those categories and informally sought heterogeneity in other categories.

The target distribution for the religious affiliation dimension was proportional to the general U.S. population: approximately 20 percent mainline Protestant, 33 percent evangelical Protestant, 25 percent Catholic, and 20 percent Other/None. I initially classified respondents on this dimension with reference to denominational membership, and later adjusted each respondent's classification in response to self-identification where appropriate, for example, in cases where a respondent attended a nondenominational church or was in transition between churches. The target distribution for the occupation dimension was approximately 80 percent nonscientific/technical and 20 percent scientific/technical. I initially classified respondents on this dimension with reference to occupational categories from the Bureau of Labor Statistics, and later adjusted as necessary based on personal knowledge of a given respondent's specific occupational situation.

I recruited respondents at multiple sites to avoid skewing results toward the idiosyncrasies of one particular site.[14] But given limited resources, I limited recruitment to two U.S. cities. I recruited 75 percent of respondents in a Southern California city with a population greater than 1.5 million and a strong high-tech and military employer base. I recruited the remaining 25 percent of respondents in a South Florida city with a population of approximately 200,000, a large tourism employer base, and a large retiree population. The demographic differences provided significant heterogeneity beyond expected geographic and regional differences. For example, the South Florida site skews higher in respondent age, and the distribution of religious affiliations within the Other/None category differs substantially between the two sites.

At each site I recruited the initial set of respondents through intermediaries with access to potential respondents in the target recruitment categories. At each site I also proceeded from that initial set of respondents using a snowball strategy for further recruitment. In Southern California I started by identifying and contacting personal acquaintances with access to local organizations (both religious and nonreligious). In South Florida I started by using public information to identify and contact local congregational leaders and other civic leaders who might act as intermediaries. At both sites I asked these intermediaries to identify (and, if necessary, introduce) potential respondents. I then contacted potential respondents directly, generally by email or telephone. I continued pursuing a snowball strategy and used selective recruitment to enforce heterogeneity for religion and occupation as necessary.

As table 8 shows, the resulting sample generally met the recruitment targets within each location and within the sample as a whole. There was some variation from the exact target percentages. For example, the sample contains a slightly higher than expected number of respondents in the Other/None category.[15] This variation is not surprising given the sample size. Beyond the target categories, respondents varied widely in education (high school to PhD), age (18 to 79 years, average 40) and gender (34 women, 28 men). But the sample is not intended to be statistically representative, so there are important variations from the U.S. general population. For example, all respondents had completed high school, and a majority had earned AA/AS or BA/BS degrees. Given the limitations of the purposive sample, I do not make general claims about differences within these categories.

TABLE 8   PURPOSIVE SAMPLE BREAKDOWN BY LOCATION AND OCCUPATION
($n = 62$)

	Mainline	Evangelical	Catholic	Other/None
Southern California				
Scientific	2	3	4	2
Nonscientific	6	11	6	13
South Florida				
Scientific	1	2	—	—
Nonscientific	3	4	3	2

Interview Schedule

I used an interview schedule to guide the sequence and subject of the interview questions, particularly in the evaluation exercises. In some cases questions (or later sections) were omitted for time, or otherwise altered for clarity. In each case, however, I took care to maintain question order, avoid priming for later responses, and avoid guiding respondents in a particular direction. As Luker points out, this is often overly cautious, since respondents are generally more willing to push back than interviewers assume.[16] Note also that many of these questions are designed to prompt reflection. I sometimes asked situation-appropriate follow-up questions to provoke elaboration on brief answers (e.g., about an anecdote that a respondent recounted).

Preliminary Questions

- Your age?
- What is your educational background?
- Have you studied scientific subjects? (*if so*) At what level?
- Were you raised in a religious tradition? (*if so*) Which one?
- Do you attend church regularly? (*if so*) How often do you attend? (*if so*) Did you go last ____?
- What do you read or watch regularly?
- Do you consider yourself to be politically active? (*if so*) In what ways are you active?
- Are you a member of any clubs or organizations? (*if so*) Which ones (e.g., professional, hobby, game)?

Issues, Debates, and Media

(1.1)   We're going to go through the same set of questions for four different religion-and-science debate topics: stem cell research, human origins, environmental policy, and origins of homosexuality.

(1.2)   Can you briefly describe the ____ debate as you see it?

(1.3)   Where did you learn about ____? Can you be specific?

(1.4)   Do you talk to other people about ____. (*if so*) Whom?

(1.5)   When is the last time you talked to other people about ____?

(1.6)   Does ____ matter (to you)?

(1.7)   Do you see yourself as participating in the debate over ____?

Representatives

In this section we're going to talk about people, positions, and viewpoints in debates about the issues we discussed earlier. We'll go through the questions for each issue separately, but it's entirely possible that the answers will be similar for different issues. That's completely okay.

(2.1)   When you think of ____, who do you think is debating? Does anyone come to mind?

(2.2)   I'm now going to provide you with some profiles of people who participate in the debate, but I'm not going to identify the person. For each profile, I would like to know whom you think the person represents. Also for each profile, I'm going to ask why you think this person represents those particular people or groups.

    (2.2.1)   (*give profile on index card, read out loud for record*) Again, for ____, whom do you think this person represents?

    (2.2.2)   Why do you think this person represents them? What is it about the profile that suggests this person represents them?

(2.3)   Now I'm going to provide you with some statements from people who participate in the debate, but I'm not going to identify the person. For each statement, I will ask a series of questions about your agreement or disagreement with the statement, and I'll also ask questions about whom this person may represent. If you have any questions at all about the statement, I'm happy to try to clarify.

    (2.3.1)   (*give statement on index card, read out loud for record*) Do you agree or disagree with this statement, even partially?

    (2.3.2)   Why do you agree or disagree? (*further*) Which part of the statement makes the most or least sense to you?

    (2.3.3)   Do you think that the person who said this represents you?

    (2.3.4)   (*if not you*) Whom do you think that this person represents?

    (2.3.5)   Why do you think this person represents them?

(2.4)   Now we're going to name some names. I will provide some names of people participating in the debate. If you don't recognize them, please say so. If you do recognize them:

    (2.4.1)   What is your impression of this person?

    (2.4.2)   Whom you think this person represents? Why?

(2.5)   Okay, no more profiles or statements or lists of people. But here is a scenario: if you had to pick a five-person committee to make important decisions about ____, who would be on your committee? Why? (*if roles*) Can you think of a particular person who fills that role?

    (2.5.1)   Why would these people be the best committee members?

    (2.5.2)   (*if specific*) How did you hear about these people?

    (2.5.3)   We've discussed the committee for ____. Would you want the same people regardless of the topic?

    (2.5.4)   What changes would you make based on a topic change?

(2.6)   If you could have this committee, how would your life change? Would you do anything differently?

(2.7)   Do you think there is anything you can do to change the debate about ____, or the people involved in the debate? If so, what might that be?

Representation and Democracy

Okay, we're on the home stretch. I'm going to ask a short set of questions that are a bit more abstract. I'd like you to think not just about what is happening, but what should happen, in your opinion.

(3.1)   Let's go back to your committee, and let's say that they came up with a position on ____. If this position went against your beliefs on ____, would you want to vote democratically on the proposal, for example, in a state referendum?

(3.2)   Should the committee be allowed to override a democratic vote? Why or why not?

(3.3)   Should anyone be allowed to override a democratic vote? Why or why not?

    (3.3.1)   (*if so*) Who?

Science and Scientists

Finally, I have a last thought question for you. Let's say that someone proposed a ten-year moratorium on basic scientific research in order to assess our current data, get consensus on policy positions, and think about moral or ethical implications of science. Would you support such a plan? Why or why not? What alternative might you suggest?

Notes

CHAPTER I

1. Robertson 2005.

2. Versions of this quote are often repeated by Dawkins and others, but it originates in Dawkins 1989.

3. Important exceptions include J. Evans 2002, 2010.

4. For a helpful overview of political representation from a sociological perspective, see Perrin and McFarland 2008.

5. For other examples of a sociological approach to religion and science, see Baker 2012; Ecklund 2010; Ecklund and Scheitle 2007; J. Evans 2010, 2011, 2013; J. Evans and M. Evans 2008; M. Evans 2009; M. Evans 2012a, Longest and Smith 2011.

6. M. Evans and J. Evans 2010.

7. Zammito 2004.

8. For an explanation of this concept, see Irwin 2001.

9. For more extensive and detailed information about the simple claims I make here, see, for example, NSB 2014; Pew Research Center 2009; and the many top-level data summaries available from the Association of Religion Data Archives (ARDA; thearda.com). An excellent example of vibrant religion is American evangelicalism; see Smith 1998.

10. Draper 1874.

11. See, for example, Russell 1997 [1935].

12. A useful discussion of this point can be found in Taylor 2007.

13. Dawkins 2006; Hitchens 2007.

14. See, for example, Harris 2004.

15. There are, of course, any number of people who advocate violence against members of particular religious groups. In the United States there is substantial anti-Muslim rhetoric, for example. However, my impression is that

this is (at least) as likely to come from other religious people as from nonreligious people. See Bail 2012, 2014.

16. Gould 1999; John Paul II 1992.

17. The basic positions in these debates are described in Audi and Wolterstorff 1997 and Habermas 2006.

18. For examples of each of these activities, see Anderson 2006; Barbour 1966; F. Collins 2006; and Haught 2000.

19. Brooke 1991; Numbers 2007.

20. Bozeman 1977.

21. Livingstone 1987.

22. Shea 1986.

23. Lienesch 2007.

24. Taylor 2004:83.

25. The definitive argument can be found in Habermas 1989. Key points are helpfully summarized in Taylor 2004.

26. Habermas 1974 [1964].

27. Mitzen 2005.

28. Habermas 1974 [1964].

29. Fraser 1990.

30. For more on this "deliberative" model, see Habermas 1989.

31. For more on this "agonistic" model, see Honig 1993.

32. For more on this "interest group politics" model, see Cigler and Loomis 1983.

33. For an example of "acting up," see Epstein 1996, especially chapter 6.

34. For a brief overview of the varieties of deliberative democratic theory, see M. Evans 2012b.

35. For an overview of this trajectory, see J. Evans and M. Evans 2008.

36. Attridge 2009.

37. Ferree et al. 2002:6.

38. Epstein 1996.

39. Ferree et al. 2002. On master frames, see Snow and Benford 1992.

40. Davies and Neal 1996; Le Vay 1994; Moon 2004.

41. For an overview of the historical trajectory of this concept, see Pitkin 1967.

42. Hadden 1969; Jelen 1993.

43. Fowler, Hertzke, and Olson 1998.

44. Wynne 1992.

45. J. Evans 2011; Sturgis and Allum 2004.

46. Wagner 2007.

47. Many basic normative questions are discussed in Pitkin 1967. See also Schwartz 1988; Urbinati 2006; M. Williams 1998.

48. Pitkin 2004. But see Perrin and McFarland 2008.

49. Przeworski, Stokes, and Manin 1999.

50. These examples come from Rehfeld 2006 and Thomassen 2007.

51. For a framework for understanding politics in this broader sense, see Armstrong and Bernstein 2008. Broader theories of representation can be found in Perrin and McFarland 2011 and in Saward 2008.

52. Binder 2002; Superfine 2009.

53. J. Evans 2002.

54. Djupe and Gilbert 2003.

55. Bourdieu 1985, 1991. Hobbes's constitutive take on representation is also discussed in Pitkin 1967, esp. 14–37.

56. Thomassen 2007.

57. Fetner 2008.

58. Gitlin 1981.

59. Epstein 1996.

60. Oreskes 2004.

61. J. Evans 2002. I recognize that some ontological assumptions preclude the casual substitution of an abstract like "ethics" for the more concrete "group members." Yet this is the constitutive power of representation. Speaking for ethics is, effectively, speaking for a group of people (real, actual, imagined, or idealized) who are ethical. Similarly, speaking of representation solely in terms of "claims" or "frames" is unhelpfully reductive. If Bourdieu is right, there is always some constitutive effect whereby representatives do not just present claims but also constitute "people who make these claims."

62. Ferree et al. 2002.

63. Wilcox and Robinson 2011.

CHAPTER 2

1. For a detailed account of how I selected issues for analysis, see the methodological appendix.

2. J. Evans and M. Evans 2008.

3. J. Evans 2013.

4. I explain this process more fully in the methodological appendix. For an overview of topic discovery, see Blei 2012. For an overview of named entity recognition, see Nadeau and Sekine 2009.

5. Brockman 2006.

6. To reduce visual clutter, I omit highly infrequent and nonsubstantive topics.

7. Intelligent Design proponents claim that evolution is "just a theory" and that alternative theories should be taught in public schools as a matter of fairness and justice. Their efforts are largely centered on educational institutions such as school boards and curriculum committees. See Binder 2007.

8. This is entirely consistent with what empirical work on conservative Protestants and evolution would predict. See J. Evans 2011.

9. Gould died in 2002. As with the death of Jerry Falwell, this is a case in which a prominent figure died during the time period covered by the newspaper sample. This coincidence brings up the possibility that the person figures prominently because of attention paid to him on the occasion of his death, in terms of obituaries, feature articles, and so forth. I think it is difficult to argue that Gould, as the most cited paleontologist in history after Darwin and G. G. Simpson, is on the list only because of media coverage spikes following his death. To give two specific examples from among the multiple reasons he shows up, he served as an expert witness in the *McLean v. Arkansas* case, and he wrote

popular science books putting forth the idea that religion and science were "nonoverlapping magisteria" (NOMA).

10. At the time of data collection Bush was the sitting president.

11. This "enrollment" of representatives is part of a broader and more complex process of "translation." See Callon 1986.

12. Rudoren 2006.

13. Goodstein 2000.

14. For a broader theoretical context, see Bourdieu 1991.

15. Scott 1997.

16. J. Evans 2010; Nisbet 2005.

17. J. Evans 2010.

18. Most of the articles in this debate predate Pope Benedict XVI, and all of them predate Pope Francis.

19. J. Evans 2010.

20. Politicians try to avoid alienating voters who are not co-religionists. See Domke and Coe 2010.

21. Quoted in Hopkins 2005.

22. Quoted in Barton 2004.

23. Grossman 2004.

CHAPTER 3

1. In theory this question should center on the origins of sexuality. In practice it focuses on the origins of homosexuality. Few bother to ask what makes a person heterosexual.

2. Jordan 1997.

3. Hamer et al. 1993.

4. See, for example, Aratani 2005.

5. See, for example, Associated Press 1999; Brelis 1999.

6. Swidey 2005.

7. That being said, distribution of persons tends to follow a Zipf distribution (that is, a straight line on a log-log plot), so even being in the top ten is a big deal as there is a fairly steep drop-off after the top group of representatives.

8. See Weiner 2000.

9. Hamer et al. 1993.

10. Exodus International ceased operations in 2013.

11. There is also a coincidental aspect of this story: Falwell's former speechwriter is a gay activist. On the rare occasions when he appears in media, the writers inevitably play up the Falwell connection. Since this is effective only as ironic contrast, I take it to be similar in rhetorical effect to explicitly invoking Falwell as the exemplar of antigay religious people.

12. Oreskes 2004.

13. See examples in Mooney 2005.

14. This debate resists keyword searches, so I added categorical restrictions from Lexis-Nexis standard categories. Further details are available in the methodological appendix.

15. Quoted in Morford 2007.

16. From an open letter to the NAE dated March 1, 2007, and widely cited across newspaper articles.

17. I discuss this point in more detail in chapter 7.

18. Wilcox and Robinson 2011; D. Williams 2010.

CHAPTER 4

1. See the methodological appendix for details on sample selection and analytical techniques.

2. Other examples of representatives in the sample who use the "public crusade" approach are religious leaders Pat Robertson and Michael Sheridan; policy activists Eugenie Scott, Janet Folger, Wayne Besen, and Samantha Smoot; politicians Sam Brownback, James Inhofe, and Arnold Schwarzenegger; and scientist Gerald Schatten.

3. Harding 2000.

4. Quoted in Falwell 2008:114.

5. An example of the former is Anita Bryant, see Fetner 2008. An example of the latter is Phyllis Schlafly; see Critchlow 2005.

6. Quoted in Falwell 2008:116.

7. See, for example, Wilcox 1989; Wilcox and Robinson 2011.

8. Quoted in Burke 2007.

9. Quoted in Inskeep 2006.

10. Focus on the Family n.d.

11. James Dobson, in July 1, 2004, interview with Stan Guthrie; transcript at http://www.christianitytoday.com/ct/2004/july/20.19.html (last retrieved July 26, 2015).

12. On the "most influential evangelical" claim, see Gilgoff 2007.

13. As best I can tell, "moral Esperanto" originates in Dunn 1979. In the scholarly study of religion it is most closely associated with Jeffrey Stout (1988).

14. In practice, talk of values is treated as a signal for conservative Protestantism. I discuss this phenomenon in chapter 7.

15. James Dobson, in October 8, 2007, interview with Sean Hannity; transcript at http://www.foxnews.com/printer_friendly_story/o,3566,300457,oo html (last retrieved July 26, 2015).

16. Moen 1992.

17. James Dobson, in November 22, 2006, interview with Larry King; transcript at http://transcripts.cnn.com/TRANSCRIPTS/0611/22/lkl.01.html.

18. George W. Bush, in January 29, 2007, National Public Radio interview with Juan Williams; transcript at http://www.npr.org/templates/story/story .php?storyId=7065633 (last retrieved July 26, 2015).

19. George W. Bush, in February 14, 2008, interview with Matt Frie; transcript at http://news.bbc.co.uk/2/hi/americas/7245670.stm (last retrieved July 26, 2015).

20. Bush, January 29, 2007, interview.

21. George W. Bush, in August 1, 2006, roundtable interview with members of Texas press; transcript at http://www.washingtonpost.com/wp-dyn/content /article/2005/08/02/AR2005080200899.html (last retrieved July 26, 2015).

22. George W. Bush, in December 8, 2008, ABC News interview with Cynthia McFadden; transcript at http://abcnews.go.com/Nightline/Politics/story?id=6418908&page2 (last retrieved July 26, 2015).

23. Quoted in Slack 2005.

24. Richard Dawkins, in October 2005, interview with Laura Sheahen; transcript at http://www.beliefnet.com/News/Science-Religion/2005/11/The-Problem-With-God-Interview-With-Richard-Dawkins.aspx (last retrieved July 26, 2015).

25. Dawkins 1989.

26. Richard Dawkins, undated interview with Lanny Swerdlow; transcript at http://www.positiveatheism.org/writ/dawkinso.htm (last retrieved July 26, 2015).

27. Dawkins 2006:15.

28. Other examples of representatives who use the "elevating the conversation" approach are scientists such as Julia Parrish, Kenneth Miller, Robert Spitzer, and Dean Hamer.

29. John Haught, in April 19, 2006, interview with Adam Shapiro; transcript at http://www.metanexus.net/essay/conversation-john-haught-evolution-intelligent-design-and-recent-dover-trial (last retrieved July 26, 2015).

30. Quoted in Paulson 2007.

31. Quoted in Paulson 2007.

32. Haught, April 19, 2006, interview.

33. See Schmidt's official bio page at http://www.giss.nasa.gov/staff/gschmidt/.

34. All quotes from Gavin Schmidt, in June 26, 2009, interview with Russell Weinberger; transcript at http://www.edge.org/3rd_culture/schmidt09/schmidt09_index.html (last retrieved July 26, 2015).

35. On the question of media strategies and visibility, see Bail 2012, 2014; Sobieraj 2011.

CHAPTER 5

1. Przeworski, Stokes, and Manin 1999. On substantive similarities, see Downs 1957; Enelow and Hinich 1984; and Rabinowitz and Macdonald 1989. On interests, see Dahl 1956; Denzau and Munger 1986; and Schattschneider 1960. On evaluative shortcuts, see Jelen 1993; Koch 2000; and Sigelman et al. 1995.

2. For a broader literature review and discussion, see M. Evans 2012b.

3. Details on the sample selection, sample composition, and interview schedule can be found in the methodological appendix.

4. A more technical definition is that evaluation is granting or withholding symbolic power based on comparison of activity to norms. Consider Bourdieu (1991:192): "Political capital is a form of symbolic capital, *credit* founded on *credence* or belief and *recognition* or, more precisely, on the innumerable operations of credit by which agents confer on a person (or on an object) the very powers that they recognize in him (or it). . . . Symbolic power is a power which the person submitting to *grants* to the person who exercises it. . . . It is a power which exists because the person who submits to it believes that it exists."

5. See also Baker 2012; Ecklund and Park 2009; Ecklund, Park, and Sorrell 2011; J. Evans 2011; Longest and Smith 2011; and Scheitle 2011.

6. See J. Evans 2010; and M. Evans and J. Evans 2010.

7. I do not address here the relationship between policy preferences and process preferences. Assumptions about this relationship underpin most liberal democratic (e.g., Habermasian) arguments about the role of religion in public life. Limited empirical research suggests that there is no predictable relationship. See M. Evans 2014a; Hibbing and Theiss-Morse 2002.

8. Hetherington 2005.

CHAPTER 6

1. Epstein 1996:3.

2. Shapin and Schaffer 1985.

3. Binder 2007; M. Evans and J. Evans 2010.

4. Green, Rozell, and Wilcox 2003; Greeley and Hout 2006; Wilcox and Robinson 2011; Wuthnow 1983.

5. I say "apparently unprecedented" because it remains unclear whether the Religious Right is a new insertion of evangelical religion into national politics. Michael Lienesch (1993), for example, traces activism back to Federalists such as Jedediah Morse.

6. "Neutrality" meaning either formally explicit neutrality toward religious expression or apparent neutrality based on shared religious premises that therefore do not cause division.

7. On the former claim, see Casanova 1994. On the latter, see Herberg 1955; Wuthnow 1983.

8. Influential versions of this claim can be found in Wuthnow 1988 and Hunter 1991.

9. There are many variations on this argument. Examples include Goldberg 2007; Hedges 2006; Phillips 2006; Schaeffer 2007; Sharlet 2008.

10. This of course resonates with fears in the 1960s about JFK's potentially split allegiance to the nation and the Pope.

11. On resource mobilization, see McCarthy and Zald 1977.

12. Hadden and Shupe 1988

13. Wilcox and Robinson 2011.

14. Lindsay 2007; Medvetz 2012; Sharlet 2008; Teles 2008.

15. J. Evans 2009.

16. Blake 2005.

17. Media Matters 2007.

18. Lindsay 2007. A related point is that electoral mobilization is a bit easier for conservative religious movements because conservative religious people actually go to church, so it's fairly easy to find them on Sunday morning if you want to tell them something. This point is emphasized in Smidt 2007.

19. For numerous examples, see "Endorsements" on the FRC Action PAC website at http://www.frcaction.org/endorsements (last retrieved July 29, 2015).

20. Lindsay 2006; Sharlet 2008.

21. Two notable exceptions are Jesse Jackson and Al Sharpton, who are often considered liberal or moderate religious figures and who are very prominent in media coverage. However, this is highly issue-specific. If you sample media coverage based on finding religious figures, Jackson and Sharpton show up prominently (see, for example, Media Matters 2007:5). But if you sample media coverage based on particular issues, they show up a lot on some issues (e.g., those related to race, poverty, and education) and not at all on others. They do not show up prominently on the debates I discuss in this study.

22. J. Evans 2009.

23. To be clear, the Protestant mainline churches have nothing close to the amount of resources the Christian Right has to spend on political and social activity.

24. Lindsay and Wuthnow 2010.

25. Olson 2007.

26. There are but few exceptions. John Quincy Adams used a book of law. Theodore Roosevelt did not use a Bible for his first term, but did for his second term. Other presidents have sworn the oath of office with their hand on multiple Bibles.

27. Bellah 1967.

28. Of course, in practice such references tend to be to Christian or Jewish religious concepts, reflecting U.S. religious history.

29. Hart 2001.

30. Stout 1988.

31. See, for example, Hunter 1983; Marsden 1980; and Smith 1998.

32. J. Evans 2009; Stout 1988.

33. J. Evans 1997; Fetner 2008; Mueller 1983.

CHAPTER 7

1. Because of the structure of the interviews, not every respondent had opportunity to recognize or identify (by name) every person in the top ten of each debate. The percentages here are calculated by dividing the number of hits (clear recognition) by the number of opportunities. So for George W. Bush, 61 respondents had the opportunity to recognize him by name, and 61 did so successfully. For Pat Robertson, by contrast, 51 respondents had the opportunity to recognize him by name, and 40 did so successfully. Successful recognition here means that they were able to generate a brief description that mostly matches known information about the representative. If someone said, "Yeah, Pat Robertson, the car dealer," I would not count that as recognition, but if they said, "Yeah, Reverend James Dobson, from Focus on the Family; I listen to his radio show," I would mark it as recognition even though Dobson is not an ordained minister. Let me anticipate two additional methodological critiques. The first concerns sequence and the possibility that I primed respondents by asking questions about specific names first, thus creating an association that is showing up here rather than finding an association that already existed. To be clear, then, I asked questions about anonymized résumés and statements of representatives first, then later asked about recognition of particular names. The

second anticipated critique is that variation in recognition is just a function of whether or not people pay attention to the news (or vary importantly in how they get it). I did not see any significant association between a person's news sources (I asked this question specifically) and his or her approval or disapproval of moral issues. For example, even among my conservative Protestant respondents, few watched Fox News, or at least only Fox News. Most people like sitcoms and reality TV, it turns out, and I cannot easily ascribe patterns in the data to variation in entertainment TV tastes.

2. "Top of mind" surveys that ask respondents to name a particular person show even worse results. For example, a Barna Group study asked a sample of Americans (not just religious) to name "the most influential Christian leader." Forty-one percent of respondents said "not sure," "no one," or "none," while the top name, given by 19 percent of respondents, was evangelist Billy Graham. See report results at http://www.barna.org/culture-articles/536-us-lacks-notable-christian-leaders (last retrieved July 29, 2015).

3. See the methodological appendix for sample details.

4. As I use the category, Other/None includes atheist, agnostic, disaffiliated, so-called "other theology" such as Unitarian Universalism, and the small-minority religious groups such as Judaism, Islam, and Buddhism. In this sample it is primarily atheist, disaffiliated, and "other theology."

5. I say this because of Gore's statement in a 2004 interview (Remnick 2004): "The influx of fundamentalist preachers have pretty much chased us out with their right-wing politics."

6. Though not as prominent in this data set because of his fairly meteoric rise to national politics in a short period of time, Barack Obama is an interesting case, not because of his denominational affiliation (UCC), but because his particular congregation (Trinity, UCC's largest) is known for activism, as several widely distributed statements by pastor Jeremiah Wright suggested. Note that this association with Trinity means that the conservatives were able to portray Obama to some extent as less religious because his church was "really" about political activism, not religion.

7. Identification as religious could be explained as the result of priming based on the presumption that people in "religion and science" debates should be evaluated in "religious" terms. But this does not suggest a direction for that evaluation. Thus it is less interesting that the word "religious" is used at all than that it is used primarily to describe conservatives and not moderates or liberals.

8. This is a different claim than "religious language should not be used" (the normative Rawlsian/Audi claim). As John Evans (2010) has found, people see the ability to use religious language as important and necessary, which he partly attributes to a preference for sincerity in discourse. See also Trilling 1972.

9. Rawls 1971, 2005. Of course I simplify Rawls to illustrate what respondents are doing. Rawls is more concerned with how to underpin a theory of justice. Since religion is not accessible to every citizen (that is, not everyone shares the same commitments or prior beliefs), it cannot serve as a basis for public reason in a pluralistic society. It is unfair to include religion, so it is unjust. Of course, religion can remain as "background culture."

10. This is true in some respects, notably that some of the most famous scandals involve conservative televangelists. On this point, see Buddenbaum 2009. However, I note that one of the largest religious media networks is actually EWTN, the 24/7 Catholic television network. Moreover, many religious cable channels are, on one hand, sufficiently eclectic in their programming to avoid an automatic "conservative" label and, on the other hand, completely indeterminate in their political orientation (e.g., Joel Osteen's policy of refusing recognition to any political candidate who visits his church).

11. Djupe and Gwiasda 2010.

CHAPTER 8

1. Mooney and Kirshenbaum 2009:125–30.
2. Epstein 1996; Gieryn 1999; Gregory and Miller 1998; Shapin 1995.
3. On the inadequacy of methods for scientific demarcation, see Feyerabend 1975; Kuhn 1996; Latour 1987.
4. Gieryn 1999.
5. Shapin 2008.
6. On virtuous scientists, see Shapin 2008. On the promulgation of a particular scientific narrative through public education, see Rudolph 2002. For data on scientific support, see the National Science Board's "Science and Engineering Indicators 2014" (NSB 2014).
7. For an overview, see Burns, O'Connor, and Stocklmayer 2003.
8. Kirby 2011; Morrison 2011.
9. Such translation is often criticized. On the failure of media translation in climate science debates, for example, see Bell 1994; and Corbett and Durfee 2004.
10. Star and Griesemer 1989.
11. Merton 1973.
12. Shapin 2010.
13. Gregory and Miller 1998; Mellor 2010.
14. Kirby 2003.
15. Star 1985.
16. H. M. Collins 1974; Mol and Law 1994.
17. Metlay 2006.
18. H. Collins 2004.
19. Gooding 1990; Latour 1987.
20. Star 1985.
21. Bruner 1991:4, 1986:25.
22. Bruner 1991:4.
23. For more on the links between science, scientists, and fictional narrative, see Morrison 2011. For more on the creation story, see Genesis 1.
24. On the link between cognition and social interaction, see Vygotsky 1978. Sociologists of religion and science are increasingly discovering that surveys of scientific knowledge are actually experienced differently depending on the extent to which the questions invoke issues of identity and social conflict. See Gauchat 2011; Roos 2014; and Rughiniş 2011.

25. M. Evans 2010.

26. Shapin 1994.

27. Shapin 2008. The canonical example in science studies is the famous "air-pump" controversy recounted in Shapin and Schaffer 1985.

28. Bruner 1991.

29. Knorr-Cetina 1981; Latour 1987.

30. Curtis 1994.

31. See, for example, Kim 2009.

32. Weingart 1998. See also Peters et al. 2008.

33. For example, see Nisbet and Lewenstein 2002; Nisbet, Brossard, and Kroepsch 2003.

34. Besley and Tanner 2011; Peters et al. 2008.

35. Shapin 2008.

36. But see Goodell 1977.

37. Shermer 2002.

38. Johnson, Ecklund, and Lincoln 2014.

39. Kirby 2011.

40. Gould 1993.

41. J. Evans and M. Evans 2008; Lawson and Worsnop 1992; Verhey 2005.

42. See, for example, Ellison and Musick 1995; J. Evans 2013; M. Evans and J. Evans 2010.

43. See, for example, Beyerlein 2004; Sherkat 2010.

44. NSB 2014.

45. See the overview in Holton 1993.

46. Forrest and Gross 2004; Mooney 2005.

47. Other attempts to explain this paradox can be found in Epstein 1996; J. Evans 2011, 2013; Gauchat 2011; Locke 1999; Wagner 2007.

48. For data on science support, see National Science Board, "Science and Engineering Indicators 2014" (NSB 2014), and see ARDA summaries at http://thearda.com for data on religious affiliation. To say anything more specific than this without additional data runs afoul of the ecological inference problem (see King 1997), but as long as one quantity cannot fit into the remainder of the other quantity (with reference to the same population), there must be some overlap between people who are religious and people who support science in that population.

49. Ellison and Musick 1995.

50. I sometimes used the term "ban" rather than "moratorium" for the sake of those respondents who were unfamiliar with the latter term. However, I made clear that the "ban" would be time-limited, which would technically be a moratorium.

51. Not all evangelical Protestants are fundamentalists, though they are often counted together because of the conventional emphasis on denominational membership rather than theological commitments. See the Association of Religion Data Archives at http://www.thearda.com for a wide range of estimates.

52. See, for example, Marty and Appleby 1991.

53. J. Evans 2011, 2013.

CHAPTER 9

1. Sociologist Kristin Luker (2008) describes a number of similar interview techniques for eliciting out-loud thinking from respondents about why something is not happening or not working.

2. Incidentally, this respondent desire for a range of expertise suggests that one of the reasons that social movements can successfully redefine scientific credibility to include "lay expertise" (e.g., as described in Epstein 1996) is that this approach aligns with preferences that ordinary persons already hold.

3. Note that respondents had multiple opportunities to suggest representatives in each interview. Only 37 percent named any person at any point, and many of these did so only on a single occasion. In other words, even when a respondent suggested a name, it was often the only time he or she did so despite multiple opportunities within the interview.

4. A methodological note: this prompt leaves me open to the accusation of asking "leading questions" or "priming the respondent." Of course, as Kristin Luker (2008) points out, this criticism makes some faulty assumptions about the agency of interview respondents. Luker shows that "leading questions" often get push-back from respondents, either because they fail to capture the meaning that the respondent intends, or more basically, because they are incorrect suggestions. In these interviews, I sometimes suggested names to keep the conversation going when I thought that I understood that the respondent had a person in mind *and* wanted my help with the name. But even in these cases, if I guessed the wrong name, the respondent would say so. For example, I once suggested the wrong UN secretary-general name, suggesting Boutros Boutros-Ghali, and the respondent looked at me as if I was an idiot and said "no, the Korean guy," meaning Ban Ki-Moon. So, while I understand the potential criticism about "leading questions" or "priming the respondents," as an interviewer I am keenly conscious of when such suggestions cross the line, and given the ability and willingness of respondents to suggest that I am some kind of idiot, I do not omit the use of such questions or suggestions on principle.

5. Let me anticipate an obvious methodological criticism, which is that I somehow selected a statement from Dawkins that is atypical and therefore skewed respondent answers away from a fair assessment. I have two responses. First, having looked at the many polemical statements Dawkins has made in interviews and written for public consumption, my personal judgment is that this statement is typical. Second, Dawkins himself has pointed out repeatedly that "hostility" toward religion in particular is necessary if one is to intervene in public life successfully (see Dawkins 2006, especially chapter 8). One might still say that Dawkins does not intend to sound as harsh as he sometimes does, but like any other public speaker's intentions, his are evaluated through his words.

6. To be sure, Teresa indicated that this was a problem that other scientists had.

CHAPTER 10

1. Shields 2009. See also Klemp 2010.

2. I take this phrase from Wuthnow and J. Evans 2002.

3. Shields 2009. On developing political apathy, see Eliasoph 1998.

4. Similarly, any efforts to promote religion in public life are, in practice, efforts to promote the Religious Right. I do not engage this point further here, but it presents a challenge to recent theoretical approaches to religion in the public sphere, as, for example, offered by Habermas (2006).

5. For example, strategic storytelling offers a promising alternative to "public crusade." See Braunstein 2012.

6. Binder 2007; Superfine 2009.

7. Rudolph 2002; Thorpe 2006.

8. Binder 2007.

9. M. Evans and J. Evans 2010.

10. Mooney 2005.

11. See, for example, MacLean and Burgess 2010; Powell and Kleinman 2008; S. N. Williams 2010.

12. I do not mean to suggest that scientists are not inherently capable of this, but simply that they might not have developed, or trained in, the necessary skills to do this successfully, or may instead be focused on other aspects of participation, such as correcting errors of accuracy and description; see Gregory and Miller 1998.

13. See also Brown 2009.

14. See, for example, Ramanathan 2010.

15. See also Honig 1993.

METHODOLOGICAL APPENDIX

1. I say "significant" only to guard against the possibility that someone, somewhere, has generated a claim about these issues that I have not seen emerge into public life.

2. Southerton 2004.

3. For discussion of newspapers as the "master forum," see Ferree et al. 2002.

4. Cunningham et al. 2002.

5. Blei 2012.

6. Blei, Ng, and Jordan 2003; Griffiths and Steyvers 2004.

7. Griffiths, Steyvers, and Tenenbaum 2007.

8. Griffiths and Steyvers 2004.

9. For a discussion of how and why topics can be generated that are not relevant to the substantive analysis, see Ramage, Dumais, and Liebling 2010.

10. See also M. Evans 2014b.

11. Sociologist Michael Lindsay (2007) gained access to hundreds of elite respondents in government and industry, primarily by leveraging religious networks. But this feat is exceptionally difficult and rare. Consider that even top-level journalists rarely get the opportunity to interview more than one of the persons I cited as examples.

12. Glaser and Strauss 1967; Luker 2008.

13. As Weiss (1994) notes, a random sample at this size might not actually capture enough different cases to derive useful theoretical insight.

14. Weiss 1994.

15. This variation is actually consistent with recent findings about the non-religious in the U.S. general population. See, for example, Hout and Fischer 2002; Baker and Smith 2009.

16. Luker 2008.

References

Anderson, Lisa. 2006. "Churches to Mark Darwin's Birthday." *Los Angeles Times,* February 11.

Aratani, Lori. 2005. "Weast Halts Launch of Sex-Ed Program; Decision Comes after Setback in Court." *Washington Post,* May 6.

Armstrong, Elizabeth A., and Mary Bernstein. 2008. "Culture, Power, and Institutions: A Multi-institutional Politics Approach to Social Movements." *Sociological Theory* 26 (1): 74–99.

Associated Press. 1999. "New Research Questions Findings of 'Gay Gene' Study." *Atlanta Journal and Constitution,* April 23.

Attridge, Harold W., ed. 2009. *The Religion and Science Debate: Why Does It Continue?* New Haven: Yale University Press.

Audi, Robert, and Nicholas Wolterstorff. 1997. *Religion in the Public Square: The Place of Religious Conviction in Political Debate.* Lanham, MD: Rowman and Littlefield.

Bail, Christopher A. 2012. "The Fringe Effect: Civil Society Organizations and the Evolution of Media Discourse about Islam since the September 11th Attacks." *American Sociological Review* 77 (6): 855–79.

———. 2014. *Terrified: How Anti-Muslim Fringe Organizations Became Mainstream.* Princeton, NJ: Princeton University Press.

Baker, Joseph O. 2012. "Public Perceptions of Incompatibility between 'Science and Religion.'" *Public Understanding of Science* 21 (3): 340–53.

Baker, Joseph O., and Buster G. Smith. 2009. "The Nones: Social Characteristics of the Religiously Unaffiliated." *Social Forces* 87 (3): 1251–63.

Barbour, Ian G. 1966. *Issues in Science and Religion.* Englewood Cliffs, NJ: Prentice-Hall.

Barton, Paul. 2004. "Bush Hears Praise for Policies." *Arkansas Democrat-Gazette,* September 1.

Bell, Allan. 1994. "Media (Mis)communication on the Science of Climate Change." *Public Understanding of Science* 3 (3): 259–75.

Bellah, Robert. 1967. "Civil Religion in America." *Daedalus* 96 (1): 1–21.

Besley, John C., and Andrea H. Tanner. 2011. "What Science Communication Scholars Think about Training Scientists to Communicate." *Science Communication* 33 (2): 239–63.

Beyerlein, Kraig. 2004. "Specifying the Impact of Conservative Protestantism on Educational Attainment." *Journal for the Scientific Study of Religion* 43 (4): 505–18.

Binder, Amy J. 2002. *Contentious Curricula: Afrocentrism and Creationism in American Public Schools*. Princeton, NJ: Princeton University Press.

———. 2007. "Gathering Intelligence on Intelligent Design: Where Did It Come From, Where Is It Going, and How Should Progressives Manage It?" *American Journal of Education* 113 (4): 549–76.

Blake, Mariah. 2005. "Stations of the Cross: How Evangelical Christians Are Creating an Alternative Universe of Faith-Based News." *Columbia Journalism Review* 44 (1): 32–39.

Blei, David M. 2012. "Probabilistic Topic Models." *Communications of the ACM* 55 (4): 77–84.

Blei, David M., Andrew Y. Ng, and Michael I. Jordan. 2003. "Latent Dirichlet Allocation." *Journal of Machine Learning Research* 3: 993–1022.

Bourdieu, Pierre. 1985. "The Social Space and the Genesis of Groups." *Theory and Society* 14 (6): 723–44.

———. 1991. *Language and Symbolic Power*. Cambridge, MA: Harvard University Press.

Bozeman, Theodore Dwight. 1977. *Protestants in an Age of Science: The Baconian Ideal and Antebellum American Religious Thought*. Chapel Hill: University of North Carolina Press.

Braunstein, Ruth. 2012. "Storytelling in Liberal Religious Advocacy." *Journal for the Scientific Study of Religion* 51 (1): 110–27.

Brelis, Matthew. 1999. "The Fading 'Gay Gene.'" *Boston Globe*, February 7.

Brockman, John, ed. 2006. *Intelligent Thought: Science versus the Intelligent Design Movement*. New York: Vintage Books.

Brooke, John Hedley. 1991. *Science and Religion: Some Historical Perspectives*. Cambridge: Cambridge University Press.

Brown, Mark B. 2009. *Science in Democracy: Expertise, Institutions, and Representation*. Cambridge, MA: MIT Press.

Bruner, Jerome. 1986. *Actual Minds, Possible Worlds*. Cambridge, MA: Harvard University Press.

———. 1991. "The Narrative Construction of Reality." *Critical Inquiry* 18 (1): 1–21.

Buddenbaum, Judith M. 2009. *Religious Scandals*. Santa Barbara, CA: Greenwood Press.

Burke, Heather. 2007. "Jerry Falwell, Evangelist, Political Activist, Dies." *Bloomberg.com*, May 16. Last retrieved April 22, 2015, from http://www.bloomberg.com/apps/news?pid=20601103&sid=auX3.SI9QH2M.

Burns, Terry W., D. John O'Connor, and Susan M. Stocklmayer. 2003. "Science Communication: A Contemporary Definition." *Science Communication* 12 (2): 183–202.

Callon, Michel. 1986. "Some Elements of a Sociology of Translation: Domestication of the Scallops and the Fishermen of St. Brieuc Bay." In *Power, Action and Belief: A New Sociology of Knowledge?* Edited by John Law, 196–233. London: Routledge and Kegan Paul.

Casanova, José. 1994. *Public Religions in the Modern World.* Chicago: University of Chicago Press.

Cigler, Allan J., and Burdett A. Loomis, eds. 1983. *Interest Group Politics.* Washington, DC: CQ Press.

Collins, Francis S. 2006. *The Language of God: A Scientist Presents Evidence for Belief.* New York: Free Press.

Collins, Harry M. 1974. "The TEA Set: Tacit Knowledge and Scientific Networks." *Science Studies* 4: 165–86.

———. 2004. *Gravity's Shadow: The Search for Gravitational Waves.* Chicago: University of Chicago Press.

Corbett, Julia B., and Jessica L. Durfee. 2004. "Testing Public (Un)certainty of Science: Media Representations of Global Warming." *Science Communication* 26 (2): 129–51.

Critchlow, Donald T. 2005. *Phyllis Schlafly and Grassroots Conservatism: A Woman's Crusade.* Princeton, NJ: Princeton University Press.

Cunningham, Hamish, Diana Maynard, Kalina Bontcheva, and Valentin Tablan. 2002. "GATE: An Architecture for Development of Robust HLT Applications." In *Proceedings of the 40th Anniversary Meeting of the Association for Computational Linguistics.* Stroudsburg, PA: Association for Computational Linguistics.

Curtis, Ron. 1994. "Narrative Form and Normative Force: Baconian Story-Telling in Popular Science." *Social Studies of Science* 24 (3): 419–61.

Dahl, Robert A. 1956. *A Preface to Democratic Theory.* University of Chicago Press.

Davies, Dominic, and Charles Neal. 1996. "An Historical Overview of Homosexuality and Therapy." In *Pink Therapy.* Edited by Dominic Davies and Charles Neal, 11–23. Buckingham, UK: Open University Press.

Dawkins, Richard. 1989. "Review of *Blueprints: Solving the Mystery of Evolution.*" *New York Times,* April 9.

———. 2006. *The God Delusion.* New York: Houghton Mifflin.

Denzau, Arthur T., and Michael C. Munger. 1986. "Legislators and Interest Groups: How Unorganized Interests Get Represented." *American Political Science Review* 80 (1): 89–106.

Djupe, Paul A., and Christopher P. Gilbert. 2003. *The Prophetic Pulpit: Clergy, Churches, and Communities in American Politics.* Lanham, MD: Rowman and Littlefield.

Djupe, Paul A., and Gregory W. Gwiasda. 2010. "Evangelizing the Environment: Decision Process Effects in Political Persuasion." *Journal for the Scientific Study of Religion* 49 (1): 73–86.

Domke, David, and Kevin Coe. 2010. *The God Strategy: How Religion Became a Political Weapon in America.* New York: Oxford University Press.

Downs, Anthony. 1957. *An Economic Theory of Democracy.* New York: Harper and Row.

Draper, John William. 1874. *History of the Conflict Between Religion and Science.* New York: D. Appleton and Company.

Dunn, John. 1979. *Western Political Theory in the Face of the Future.* Cambridge: Cambridge University Press.

Ecklund, Elaine Howard. 2010. *Science vs. Religion: What Scientists Really Think.* Oxford: Oxford University Press.

Ecklund, Elaine Howard, and Jerry Z. Park. 2009. "Predicting Conflict between Religion and Science among Academic Scientists." *Journal for the Scientific Study of Religion* 48 (2): 276–92.

Ecklund, Elaine Howard, and Christopher P. Scheitle. 2007. "Religion among Academic Scientists: Distinctions, Disciplines, and Demographics." *Social Problems* 54 (2): 263–88.

Ecklund, Elaine Howard, Jerry Z. Park, and Katherine Sorrell. 2011. "Scientists Negotiate Boundaries between Religion and Science." *Journal for the Scientific Study of Religion* 50 (3): 552–69.

Eliasoph, Nina. 1998. *Avoiding Politics: How Americans Produce Apathy in Everyday Life.* New York: Cambridge University Press.

Ellison, Christopher G., and Marc A. Musick. 1995. "Conservative Protestantism and Public Opinion toward Science." *Review of Religious Research* 36 (3): 245–62.

Enelow, James M., and Melvin J. Hinich. 1984. *The Spatial Theory of Voting: An Introduction.* New York: Cambridge University Press.

Epstein, Steven. 1996. *Impure Science: AIDS, Activism, and the Politics of Knowledge.* Berkeley: University of California Press.

Evans, John H. 1997. "Multi-organizational Fields and Social Movement Organization Frame Content: The Religious Pro-choice Movement." *Sociological Inquiry* 67 (4): 451–69.

———. 2002. *Playing God? Human Genetic Engineering and the Rationalization of Public Bioethical Debate.* Chicago: University of Chicago Press.

———. 2009. "Where Is the Counterweight? Explorations of the Decline in Mainline Protestant Participation in Public Debates over Values." In *Evangelicals and Democracy in America: Religion and Society.* Edited by Steven G. Brint and Jean Reith Schroedel, 221–47. New York: Russell Sage.

———. 2010. *Contested Reproduction: Genetic Technologies, Religion, and Public Debate.* Chicago: University of Chicago Press.

———. 2011. "Epistemological and Moral Conflict between Religion and Science." *Journal for the Scientific Study of Religion* 50 (4): 707–27.

———. 2013. "The Growing Social and Moral Conflict between Conservative Protestants and Science." *Journal for the Scientific Study of Religion* 52 (2): 368–85.

Evans, John H., and Michael S. Evans. 2008. "Religion and Science: Beyond the Epistemological Conflict Narrative." *Annual Review of Sociology* 34: 87–105.

Evans, Michael S. 2009. "Defining the Public, Defining Sociology: Hybrid Science-Public Relations and Boundary-Work in Early American Sociology." *Public Understanding of Science* 18 (1): 5–22.

———. 2010. "Achieving Continuity: A Story of Stellar Magnitude." *Studies in History and Philosophy of Science* 41 (1): 1026–41.

———. 2012a. "Supporting Science: Reasons, Restrictions, and the Role of Religion." *Science Communication* 34 (3): 334–62.

———. 2012b. "Who Wants a Deliberative Public Sphere?" *Sociological Forum* 27 (4): 872–95.

———. 2014a. "Religion and Political Decision Making." *Journal for the Scientific Study of Religion* 53 (1): 145–63.

———. 2014b. "A Computational Approach to Qualitative Analysis in Large Textual Datasets." *PLOS ONE* 9 (2): e87908.

Evans, Michael S., and John H. Evans. 2010. "Arguing against Darwinism: Religion, Science, and Public Morality." In *The New Blackwell Companion to the Sociology of Religion*. Edited by Bryan S. Turner. Oxford: Wiley-Blackwell.

Falwell, Macel. 2008. *Jerry Falwell: His Life and Legacy*. New York: Howard Books.

Ferree, Myra Marx, William Anthony Gamson, Jürgen Gerhards, and Dieter Rucht. 2002. *Shaping Abortion Discourse: Democracy and the Public Sphere in Germany and the United States*. Cambridge: Cambridge University Press.

Fetner, Tina. 2008. *How the Religious Right Shaped Lesbian and Gay Activism*. Social Movements, Protest, and Contention, Vol. 31. Minneapolis: University of Minnesota Press.

Feyerabend, Paul. 1975. *Against Method: Outline of an Anarchistic Theory of Knowledge*. Atlantic Highlands, NJ: Humanities Press.

Focus on the Family. n.d. "Focus on the Family's Foundational Values." Last retrieved August 21, 2015, from http://www.focusonthefamily.com/about_us/guiding-principles.aspx.

Forrest, Barbara, and Paul R. Gross. 2004. *Creationism's Trojan Horse: The Wedge of Intelligent Design*. New York: Oxford University Press.

Fowler, Robert Booth, Allen D. Hertzke, and Laura R. Olson. 1999. *Religion and Politics in America: Faith, Culture, and Strategic Choices*. 2nd ed. Boulder, CO: Westview Press.

Fraser, Nancy. 1990. "Rethinking the Public Sphere: A Contribution to the Critique of Actually Existing Democracy." *Social Text* 25–26: 56–80.

Gauchat, Gordon. 2011. "The Cultural Authority of Science: Public Trust and Acceptance of Organized Science." *Public Understanding of Science* 20 (6): 751–70.

Gieryn, Thomas F. 1999. *Cultural Boundaries of Science: Credibility on the Line*. Chicago: University of Chicago Press.

Gilgoff, Dan. 2007. *The Jesus Machine: How James Dobson, Focus on the Family, and Evangelical America Are Winning the Culture War*. New York: St. Martin's Press.

Gitlin, Todd. 1981. *The Whole World Is Watching: Mass Media in the Making and Unmaking of the New Left*. Berkeley: University of California Press.

Glaser, Barney G., and Anselm L. Strauss. 1967. *The Discovery of Grounded Theory: Strategies for Qualitative Research.* Chicago: Aldine.

Goldberg, Michelle. 2007. *Kingdom Coming: The Rise of Christian Nationalism.* New York: W. W. Norton.

Goodell, Rae. 1977. *The Visible Scientists.* New York: Little, Brown.

Gooding, David. 1990. "Mapping Experiment as a Learning Process: How the First Electromagnetic Motor Was Invented." *Science, Technology, and Human Values* 15 (2): 165–201.

Goodstein, Laurie. 2000. "Conservative Church Leaders Find a Pillar in Bush." *New York Times,* January 23, sec. 1, p. 16.

Gould, Stephen Jay. 1993. "Dinomania." *New York Review of Books,* no. 23 (August): 51–56.

———. 1999. *Rocks of Ages: Science and Religion in the Fullness of Life.* New York: Ballantine.

Greeley, Andrew, and Michael Hout. 2006. *The Truth about Conservative Christians: What They Think and What They Believe.* Chicago: University of Chicago Press.

Green, John C., Mark J. Rozell, and Clyde Wilcox, eds. 2003. *The Christian Right in American Politics: Marching to the Millennium.* Washington, DC: Georgetown University Press.

Gregory, Jane, and Steve Miller. 1998. *Science in Public: Communication, Culture, and Credibility.* New York: Basic Books.

Griffiths, Thomas L., and Mark Steyvers. 2004. "Finding Scientific Topics." *Proceedings of the National Academy of Sciences* 101 (suppl. 1) (April 6): 5228–35.

Griffiths, Thomas L., Mark Steyvers, and Joshua B. Tenenbaum. 2007. "Topics in Semantic Representation." *Psychological Review* 114 (2): 211–44.

Grossman, Cathy Lynn. 2004. "Can Politics Be a Litmus Test for Communion?" *USA Today,* June 15, 10D.

Habermas, Jürgen. 1974 [1964]. "The Public Sphere: An Encyclopedia Article." *New German Critique* 3: 49–55.

———. 1989. *The Structural Transformation of the Public Sphere.* Cambridge, MA: The MIT Press.

———. 2006. "Religion in the Public Sphere." *European Journal of Philosophy* 14 (1): 1–25.

Hadden, Jeffrey K. 1969. *The Gathering Storm in the Churches.* Garden City, NY: Doubleday.

Hadden, Jeffrey K., and Anson D. Shupe. 1988. *Televangelism, Power, and Politics on God's Frontier.* New York: Henry Holt.

Hamer, Dean H., S. Hu, V. L. Magnuson, N. Hu, and A. M. Pattatucci. 1993. "A Linkage between DNA Markers on the X Chromosome." *Science* 261 (5119): 321–27.

Harding, Susan Friend. 2000. *The Book of Jerry Falwell: Fundamentalist Language and Politics.* Princeton, NJ: Princeton University Press.

Harris, Sam. 2004. *The End of Faith: Religion, Terror, and the Future of Reason.* New York: W. W. Norton.

Hart, Stephen. 2001. *Cultural Dilemmas of Progressive Politics: Styles of Engagement among Grassroots Activists.* Chicago: University of Chicago Press.

Haught, John F. 2000. *God after Darwin: A Theology of Evolution.* Boulder, CO: Westview Press.

Hedges, Chris. 2006. *American Fascists: The Christian Right and the War on America.* New York: Simon and Schuster.

Herberg, Will. 1955. *Protestant, Catholic, Jew: An Essay in American Religious Sociology.* New York: Doubleday.

Hetherington, Marc J. 2005. *Why Trust Matters: Declining Political Trust and the Demise of American Liberalism.* Princeton, NJ: Princeton University Press.

Hibbing, John R., and Elizabeth Theiss-Morse. 2002. *Stealth Democracy: Americans' Beliefs about How Government Should Work.* Cambridge: Cambridge University Press.

Hitchens, Christopher. 2007. *God Is Not Great: How Religion Poisons Everything.* New York: Twelve Books.

Holton, Gerald. 1993. *Science and Anti-science.* Cambridge, MA: Harvard University Press.

Honig, Bonnie. 1993. *Political Theory and the Displacement of Politics.* Ithaca, NY: Cornell University Press.

Hopkins, Jim. 2005. "Stem Cells' Promise Pits Jobs vs. Values." *USA Today,* February 16, 1B.

Hout, Michael, and Claude S. Fischer. 2002. "Why More Americans Have No Religious Preference: Politics and Generations." *American Sociological Review* 67: 165–90.

Hunter, James Davison. 1983. *American Evangelicalism: Conservative Religion and the Quandary of Modernity.* New Brunswick, NJ: Rutgers University Press.

———. 1991. *Culture Wars: The Struggle to Define America.* New York: Basic Books.

Inskeep, Steve. 2006. "Religion, Politics a Potent Mix for Falwell." *NPR Morning Edition,* June 30. Last retrieved April 22, 2015, from http://www.npr.org/templates/story/story.php?storyId=5522064.

Irwin, Alan. 2001. "Constructing the Scientific Citizen: Science and Democracy in the Biosciences." *Public Understanding of Science* 10 (1): 1–18.

Jelen, Ted G. 1993. *The Political World of the Clergy.* Westport, CT: Praeger.

John Paul II. 1992. "Lessons of the Galileo Case." *Origins* 22 (2): 371.

Johnson, David R., Elaine Howard Ecklund, and Anne E. Lincoln. 2014. "Narratives of Science Outreach in Elite Contexts of Academic Science." *Science Communication* 36 (1): 81–105.

Jordan, Mark D. 1997. *The Invention of Sodomy in Christian Theology.* Chicago: University of Chicago Press.

Kim, Jongyoung. 2009. "Public Feeling for Science: The Hwang Affair and Hwang Supporters." *Public Understanding of Science* 18 (6): 670–86.

King, Gary. 1997. *A Solution to the Ecological Inference Problem: Reconstructing Individual Behavior from Aggregate Data.* Princeton, NJ: Princeton University Press.

Kirby, David A. 2003. "Scientists on the Set: Science Consultants and the Communication of Science in Visual Fiction." *Public Understanding of Science* 12 (3): 261–78.

———. 2011. *Lab Coats in Hollywood: Science, Scientists, and Cinema*. Cambridge, MA: MIT Press.

Klemp, Nathaniel J. 2010. "The Christian Right: Engaged Citizens or Theocratic Crusaders?" *Politics and Religion* 3 (1): 1–27.

Knorr-Cetina, Karin. 1981. *The Manufacture of Knowledge: An Essay on the Constructivist and Contextual Nature of Science*. Oxford: Pergamon Press.

Koch, Jeffrey W. 2000. "Do Citizens Apply Gender Stereotypes to Infer Candidates' Ideological Orientations?" *Journal of Politics* 62 (2): 414–29.

Kuhn, Thomas S. 1996. *The Structure of Scientific Revolutions*. 3rd ed. Chicago: University of Chicago Press.

Latour, Bruno. 1987. *Science in Action*. Cambridge, MA: Harvard University Press.

Lawson, Anton E., and William A. Worsnop. 1992. "Learning about Evolution and Rejecting a Belief in Special Creation: Effects of Reflective Reasoning Skill, Prior Knowledge, Prior Belief, and Religious Commitment." *Journal of Research in Science Teaching* 29 (2): 143–66.

Le Vay, Simon. 1994. *The Sexual Brain*. London: A Bradford Book.

Lienesch, Michael. 1993. *Redeeming America: Piety and Politics in the New Christian Right*. Chapel Hill: University of North Carolina Press.

———. 2007. *In the Beginning: Fundamentalism, the Scopes Trial, and the Making of the Antievolution Movement*. Chapel Hill: University of North Carolina Press.

Lindsay, D. Michael. 2006. "Is the National Prayer Breakfast Surrounded by a 'Christian Mafia'? Religious Publicity and Secrecy within the Corridors of Power." *Journal of the American Academy of Religion* 74 (2): 390–419.

———. 2007. *Faith in the Halls of Power: How Evangelicals Joined the American Elite*. Oxford: Oxford University Press.

Lindsay, D. Michael, and Robert Wuthnow. 2010. "Financing Faith: Religion and Strategic Philanthropy." *Journal for the Scientific Study of Religion* 49 (1): 87–11.

Livingstone, David. 1987. *Darwin's Forgotten Defenders: The Encounter between Evangelical Theology and Evolutionary Thought*. Grand Rapids, MI: Eerdmans.

Locke, Simon. 1999. "Golem Science and the Public Understanding of Science: From Deficit to Dilemma." *Public Understanding of Science* 8 (2): 75–92.

Longest, Kyle C., and Christian Smith. 2011. "Conflicting or Compatible: Beliefs about Religion and Science among Emerging Adults in the United States." *Sociological Forum* 26 (4): 846–69.

Luker, Kristin. 2008. *Salsa Dancing into the Social Sciences: Research in an Age of Info-Glut*. Cambridge, MA: Harvard University Press.

MacLean, Samantha, and Michael M. Burgess. 2010. "In the Public Interest: Assessing Expert and Stakeholder Influence in Public Deliberation about Biobanks." *Public Understanding of Science* 19 (4): 486–96.

Marsden, George. 1980. *Fundamentalism and American Culture: The Shaping of Twentieth-Century Evangelicalism, 1870–1925*. Oxford: Oxford University Press.

Marty, Martin E., and R. Scott Appleby, eds. 1991. *Fundamentalisms Observed*. Vol. 1. The Fundamentalism Project. Chicago: University of Chicago Press.

McCarthy, John D., and Mayer N. Zald. 1977. "Resource Mobilization and Social Movements: A Partial Theory." *American Journal of Sociology* 82 (6): 1212–41.

Media Matters. 2007. *Left Behind: The Skewed Representation of Religion in Major News Media*. Special Report. Washington, DC: Media Matters for America.

Medvetz, Thomas. 2012. *Think Tanks in America*. Chicago: University of Chicago Press.

Mellor, Felicity. 2010. "Negotiating Uncertainty: Asteroids, Risk, and the Media." *Public Understanding of Science* 19 (1): 16–33.

Merton, Robert K. 1973. "The Normative Structure of Science." In *The Sociology of Science: Theoretical and Empirical Investigations*, 267–80. Chicago: University of Chicago Press.

Metlay, Grischa. 2006. "Reconsidering Renormalization: Stability and Change in 20th-Century Views on University Patents." *Social Studies of Science* 36 (4): 565–97.

Mitzen, Jennifer. 2005. "Reading Habermas in Anarchy: Multilateral Diplomacy and Global Public Spheres." *American Political Science Review* 99 (3): 401–17.

Moen, Matthew C. 1992. *The Transformation of the Christian Right in the 1980s*. Tuscaloosa: University of Alabama Press.

Mol, Annemarie, and John Law. 1994. "Regions, Networks and Fluids: Anaemia and Social Topology." *Social Studies of Science* 24 (4): 641–71.

Moon, Dawne. 2004. *God, Sex, and Politics: Homosexuality and Everyday Theologies*. Chicago: University of Chicago Press.

Mooney, Chris. 2005. *The Republican War on Science*. New York: Basic Books.

Mooney, Chris, and Sheril Kirshenbaum. 2009. *Unscientific America: How Scientific Illiteracy Threatens Our Future*. New York: Basic Books.

Morford, Mark. 2007. "Remembering Rev. Jerry Falwell in His Own Words." *San Francisco Chronicle*, May 18, F8.

Morrison, Grant. 2011. *Supergods*. New York: Spiegal and Grau.

Mueller, Carol. 1983. "In Search of a Constituency for the 'New Religious Right.'" *Public Opinion Quarterly* 47: 213–29.

Nadeau, David, and Satoshi Sekine. 2009. "A Survey of Named Entity Recognition and Classification." In *Named Entities*. Edited by Satoshi Sekine and Elisabete Ranchhod, 3–28. Philadelphia: John Benjamins.

Nisbet, Matthew C. 2005. "The Competition for Worldviews: Values, Information, and Public Support for Stem Cell Research." *International Journal of Public Opinion Research* 17 (1): 90–112.

Nisbet, Matthew C., and Bruce V. Lewenstein. 2002. "Biotechnology and the American Media: The Policy Process and the Elite Press, 1970 to 1999." *Science Communication* 23 (4): 359–91.

Nisbet, Matthew C., Dominique Brossard, and Adrianne Kroepsch. 2003. "Framing Science: The Stem Cell Controversy in an Age of Press/Politics." *Press/Politics* 8 (2): 36–70.

NSB (National Science Board). 2014. *Science and Engineering Indicators 2014.* Arlington, VA: National Science Foundation. Last retrieved August 25, 2015, from http://www.nsf.gov/statistics/seind14/index.cfm/chapter-7/c7s3.htm.

Numbers, Ronald L. 2007. *Science and Christianity in Pulpit and Pew.* Oxford: Oxford University Press.

Olson, Laura R. 2007. "Whither the Religious Left? Religiopolitical Progressivism in Twenty-First-Century America." In *From Pews to Polling Places: Faith and Politics in the American Religious Mosaic.* Edited by J. Matthew Wilson, 53–80. Washington, DC: Georgetown University Press.

Oreskes, Naomi. 2004. "The Scientific Consensus on Climate Change." *Science* 306 (3 December): 1686.

Paulson, Steve. 2007. "The Atheist Delusion." *Salon.com,* December 18. Last retrieved April 22, 2015, from http://www.salon.com/books/feature/2007/12/18/john_haught/.

Perrin, Andrew J., and Katherine McFarland. 2008. "The Sociology of Political Representation and Deliberation." *Sociology Compass* 2 (4): 1228–44.

———. 2011. "Social Theory and Public Opinion." *Annual Review of Sociology* 37: 87–107.

Peters, Hans Peter, Dominique Brossard, Suzanne de Cheveigné, Sharon Dunwoody, Monika Kallfass, Steve Miller, and Shoji Tsuchida. 2008. "Science-Media Interface: It's Time to Reconsider." *Science Communication* 30 (2): 266–76.

Pew Research Center. 2009. *Public Praises Science; Scientists Fault Public, Media.* Washington, DC: Pew Research Center for the People and the Press.

Phillips, Kevin. 2006. *American Theocracy: The Peril and Politics of Radical Religion, Oil, and Borrowed Money in the 21st Century.* New York: Viking.

Pitkin, Hanna Fenichel. 1967. *The Concept of Representation.* Berkeley: University of California Press.

———. 2004. "Representation and Democracy: Uneasy Alliance." *Scandinavian Political Studies* 27 (3): 335–42.

Powell, Maria, and Daniel Lee Kleinman. 2008. "Building Citizen Capacities for Participation in Nanotechnology Decision-Making: The Democratic Virtues of the Consensus Conference Model." *Public Understanding of Science* 17 (3): 329–48.

Przeworski, Adam, Susan C. Stokes, and Bernard Manin, eds. 1999. *Democracy, Accountability, and Representation.* Cambridge: Cambridge University Press.

Rabinowitz, George, and Stuart Elaine Macdonald. 1989. "A Directional Theory of Issue Voting." *American Political Science Review* 83 (1): 93–121.

Ramage, Daniel, Susan Dumais, and Dan Liebling. 2010. "Characterizing Microblogs with Topic Models." In *Proceedings of the Fourth International*

AAAI Conference on Weblogs and Social Media, 130–37. Association for the Advancement of Artificial Intelligence.

Ramanathan, G. V. 2010. "How Much Math Do We Really Need?" *Washington Post*, October 23, A15.

Rawls, John. 1971. *A Theory of Justice*. Cambridge, MA: Harvard University Press.

———. 2005. *Political Liberalism*. Expanded edition. New York: Columbia University Press.

Rehfeld, Andrew. 2006. "Towards a General Theory of Political Representation." *Journal of Politics* 68 (1): 1–21.

Remnick, David. 2004. "The Wilderness Campaign." *The New Yorker*, September 13. Last retrieved April 22, 2015, from http://www.newyorker.com /magazine/2004/09/13/the-wilderness-campaign.

Robertson, Pat. 2005. *The 700 Club*. Episode originally aired November 10, 2005.

Roos, J. Micah. 2014. "Measuring Science or Religion? A Measurement Analysis of the National Science Foundation Sponsored Science Literacy Scale, 2006–2010." *Public Understanding of Science* 23 (7): 797–813.

Rudolph, John L. 2002. *Scientists in the Classroom: The Cold War Reconstruction of American Science Education*. New York: Palgrave.

Rudoren, Jodi. 2006. "Ohio Board Undoes Stand on Evolution." *New York Times*, February 16, A6.

Rughiniş, Cosima. 2011. "A Lucky Answer to a Fair Question: Conceptual, Methodological, and Moral Implications of Including Items on Human Evolution in Scientific Literacy Surveys." *Science Communication* 33 (4): 501–32.

Russell, Bertrand. 1997 [1935]. *Religion and Science*. New York: Oxford University Press.

Saward, Michael. 2008. "Representation and Democracy: Revisions and Possibilities." *Sociology Compass* 2 (3): 1000–1013.

Schaeffer, Frank. 2007. *Crazy for God: How I Grew Up as One of the Elect, Helped Found the Religious Right, and Lived to Take All (or Almost All) of It Back*. Cambridge, MA: Da Capo Press.

Schattschneider, E. E. 1960. *The Semisovereign People: A Realist's View of Democracy in America*. New York: Holt, Rinehart and Winston.

Scheitle, Christopher P. 2011. "U.S. College Students' Perception of Religion and Science: Conflict, Collaboration, or Independence? A Research Note." *Journal for the Scientific Study of Religion* 50 (1): 175–86.

Schwartz, Nancy L. 1988. *The Blue Guitar: Political Representation and Community*. Chicago: University of Chicago Press.

Scott, Eugenie C. 1997. "Antievolution and Creationism in the United States." *Annual Review of Anthropology* 26: 263–89.

Shapin, Steven. 1994. *A Social History of Truth: Civility and Science in Seventeenth-Century England*. Chicago: University of Chicago Press.

———. 1995. "Cordelia's Love: Credibility and the Social Studies of Science." *Perspectives on Science* 3: 255–75.

———. 2008. *The Scientific Life: A Moral History of a Late Modern Vocation*. Chicago: University of Chicago Press.

———. 2010. "The Darwin Show." *London Review of Books* 32 (1): 3–9.

Shapin, Steven, and Simon Schaffer. 1985. *Leviathan and the Air-Pump*. Princeton, NJ: Princeton University Press.

Sharlet, Jeff. 2008. *The Family: The Secret Fundamentalism at the Heart of American Power*. New York: HarperCollins.

Shea, William R. 1986. "Galileo and the Church." In *God and Nature: Historical Essays on the Encounter between Christianity and Science*. Edited by David C. Lindberg and Ronald L. Numbers, 114–35. Berkeley: University of California Press.

Sherkat, Darren E. 2010. "Religion and Verbal Ability." *Social Science Research* 39 (1): 2–13.

Shermer, Michael B. 2002. "This View of Science: Stephen Jay Gould as Historian of Science and Scientific Historian, Popular Scientist and Scientific Popularizer." *Social Studies of Science* 32 (4): 489–524.

Shields, Jon A. 2009. *The Democratic Virtues of the Christian Right*. Princeton, NJ: Princeton University Press.

Sigelman, Carol K., Lee Sigelman, Barbara J. Walkosz, and Michael Nitz. 1995. "Black Candidates, White Voters: Understanding Racial Bias in Political Perceptions." *American Journal of Political Science* 29 (1): 243–65.

Slack, Gordy. 2005. "The Atheist." *Slate,* April 30. Last retrieved August 21, 2015, from http://www.salon.com/2005/04/30/dawkins/.

Smidt, Corwin E. 2007. "Evangelical and Mainline Protestants at the Turn of the Millennium: Taking Stock and Looking Forward." In *From Pews to Polling Places: Faith and Politics in the American Religious Mosaic*. Edited by J. Matthew Wilson, 29–52. Washington, DC: Georgetown University Press.

Smith, Christian. 1998. *American Evangelicalism: Embattled and Thriving*. Chicago: University of Chicago Press.

Snow, David A., and Robert D. Benford. 1992. "Master Frames and Cycles of Protest." In *Frontiers in Social Movement Theory*. Edited by Aldon D. Morris and Carol McClurg Mueller, 135–55. New Haven: Yale University Press.

Sobieraj, Sarah. 2011. *Soundbitten: The Perils of Media-Centered Political Activism*. New York: New York University Press.

Southerton, Simon G. 2004. *Losing a Lost Tribe: Native Americans, DNA, and the Mormon Church*. Salt Lake City: Signature Books.

Star, Susan Leigh. 1985. "Scientific Work and Uncertainty." *Social Studies of Science* 15 (3): 391–427.

Star, Susan Leigh, and James Griesemer. 1989. "Institutional Ecology, 'Translations' and Boundary Objects: Amateurs and Professionals in Berkeley's Museum of Vertebrate Zoology, 1907–39." *Social Studies of Science* 19 (3): 387–420.

Stout, Jeffrey. 1988. *Ethics after Babel: The Languages of Morals and Their Discontents*. Princeton, NJ: Princeton University Press.

Sturgis, Patrick, and Nick Allum. 2004. "Science in Society: Re-evaluating the Deficit Model of Public Attitudes." *Public Understanding of Science* 13: 55–74.

Superfine, Benjamin Michael. 2009. "The Evolving Role of the Courts in Educational Policy: The Tension between Judicial, Scientific, and Democratic

Decision Making in *Kitzmiller v. Dover.*" *American Educational Research Journal* 46 (4): 898–923.

Swidey, Neil. 2005. "What Makes People Gay?" *Boston Globe Magazine*, August 14.

Taylor, Charles. 2004. *Modern Social Imaginaries.* Durham, NC: Duke University Press.

———. 2007. *A Secular Age.* Cambridge, MA: Belknap Press of Harvard University Press.

Teles, Steven. 2008. *The Rise of the Conservative Legal Movement: The Battle for Control of the Law.* Princeton, NJ: Princeton University Press.

Thomassen, Lasse. 2007. "Beyond Representation?" *Parliamentary Affairs* 60 (1): 111–26.

Thorpe, Charles. 2006. *Oppenheimer: The Tragic Intellect.* Chicago: University of Chicago Press.

Trilling, Lionel. 1972. *Sincerity and Authenticity.* Cambridge, MA: Harvard University Press.

Urbinati, Nadia. 2006. *Representative Democracy: Principles and Genealogy.* Chicago: University of Chicago Press.

Verhey, Steven. 2005. "The Effect of Engaging Prior Learning on Student Attitudes toward Creationism and Evolution." *BioScience* 44: 996–1003.

Vygotsky, L. S. 1978. *Mind in Society: The Development of Higher Psychological Processes.* Cambridge, MA: Harvard University Press.

Wagner, Wolfgang. 2007. "Vernacular Science Knowledge: Its Role in Everyday Life Communication." *Public Understanding of Science* 16 (1): 7–22.

Weiner, Jennifer. 2000. "Making Waves: Proposed TV Show of Radio's Dr. Laura Schlessinger Causing Rift in Gay Community." *Pittsburgh Post-Gazette*, March 14, D5.

Weingart, Peter. 1998. "Science and the Media." *Research Policy* 27 (8): 869–79.

Weiss, Robert S. 1994. *Learning from Strangers: The Art and Method of Qualitative Interview Studies.* New York: Free Press.

Wilcox, Clyde. 1989. "Evangelicals and the Moral Majority." *Journal for the Scientific Study of Religion* 28 (4): 400–414.

Wilcox, Clyde, and Carin Robinson. 2011. *Onward Christian Soldiers? The Religious Right in American Politics.* 4th ed. Boulder, CO: Westview Press.

Williams, Daniel K. 2010. *God's Own Party: The Making of the Christian Right.* New York: Oxford University Press.

Williams, Melissa S. 1998. *Voice, Trust, and Memory.* Princeton, NJ: Princeton University Press.

Williams, Simon N. 2010. "A Twenty-First Century Citizens' POLIS: Introducing a Democratic Experiment in Electronic Citizen Participation in Science and Technology Decision-Making." *Public Understanding of Science* 19 (5): 528–44.

Wuthnow, Robert. 1983. "The Political Rebirth of American Evangelicals." In *The New Christian Right: Mobilization and Legitimation.* Edited by Robert C. Liebman and Robert Wuthnow, 167–85. Hawthorne, NY: Aldine Transaction.

————. 1988. *The Restructuring of American Religion*. Princeton, NJ: Princeton University Press.

Wuthnow, Robert, and John H. Evans, eds. 2002. *The Quiet Hand of God: Faith-Based Activism and the Public Role of Mainline Protestantism*. Berkeley: University of California Press.

Wynne, Brian. 1992. "Misunderstood Misunderstandings: Social Identities and Public Uptake of Science." *Public Understanding of Science* 1 (3): 281–304.

Zammito, John H. 2004. *A Nice Derangement of Epistemes: Post-positivism in the Study of Science from Quine to Latour*. Chicago: University of Chicago Press.

Index